It's Not Over
'Til It's Over

IT'S NOT OVER 'TIL IT'S OVER

Al Silverman

THE OVERLOOK PRESS
Woodstock & New York

First published in the United States in 2002 by
The Overlook Press, Peter Mayer Publishers, Inc.
Woodstock & New York

WOODSTOCK:
One Overlook Drive
Woodstock, NY 12498
www.overlookpress.com
[for individual orders, bulk and special sales, contact our Woodstock office]

NEW YORK:
141 Wooster Street
New York, NY 10012

∞The paper used in this book meets requirements for paper
permanence as described in the ANSI Z39.48-1992 standard.

Library of Congress Cataloging-in-Publication Data

Silverman, Al.
It's not over 'til it's over : the stories behind the most magnificent,
heart-stopping sports miracles of our time/Al Silverman.—1st ed.
p. cm.
1. Sports—History—20th century. 2. Sports—United States—
History—20th century. I. Title.
GV576 .S55 2002   796'.09'0904—dc21   2002072335

Book design and typeformatting by Bernard Schleifer
Manufactured in the United States of America
FIRST EDITION
10 9 8 7 6 5 4 3 2 1
ISBN 1-58567-317-X

CONTENTS

For The Children of
The New Century, who
Will Help Make it Better

Ella and Zoë
Jonathan, Erin, and Emma
And Louis

INTRODUCTION

I always think of 1946 as one of the happiest times of my life. In June I was discharged from the Navy, where I had served 26 months as a medic. I was so pumped up by my freedom that I decided to hitch-hike home from Texas, although Camp Wallace was a long way from where my family was living in Lynn, Massachusetts, just north of Boston. My first ride left me off in the border town of Texarkana, where I waited for several hours on a lonely road; I never did know whether I was thumbing a ride from Texas or Arkansas. Finally a car pulled up with two Marines who had also just been discharged. They said they were going to Boston. My new life was off to a good start.

Home in Lynn, I got another pleasant surprise. I wanted to go back to Boston University for my final three years, but I was worried that my parents wouldn't be able to find the money. That's when I learned that the G.I. Bill of Rights would pay my tuition. I also found out that I was a member of the "52-20 club"—all veterans would receive $20 a week for 52 weeks, for doing nothing. I did next to nothing that summer. I played baseball for my Jewish Community Center team, and I lolled on the beach at Swampscott, checking out which of the girls of summer had become desirable women. I also listened on the radio to the games of the Boston Red Sox as they marched regally to a pennant, only to be undone in the seventh game of the World Series against the St. Louis Cardinals, an early manifestation of the disease that would afflict them for the rest of the century. Then, in September, I did return to Boston University, to prepare myself for a career in journalism.

But the high point of that miracle year of 1946, for me, was the football game on Thanksgiving morning between my high school, Lynn English, and its traditional rival, Lynn Classical. The rivalry was mostly geographic. Lynn English was in East Lynn, where I lived; Classical was in West Lynn, the blue-collar section of the city. Now tons of fans—East Lynners on one side, West Lynners on the other side; no one was neutral—were filling Manning Bowl to its capacity of 20,000.

It was an ice-cold morning, with a fierce wind blowing. They had covered the field overnight with bales of hay to keep it from freezing. I don't remember ever feeling so much excitement in the air for a high school football game. Pom-pom girls from both English and Classical were strutting alongside the hay, which had been piled up on the sidelines. Drum and bugle corps from both English and Classical were on the field, blaring away in competition with each other. Everyone in the stadium seemed to be jumping up and down, maybe to keep warm, but also because of the electric charge in the air. During the season Lynn Classical had gone 10-0 and was considered one of the top high school teams in New England, largely because of its junior quarterback, Harry Agganis, who was known as "the Golden Greek." My team had lost three close games that fall and was a three-touchdown underdog. That didn't mean a thing, this was English vs. Classical in the Thanksgiving Game. Anything could happen.

Sure enough. Harry Agganis's first punt, buffeted by the wind, careened out of bounds on the Classical 35. Charlie Ruddock, our tailback, who also called the plays for Lynn English, knew what he had to do. That morning, his father, Charlie Ruddock, Sr, who was a milkman (he used to drop bottles at our house in his horse-drawn wagon), a gambler and a fiery athlete in his time, told his son, "Look, never mind the bullshit about giving the ball to someone else. I want you to score the first touchdown, so if you come in close, call your own play—or don't come home." The father knew that the first person to score in the game would receive a bundle of gifts—a pair of shoes, ten pounds of pastry from the New York Model Bakery, a new hat, dinner with his family at Lynn's fanciest and only hotel, and a wristwatch. So what could his son do? He called for the ball and swept 29 yards down the sideline for the touchdown.

That was the start of a thrilling seesaw game. My team would march downfield and score. Their team would strike back almost immediately and score. With three minutes left, Lynn English led by 27-20. But with Agganis's passes clicking, Classical drove downfield scoring the final touchdown and making the extra point—a surprise pass from Agganis to his end, Vic Pujo, that tied the game and kept the team undefeated. Still, I left Manning Bowl elated. The tie was a moral victory for Lynn English.

Aside from the impact of the game itself, there are other reasons why that Thanksgiving morning 1946 remains locked into my mind. One is my obsession with Harry Agganis. It developed in the spring of 1948 when, in my first issue as editor of the Boston University *News*, I broke the story that Agganis, who was being courted by more than 100 colleges, would enroll at Boston University. That fall I met BU freshman Agganis, and he laughed at me for my scoop. "I don't know how you knew I was coming here when I didn't know myself," he said. I followed his career closely— his three All-America years at BU; his decision to play professional baseball instead of football, though he had been the No. 1 draft choice of the Cleveland Browns, and his quick ascent to the Boston Red Sox after less than a year in the minors. In the late spring of 1955 he was batting .313 when he went into the hospital with pneumonia. On June 26, 1955, he died of a pulmonary embolism, leaving a severe void in many people's lives.

The other reason why that Thanksgiving day in Lynn continued to hold a special meaning for me was that the job I found in journalism, in 1951, turned out to involve sports. I went to work at *Sport* magazine as an apprentice editor, left in 1954 to become a freelance writer, and came back to *Sport* in 1960 as its editor.

Those were ideal years for a young man who had loved sports since he was a kid. Even after I left the magazine and went on to senior positions in book publishing, people kept telling me what a lucky guy I was to have been with *Sport* magazine. They were mainly middle-aged jocks who remembered pulling the four-color portraits of their favorite athletes out of the magazine and pinning them to their bedroom wall. I *was* lucky. I was able to edit the magazine and also write pieces about the leading athletes of the era. I also wrote biographies. One was of Mickey Mantle, "Master Yankee." Another was of my all-time favorite athlete, the Hall of Fame pitcher, Warren Spahn. Then there was Joe DiMaggio. I still have the $500 cancelled check that I had made out to DiMaggio, who then granted me an hour's interview. Though it depleted my earnings, I needed that interview to give credibility to the book I was writing on DiMaggio's "golden" year of 1941. I also helped three stars to write their autobiographies: Paul Horning, the Green Bay Packers' quarterback; Frank Robinson, the Hall of Fame slugger; and Gale Sayers, one of the greatest runners in National Football League history. The Sayers book, *I Am Third,* was made into the television movie, *Brian's Song.* Best of all, I got to present the Corvette automobile to the most valuable player of the World Series, the NFL championship game, and the National Basketball Association and National Hockey League championships in the years our magazine picked the winners. All the athletes were thrilled when, right after the game, I informed them they had won the Corvette. But in 1969 when I went down to the locker room to tell Joe Namath the good news, Namath having just led his three-touchdown underdog New York Jets to victory over the Baltimore Colts, he looked hard at me and said, "Is that one of those cars you have to give back after a year?" I assured him it was not.

I also saw some of the greatest sports events of those years: Wilma Rudolph winning a gold medal in both the 100- and the 200-meter race at the 1960 Rome Olympics; Bill Mazeroski's home run in the last of the ninth inning of the seventh game that won the 1960 World Series for the Pittsburgh Pirates against the Yankees; and the first fight between Joe Frazier and Muhammad Ali in 1971.

All these experiences came together for me when book publisher, Peter Mayer, asked me if I would like to write a book about memorable events in twentieth century sports. Would I? He is now my publisher. One of the first things I did was to revisit that Thanksgiving game of 1946 by meeting with Charlie Ruddock and his Lynn English co-star, the running back Billy Whelan. Whelan then was 67 years old and retired. After high school he had gone on to Cornell, where he was captain of the 1952 football team and was elected to Cornell's Athletic Hall of Fame. I wanted to ask Whelan whether that 27-27 tie against Lynn Classical had been the highlight of his athletic life. He said it had been, along with a game in 1951 when Cornell upset the University of Michigan, 20-7. "But in the case of Classical," he told me, "we were playing the prime rival, who was undefeated."

There it was—Whelan had given me an excellent guideline for my book. When I began to choose the events I wanted to write about, I developed two criteria. One was the importance of the game: Was a championship at stake? Was it against a prime rival? The other was the closeness of the game: Was it a tight, breathless, down-to-the-wire struggle? Eleven of my 13 events did go down to the wire. I also wanted to achieve a representative sample of the great spectator sports, and my final lineup includes three baseball games, two boxing fights, two football games, one Olympic track race, one Olympic hockey game, a U.S. Open golf championship, a Davis Cup tennis match, a college basketball nail-biter, and a World Cup soccer final.

Altogether I spent four years on my journey into the heroic past. Many hours went into watching films or tapes of the contests I was writing about. I watched them over and over again, particularly the last climactic minutes or seconds, to help me understand exactly what was going on down on the field, or the ice, or the court, or the golf course, or in the ring.

But what I knew I needed most—to bring fresh recollections to my stories—was to talk with the athletes who were involved in those epic events, as many people as I could who were prime participants in my chosen events and were not, in Casey Stengel's words, presently dead. That eliminated only two distant events, a 1908 baseball game and a 1923 heavyweight prizefight. But the voice of Fred Merkle and the blows leveled at each other by Jack Dempsey and Luis Firpo, I believe, come through loud and clear.

I was lucky to be the last journalist to hear Don Budge's account of the greatest tennis match of his life; Budge died six months after I talked with him at his Pennsylvania home. Many other voices sustained me during my writing of this book: Bobby Thomson and Ralph Branca talking about the playoff game that perhaps ranks No. 1 in the eyes of American sports fans; Billy Mills, the 10,000-meter runner in the 1964 Tokyo Olympics telling me about his search for "positive desires" while growing up on a Native American reservation that offered no such solaces to its children; Michelle Akers, the Babe Ruth of women's soccer, reminding me of her refusal to give in to a "spaghetti knee," other serious injuries and "chronic energy syndrome" that plagued most of her career.

But the most resonant interview was probably the one I had with Frank Champi, Harvard's second-string quarterback, who came into the game against undefeated Yale when the game was seemingly out of reach. When I talked with Champi many years later in his home in Newburyport, Massachusetts, I mentioned that one of the emptiest metaphors of all was the often heard claim that sports is a metaphor for life. He agreed with me. In one of his many soliloquies during our long talk, he said, "At certain times, there is a crystal-clear clarity in sports, and it gives life the kind of clarity it doesn't otherwise have."

That clarity is what I've gone looking for in this book.

AL SILVERMAN
May 2002

1

1908
MERKLE FOREVER
New York Giants
vs. Chicago Cubs

I know. You're asking, why am I beginning a book that's about heroic acts—about winners mostly—with a loser? Please be patient. The loser I'm writing about also happens to be a romantic hero, whose name continues to stand the test of time. It was invoked as recently as 1998, in connection with the second game of the American League championship series between the New York Yankees and Cleveland Indians.

The score was tied in the top of the 12th inning, and the Yankee second baseman Chuck Knoblauch was arguing with an umpire. Meanwhile, the ball was sitting behind him, unattended, allowing a vital run to score. The Indians went on to win the game by 4-1. On its editorial page the next day, the *New York Times* warned that if the Yankees lost the series Knoblauch would "forever be remembered in the same company as Fred (Bonehead) Merkle, who failed to reach second base in a crucial game in 1908."

On that doomed afternoon of September 23, 1908, the Polo Grounds was crammed with excitable spectators, hoping against hope that the New York Giants' starting pitcher, Christy Mathewson, the fans' "best-beloved," could stop the late surge of the Chicago Cubs. On the previous day, Chicago had swept a double-header from the Giants, and now the two teams were only a whisper apart. The Cubs had a 90-53 record, the Giants were 87-50, and Pittsburgh was breathing hard on them both. It was all up to Mathewson, who was 28 years old, in his ninth and greatest year with the Giants. But the handsome 6-foot-1 righthander—"a Greek god in flannels," sportswriter Frank Graham called him—would be pitching one of the most crucial games of his life. "The race is still of the closest, fiercest pattern and no one prophet ever prophed who could foretell the finish," wrote W. A. Phelon in the *Chicago Journal*."

In those early years of the twentieth century the National League was blessed with three amazing teams: the Giants, the Cubs, and the Pittsburgh Pirates. One man had mainly kept the Pirates in contention: shortstop John Peter "Honus" Wagner, a man so bowlegged, said one writer, that "he looked like a hoop rolling down the baselines." Wagner drove the Pirates to pennants in 1901, 1902, and 1903, and now, in 1908, at 34, he was leading the league in hits, doubles, triples, and runs batted in. Time would only magnify his reputation; in 2002, a Honus Wagner base-ball card, in "near mint condition," sold for $1.2 million..

For the Chicago Cubs, their success of the early 1900s can be traced to the day in 1902 when a scorer made this notation: "Double play—Tinker to Evers to Chance." That dynamic trio would become the centerpiece of a mighty major league dynasty.

Frank Chance began his career with the Cubs in 1898 as a catcher, and he switched to first base in 1902. Three years later, he added the title, player-manager, and took the Cubs to three straight pennants—an achievement for which he became forever known as "the peerless leader." Second baseman Johnny Evers and shortstop Joe Tinker both started with the Cubs in 1902. The fourth member of the infield, third baseman Harry Steinfeldt, didn't have rhythm in his name so he lost his shot at immor-tality when, in 1908, the New York newspaper columnist Franklin P. Adams sanctified the trio with a verse that he himself came to hate:

> *These are the saddest of possible words.*
> *Tinker to Evers to Chance.*
> *Trio of bear cubs and fleeter than birds.*
> *Tinker to Evers to Chance.*
>
> *Thoughtlessly pricking our gonfalon bubble.*
> *Making a Giant hit into a double.*
> *Words that are weighty with nothing but trouble—*
> *Tinker to Evers to Chance.*

Although the three men sang in harmony on the field, out of uniform they couldn't carry a tune together. Even Steinfeldt tended towards animosity; once, after a shouting match in the clubhouse, he went after Tinker with a pair of scissors. The chemistry was the worst between Tinker and Evers. "Every time something went wrong on the field," Johnny Evers told a New York sportswriter, "Joe would rush at me and get me by the throat and I'd punch him in the belly and try to cut him with my spikes. We didn't speak to each other friendly until we'd been out of baseball for years." In 1946, all three were voted into the Hall of Fame. By then Chance was gone, but Tinker and Evers were there for the ceremonies, and the two old men cried on each other's shoulders.

The New York Giants didn't require a trio to get them going, only a soloist: John Joseph "Little Napoleon" McGraw. In 1902, McGraw was stolen away from Baltimore, where he was managing the Orioles, by the Giants' owner, Andrew Freedman, the George Steinbrenner of his day, and then some. Freedman, a political ally of New York's Boss Tweed and the corrupt Tammany Hall gang, was arrogant and ruthless. When newspapermen covering the Giants criticized him in print, he would ban them from the ballpark. One sportswriter, Charlie Dryden of the *Chicago Tribune*, was exiled after he ran this quote verbatim from the Giants' owner: "I don't like what you have been writing about me. You are standing on the brink of an abscess and if you ain't careful I'll push you in."

But Freedman was never able to to push John McGraw around, as he found out almost as soon as he hired him, and he sold the club to a less excitable man named John T. Brush. McGraw may have missed the tempestuous Freedman, because they were two of a kind. The Giants' manager believed that his players should be rowdy as well as skilled. He encouraged them to engage in street battles on the field. When one of his sturdiest pitchers, "Iron Man" Joe McGinnity, got too old to pitch regularly, McGraw kept him around to goad players on the other team to fight, hoping some of them would be thrown out of the game. It didn't matter if the Iron Man also got the heave.

In 1903, his first full year as manager, McGraw's Giants won 84 games and finished second to the Pirates. In 1904, with McGinnity winning 35 games and Mathewson winning 33, the Giants won the pennant. In 1905, they won 105 games and took the pennant again, with Mathewson winning 31, along with a 1.28 earned run average. In the World Series against the Philadelphia Athletics, Matty threw three shutouts in six days. Joe McGinnity won the other game, and the Giants were world champions.

The batting star of the team was Mike Donlin; in 1904, his .356 average was third in the league and he led in runs scored, 124. "Turkey Mike" was a typical McGraw acquisition. He had earned a reputation as a man who liked to dance and drink by candlelight; showgirls particularly attracted his attention. Some years later, when night baseball was being played in the minors, he was heard to say, "Gee, imagine taking a ballplayer's nights away from him!" In 1906, Donlin broke his leg and played in only 39 games. He spent the rest of the season limping after a vaudeville actress named Mabel Hite. She, fully mobile, allowed him to catch up with her and they were married.

That same year, Mathewson came down with diphtheria and won only 22 games. In 1907, still not fully recovered, he won only 24. Other veteran Giants slumped that year, too, and McGraw decided to make some changes. He signed two minor league infielders, Larry Doyle and Charles "Buck" Herzog, and, in a blockbuster trade with Boston, he acquired the Red Sox player-manager, Fred Tenney, not to manage—McGraw would take care of that, thank you—but to play first base. In the same deal, McGraw picked up a promising young shortstop, Al Bridwell. The other new face, signed late in the season, was 18-year-old Fred Merkle.

"Here is something to consider," wrote a sportswriter named Bozeman Bulger of the *Chicago Tribune* near the end of the 1908 season. "Suppose Fred Tenney should be crippled, that would be a calamity, wouldn't it? Yes, it would in one way, but it wouldn't keep the Giants from winning the pennant. There is a young fellow on the bench named Fred Merkle who can fill that job better than nine-tenths of the first basemen in the league."

When Fred Merkle, a tall and polite Midwesterner, reached the Polo Grounds on the morning of September 23, he almost keeled over, for he saw his name in a major league starting lineup for the first time. Fred Tenney had awakened with a severe backache and couldn't play. Merkle was excited. Although he had never started a game, he had done his share for the team. In 1907, he played in 15 games, got 12 hits and impressed at first base. In 1908, he was in 38 games and hit one home run as a pinch-hitter. "The youngster is of splendid proportion," wrote a New York reporter. "Best of all, he has plenty of nerve and a cool head."

As the game was about to begin, Merkle watched his idol Christy Mathewson stride to the mound to face the Cubs. The crowd roared its adoration. Matty's opponent would be Jack Pfiester, who in 1907 had led the league with a 1.15 earned run average. Pfiester was remembered mostly for the way he roused himself when facing the Giants, thereby earning his nickname "the Giant killer."

Both men pitched brilliantly. The game was scoreless until the fifth inning, when Joe Tinker drove one through the infield onto the grass in right center. Rightfielder Turkey Donlin rushed over and made a desperate stab at the ball with his foot—hardly an orthodox move. But this dance step failed, and the ball carried to the ropes that kept spectators off the field. Tinker's inside-the-park home run gave the Cubs the lead.

The Giants fought back an inning later. Buck Herzog smashed a ball that handcuffed third baseman Steinfeldt, who then made a wild throw to first base that allowed Herzog to go to second. Catcher Roger Bresnahan sacrificed him to third. Up came Donlin, hoping to atone for his soft-shoe routine, and he did, lashing a pitch between two infielders to score Herzog. The game was tied, 1-1.

Through eight innings, it was a classic pitching battle. Mathewson had held the Cubs to five hits and struck out nine. Jack the Giant Killer had allowed the Giants only four hits. Then came the fateful bottom of the ninth—and a trap that the Cubs had set for the Giants three weeks earlier.

The date was September 4, and the two teams that were chasing New York—the Cubs and Pirates—were involved in a memorable game of their own in Pittsburgh. The Cubs' ace, Mordecai

"Three Finger" Brown, who would win 29 games that year, was pitching a shutout going into the last of the tenth. His nickname came from an accident at the age of seven in which a farm machine mangled two fingers on his right hand—a disfigurement that caused his pitches to dip and swerve in unexpected ways.

Player-manager Frank Chance opened the tenth with a single. Tommy Leach sacrificed him to second. Honus Wagner singled sharply, though Johnny Evers was able to slow up the ball enough so that Clarke couldn't score. Then Brown hit rookie first baseman Warren Gill, loading the bases. After a strikeout for the second out, John Wilson, who had recently been recalled from the minors, embarrassed Three Finger by singling into centerfield. Clarke scored, and the game was over—or so everyone thought.

But the Cubs' second baseman, Johnny Evers, saw that the runner on first had dashed off the field instead of running down to second base and touching the bag. "Throw me the ball," Evers hollered to his centerfielder, Art Hofman. Then, with the ball in his hand and one foot on the base, he yelled to umpire Hank O'Day that Gill was the third out. O'Day didn't respond; he later said he never heard Evers because of the noise of the crowd. The next day, the Cubs protested the loss to National League president Harry C. Pulliam. Umpire O'Day had previously told Pulliam that "the game was fairly won." Pulliam rejected the protest, saying, "I think the baseball public prefers to see games settled on the field and not in this office."

Now, on September 23, centerfielder Cy Seymour led off the last half of the ninth inning for the Giants with a hot groundball to Evers, who swallowed it up, Evers to Chance, for the out. Third baseman Art Devlin singled into centerfield but was forced at second when leftfielder Moose McCormick grounded to Evers. That made two outs, and up stepped Fred Merkle, deep in his debut role as a starter.

In the *New York Times'* account of the game, W. W. Aulick, wrote, "Merkle, who failed us the day before in an emergency, is at bat, and we pray of him that he mend his ways." Aulick was referring to Merkle's unsuccessful effort as a pinch-hitter. The *Times'* reporter then followed with a sentence that still rings with irony almost a century later: "If he will only single we will ignore any errors he may make in the rest of his natural life." The kid came through for Aulick, blasting a single down the rightfield line. Now, with McCormick on third and Merkle on first, it was up to Al Bridwell. This was Bridwell's first year with the Giants, and he was enjoying himself. He was a spectacular shortstop and was batting .285, a respectable average for a number eight hitter. Bridwell scorched a single over second base into centerfield—a ball hit so hard that umpire Bob Emslie had to dive to the ground to get out of the way. He was thus flat on his back in the ten seconds that shook the world.

But various other principals understood what was happening, especially a Giant benchwarmer named Fred Snodgrass. I've listened many times to Snodgrass's voice on tape reconstructing that incident. Many of baseball's oldtimers can be heard on Lawrence S. Ritter's audio edition of his classic book, *The Glory of Their Times,* but none of the voices are as sonorous as Snodgrass's—a deep, melodic John Wayne timbre. He could have been a world-class preacher.

"In those days, as soon as a game ended at the Polo Grounds," Snodgrass says, "ushers would open the gates from the stands in the field, and the people would pour out and rush at you. Because of that, as soon as a game was over we benchwarmers all made it a practice to sprint to the clubhouse as fast as we could. And that was precisely the reason why Fred Merkle got in that awful jam. He was so used to sitting on the bench all during the game, and then jumping up with the rest of us and taking off as fast as we could for the clubhouse, that on this particular day he did it by force of habit and never gave it another thought. McCormick scored easily from first on Bridwell's single. He could have walked in. The game was won and over, and Merkle lit out for the clubhouse, as he had been doing all season long. That was Merkle's downfall. Because, technically, the rules of baseball are that to formally complete the play he had to touch second base, which was unoccupied, since Bridwell had moved on to third."

The crowd knew none of this. All they knew was that Bridwell had slashed a single that brought in the winning run, and the first wave of fans began vaulting out of the stands onto the field.

Like them, Merkle thought the game was over. Halfway between first and second base, seeing the winning run about to cross the plate, he changed directions and sprinted towards the clubhouse. He wanted to get there before the crowd had a chance to grab at him and choke him half to death—that's what he had done all year long at the Polo Grounds, run like the dickens for the clubhouse when the game was over, or risk being mashed to pulp.

But one person in the Polo Grounds kept his head when everyone else was going crazy. Johnny Evers remembered that game in Pittsburgh, back on September 4, when his team lost to the Pirates even though the runner on first had run off the field without touching second base. Umpire Hank O'Day refused to change the call. But afterward, Evers had put him on notice that Rule 59 had to be obeyed, and he knew that the umpire-in-chief remembered. Now, standing on second base, defying the howling crowd, he hollered frantically for the ball.

Gridlock continued to prevail between the pitcher's mound and second base. Players from both teams were milling around along with fans, yelling at each other. Finally the telltale ball was thrown back into the mob and was intercepted by the Giants' Iron Man Joe McGinnity, who threw it into the stands.

In 1999, a letter from McGinnity, written in 1926, turned up at a Sotheby's auction of baseball memorabilia. It explained for the first time what had really happened at that feverish moment. "Contrary to common belief," McGinnity wrote, "I was not trying to 'break up' any play that Mr. Evers may have had when Merkle failed to advance to second base. Only a few weeks earlier, umpire O'Day ruled against Mr. Evers on this very same play and I assumed he would not honor it again. However, it seems umpire O'Day realized his error after checking the rules book, and this time he correctly called Merkle out and did not allow the run to score. My throwing of the baseball into the seats was an act of jubilation, brought on by the belief that we had just won the pennant."

Evers had somehow found another baseball—no one ever knew where it came from—and holding it aloft, his foot planted on second base, he demanded of the umpires that the runner, Fred Merkle, be called out.

The two umpires looked at each other. Bob Emslie, the umpire on the bases, told O'Day he hadn't seen the play—he had been flat on the ground. "Did *you* see what happened?" he asked.

"I did," said O'Day with Biblical certainty, though in fact he hadn't seen anything; he had been covering home plate. But O'Day, as McGinnity suggested, did remember that September 4 game, when Johnny Evers hollered at him to call the play correctly. This time he would call it Evers's way. "Merkle did not touch second base," O'Day said. "The runner is forced at second and the game is a tie."

A tie? That being the case, the umpires should have resumed the game on the spot. But how could they clear the field of a horde that was growling in rage? A photograph taken at that moment shows that all the smiling faces in the crowd have been replaced by uncertainty and menace. Something was up, and the fans who had been wet-nursed in the John McGraw style—scratching and clawing and snarling and battling, always seeking an edge—weren't going to stand for it. Many fans who had heard Evers calling for the ball began to maul the Cub players. Then even the umpires began to get roughed up. Finally, under police escort, O'Day and Emslie were hustled into the clubhouse.

The Giants declared the game theirs, 2-1. Cubs manager Frank Chance declared it a forfeit because the game should have continued. Two days later, National League president Pulliam confirmed the umpire's decision and declared that the game had ended in a tie. But it wasn't until October 5 that he called for a playoff game if the National League season ended in a tie between the Giants and the Cubs, to be held in New York.

The players didn't know any of this as they gathered at the Polo Grounds the next day for the fourth game of the series. A rumor had spread during the night that young Fred Merkle had committed suicide. But here he was at the Polo Grounds, alive but unwell—inconsolable, in fact; he squirreled himself away at the furthest end of the dugout.

Thanks again to Christy Mathewson, the Giants beat the Cubs, 5-4. After his nine-inning heroics of the previous day, Matty came into the game and saved it with three stout innings of relief.

But odd things began to happen to the Giants after that. First, they lost a doubleheader to the lowly Cincinnati Reds. Then, they went to Philadelphia to play a team they had beaten 11 out of 14 times, and lost all three games. The Cubs finished their season three days ahead of New York, beating the Pirates 5-2 and eliminating them from the race. The Giants needed to sweep their last three games against the Boston Braves, and they did.

So here the two teams were, 98-55. The playoff decreed by president Pulliam because of Merkle's mistake would take place on October 8 at the Polo Grounds. Christy Mathewson, in his auto-biography, *Pitching In A Pinch*, compared the game to "the battle of Waterloo and the assassination of President Lincoln."

"Fred Merkle's best chance to go down in baseball history," wrote John E. Wray of the *St. Louis Post Dispatch* on the morning of the game, "is for the Giants to lose today. At least a dozen persons will remember him for life." Ever since the incident, Merkle had begged McGraw to send him back to the minors, send him any-where but here. McGraw wouldn't hear of it; he thought highly of his plucky 19-year-old. Besides, he had other things to think about. Christy Mathewson would be his starting pitcher. Who else could it be? It had been Matty's greatest year—a league-leading 37 wins (in 56 games); a league-leading five saves, a league-leading 259 strike-outs, a league-leading 1.43 earned run average. But also a league-leading and exhausting 390 innings pitched. The Mathewsons lived near the Polo Grounds, and their sleep had been interrupted by a crowd outside the ballpark that hollered and tooted horns through the night and would be a considerable trial for the police the next day. When Matty struggled out of bed that morning he told his wife, Jane, that he didn't think he could make it. "There's no life in my arm," he said. "It feels as heavy as a board."

When he got to the clubhouse he told his manager, who was also one of his closest friends, the same thing. "You've got to do it, Christy," John McGraw said. "I wouldn't trust this game to anyone else."

"Well, I'll start and go as far as I can," Matty told him.

October 8 was as warm as a perfect day in July, and an estimated 35,000 people turned out, the largest crowd at that time for a baseball game anywhere. But it was a riotous crowd. Thousands of fans who had tickets found it impossible to force their way through the mobs to the entrances. Outside the park, the mob set fire to the leftfield fence, ready to dash through as soon as the flames weakened the boards. Firemen arrived and trained their hoses on the fire and then on the crowd. Those who escaped ran into the stands dripping wet. Mounted police galloped into the fray to scatter the spectators. Various Cubs players received death threats. Mordecai Brown said he had gotten phone and mail messages saying that he would be killed if he pitched and beat the Giants. "The crowds fought the police all the time, it seemed to us as we sat in the dugout," Brown said. "From the stands, there was a steady roar of abuse. I never heard anybody or any set of men called as many foul names as the Giants fans called us that day from the time we showed up till it was over." Just before the start of the game, someone hurled a bottle that struck Frank Chance in the neck. He went down to his knees, gasping for breath. He was not examined until after the game—the blow had broken a cartilage in his neck. The player-manager would not leave the playing field.

He decided he would start Jack "the Giant killer" Pfiester. It was almost a fatal mistake. In the last of the first inning, the Giants had a chance to put him away. Pfiester's first pitch caught Fred Tenney in the leg. Buck Herzog walked. With men on first and second, Roger Bresnahan struck out and Herzog was picked off first by a rifle throw from catcher John Kling. But Mike Donlin followed with a smash down the rightfield line and Tenney scored the first run of the game. When Pfiester walked Cy Seymour, Chance had seen enough. He replaced the ex-Giant killer with his ace, Three Finger Brown, who struck out Art Devlin to end the inning.

In the top of the third, Tinker tripled and John Kling singled him home with the tying run. Mathewson got the next two batters, then walked Johnny Evers. Frank Schulte, the rightfielder, doubled to right, scoring Kling, and the peerless Frank Chance, defying his neck injury, stroked a double that scored two more runs. The Cubs now led by 4-1, and Mathewson was disconsolate and arm weary. But he continued to pitch with guile and heart, holding the Cubs scoreless over the next four innings.

In the last of the seventh, the Giants rallied briefly. Art Devlin and Moose McCormick started it with singles, and Brown walked Bridwell. Bases loaded, nobody out. Jack Doyle came up to pinch-hit for Mathewson; the great pitcher's ordeal was over. Doyle hit a pop foul close to the stands. As Kling ran over to catch it, a whiskey glass, two beer bottles, and a derby hat sailed into his vision. Somehow, Kling held onto the ball. Tenney got Devlin home with a sacrifice fly, but Herzog grounded to Tinker for the final out.

The score was 4-2, Cubs, and that's how it would end; the Giants could do no more against Brown. In the ninth inning, he retired the last three Giants on four pitches. Then the new National League champions ran for their lives. Harry Steinfeldt was struck in the face and Art Hofman was hit on the nose by a bottle. Chance, Pfeister, and Kling ran towards the clubhouse with a half-dozen policemen around them, flailing their clubs. But not until the cops drew their revolvers did the mob give way.

Two days later, the Cubs faced Detroit in the World Series. The Cubs beat the Tigers in five games and became world champions.

As for the Giants, John McGraw had a message for the press: "My team lost something it should have won three weeks before. But—and this cannot be put too strongly—it's criminal to say that Merkle is stupid and to blame the loss of the pennant on him. He didn't cost us the pennant. We lost a dozen games that we should have won. We were robbed of it and you can't say that Merkle did it."

McGraw's words didn't work. That fall, a comedian in a vaudeville skit said, "I call my cane Merkle because it has a bone head." The epithet, "the Merkle boner," stuck in the craw of this gentle man until the end of his days.

Nevertheless Frederick Charles Merkle had a productive career that lasted 16 years. He was a key player with the Giants as they won pennants in 1911, 1912, and 1913—he hit .309 in 1912—and later became a coach for the

New York Yankees. He retired from baseball in 1927 and lived a quiet life in Florida. He didn't want to be bothered any more by people recalling his "boner."

But in 1950, Merkle accepted an invitation from Horace Stoneham, owner of the Giants, to attend an old-timer's day at the Polo Grounds. There he found a pleasant surprise awaiting him. He was lionized by fans, and the press treated him with tact and sympathy. A photograph of that occasion shows a smiling 61-year-old man sitting with the widow of John McGraw.

The reemergence of Fred Merkle inspired the Dodgers' peerless announcer, Red Barber, to ask the great umpire Bill Klem if he would review the Merkle incident. Klem said he would do it for Merkle's sake because of all the punishment he had taken.

"There was no real force on that play," Klem concluded. "It was a clean hit to the outfield. The winning run was across the plate before the ball was returned to the infield, and that should have ended it. The game was over when the winning run came over." Klem's interpretation differs from the one delivered by Fred Snodgrass; over the years other views have been offered by baseball archivists. In the end it doesn't matter who was correct. The play stands.

But Fred Merkle felt better about himself after his warm reception at the Polo Grounds. He returned to Daytona Beach, where he died six years later at the age of 67. Except that he hasn't died. The curse for all people who play in public is that their failures are celebrated, and if they are original enough they become immortal. So Fred Merkle lives forever.

2

1923
THE BATTLE OF
THE CENTURY
Dempsey vs. Firpo

The 1923 newsreel is old and grainy, and the narrator matches the film in his flat and tinny voice, a carnival barker on the sell. "Here at his training camp in Atlantic City," the voice says, "Luis Angel Firpo displays the powerful arms that have brought disaster to a long list of victims. With these weapons Firpo has clubbed his way past fighter after fighter until they now call him 'the Wild Bull of the Pampas.'"

The 26-year-old, 6-foot-3 Argentinian, naked to the waist, his back to the camera, is seen banging away at a punching bag, preparing for the fight of his life against the heavyweight champion of the world, Jack Dempsey. The fight is to be held on September 14, 1923, at the Polo Grounds in New York, and it's already sold out—"a million dollar gate," as they called it in those days.

Dempsey, at 28, was a known commodity. The scowling black-haired Irish assassin with fierce blue-black eyes, from Manassa, Colorado—"the Manassa Mauler"—had already defended his title four times and was on his way to becoming one of the emblematic figures of America's first golden age of sports, the '20s—along with Babe Ruth, Red Grange, Bill Tilden, and Bobby Jones. His opponent was something quite different—an exotic from a faraway country, relatively unknown in the world of professional boxing.

About Luis Angel Firpo, two things could be said with certainty. He had never been consumed by Jack Dempsey's desperate urge to engage in "the sweet science" of boxing. But if he could make his iron fists work for him, he, a man of surpassing frugality, would become rich. Born in Buenos Aires on October 11, 1896, to a poor family—his father was Italian, his mother Spanish—he went to work at an early age and held various jobs as a cowboy, brickyard laborer, butcher, and drugstore clerk. At 23, he joined an athletic club in Buenos Aires and took up boxing for exercise. He was an impressive looking young man, taller than anyone, trim and muscled, hairy in the arms and legs and chest, with huge fists. He didn't know quite what to do with those fists, but he enjoyed throwing roundhouse rights at those who were willing to get in the ring with him. Every once in a while his fist would connect, and the thud of an opponent hitting the floor could be heard all over the gym. His friends urged him to become a professional boxer. There was no such thing in Argentina at the time, but he was told that there was money to be made in neighboring Latin American countries. That was all he had to hear.

Firpo's only demand about turning pro was that he wouldn't pay anyone to teach him. He would teach himself—on-the-job training. After six months of self-help he felt that he was ready and traveled to Montevideo to fight the alleged heavyweight champion of Uruguay. He was knocked out in the first round. "But it did not draw me down," Firpo said afterward. "I was not chastised." He simply tried another country, Chile. There he won his first recorded fight, knocking out an American named William Daley. Then, in two years of roaming around South America, he kept winning his fights, most of them knockouts. He had no finesse, didn't know how to move in the ring, how to feint, cover, slip a punch. He just kept throwing bombs.

Argentina, noting the success of their homeboy, legalized the sport, just in time for him to fight a tough American fighter, "Gunboat" Smith, in Buenos Aires. Firpo caught Gunboat at the right time—by 1921 he had weathered 130 tough fights—and toppled him with a firecracker to the jaw in the 12th round. The local press declared Firpo "the South American heavyweight champion."

The news reached the manager of a tough New Jersey heavyweight called "Sailor" Tom Maxted. The manager had heard about Firpo—his many weaknesses and his one strength—and raced to see a Newark promoter. "Get us this bum," the manager said.

"He ain't nothin' but a bum," the promoter said.

"I know he's a bum," the manager said, "but the people around here don't."

Early in 1922, Luis Firpo set sail for New York. He traveled light, a straw hat on his head, a high mustard-yellow celluloid collar around his neck, a baggy $15 suit on his body that someone said had been derived from oatmeal. He carried all his belongings in a cardboard suitcase.

The fight was held on March 20, 1922, at the Laurel Gardens in Newark. Sailor Tom Maxted entered the ring the 14-1 favorite. Firpo was unmarked—he looked like a matinee idol. His hair was black and curly, his body long and lean and not overly muscled. His face was that of an innocent, but with calculation in his eyes. By contrast, the Sailor's face bore the marks of his trade—scars above both eyes, a bashed-in nose, and a series of tattooed crosses running from his waist to his neck. Firpo asked his second, Calvin Respress, what those crosses were all about. Each cross, Respress explained, represented a knockout by the Sailor. He told Luis it was nothing to be concerned about.

Firpo fought unconcerned, withstanding rushes from Maxted, pushing him away, and throwing rights all over the ring. In the fourth round one of them landed on Sailor Tom's jaw, and that was that. Firpo looked down at the fallen fighter with all those crosses and thought, the last cross is so heavy he will never rise again.

In his second American fight, two weeks later, he faced a confident pug named Joe McCann. "The way he throws punches," McCann said, "he won't hit me in 2000 years. I'll grab that phony title and go places with it." The only place McCann went was to sleep, in the sixth round. Afterwards, Firpo asked the promoter innocently if this victory was enough to establish him as a serious opponent for Jack Dempsey. The question was ignored, but Firpo hadn't lost heart. "Enough man I will fight and knock out so they will let me knock out Dempsey," he said. "I am of the determination."

At that moment the manager of a fighter called "Italian" Jack Herman was looking for a not-too-worthy opponent for his ambitious heavyweight, to be held at Ebbets Field, home of the Brooklyn

Dodgers. Firpo was offered $1,000 for the semi-final bout on the card. Thinking like a chief financial officer rather than a boxer, he said, "Will moving pictures be taken of the fight?" Only the main bout, he was told. Firpo said if they would take pictures of his fight and give him South American rights, he would pay the cost out of his $1,000 guarantee. The offer was accepted.

Firpo knocked out Italian Jack Herman in the fifth round. As soon as the film was developed, he put on a fresh celluloid collar and his oatmeal suit and sailed back to Argentina. Armed with the moving pictures of his "epic" victory over Herman, Firpo barnstormed all over Latin America, collected an estimated $25,000, and waited to hear from the noted promoter Tex Rickard, who had a proprietary interest in Jack Dempsey.

William Harrison Dempsey was born on June 24, 1895, in a wood cabin in Manassa, Colorado, the ninth child in a family of 11. His parents called him "Harry" but, when he was 16, jumping off freight trains to fight for nickels and dimes in the small towns of Colorado and Utah, he heard of a middleweight champion of the 1880s who was called "Jack Dempsey the Nonpareil." Jack Dempsey he would become, though not yet a nonpareil. In 1915 and 1916, he had a number of real fights under a series of Humpty-Dumpty managers who would pocket most of the money he was earning. Still, young Dempsey loved to smack his opponents, and he beat up on the likes of Chief Gordon, Two Round Gillian, Boston Bear Cat, Wild Bert Kenney.

In 1917, he met the manager of his life, Jack "Doc" Kearns. "He was devious, untruthful, unscrupulous," Paul Gallico, one of the best writers in that first golden age of sports, wrote about Kearns, "but quick-witted and everything else that a great manager of a prize fighter ought to be." By 1919, under Kearns's direction, Dempsey had won 31 of 32 fights, with 22 knockouts, 17 of them in the first round. He had cleaned out the heavyweight division. On July 4, 1919, he would fight Jess Willard, the heavyweight champion of the world. Willard, who was 38 years old and a blubbery 245 pounds, wasn't much interested in fighting anymore, but he couldn't resist the $100,000 offer from Tex Rickard, the most renowned fight promoter of the era. Dempsey would have his biggest payday, $27,500. Despite the Ohio Ministerial Association recoiling at "this invasion of our state by barbarians," the fight was held in Toledo, Ohio, in a newly built arena that could hold 60,000. Only 19,500 showed up, but they were treated to the coronation of a new American hero. In the first round, Dempsey, 24 years old, 187 pounds, eluded two jabs from Willard, then knocked down the champ six times. He eased up in the second round—the temperature was 110 degrees—but after round three Willard sat in his corner, his right eye tightly closed, six teeth gone, the right side of his face swollen to almost twice its normal size. The towels of surrender flashed into the ring. The Manassa Mauler was the heavyweight champion of the world.

In 1921, Tex Rickard staged a masterpiece for Dempsey, matching him against the Frenchman, Georges Carpentier, light heavyweight champion of the world. The fight was held at Rickard's arena, "Boyle's Thirty Acres," and attracted a new clientele to the sport—not just down-and-dirty fight fans and bettors, but legions of women, public officials, and celebrities from show business, all willing to go travel to uncouth Jersey City. More than 82,000 spectators flocked there for boxing's first million-dollar gate.

How was it that a foreigner was able to transform the sport in America? Georges Carpentier was not only a boxer: he was a war hero, a romantic Gallic figure with blond hair, sparkling gray eyes, and a slender body, weighing only 172 pounds compared to Dempsey's 188 pounds. Elmer Davis, who covered the fight for the *New York Times,* said that Carpentier's "eager intensity, his fiery slightness, gave to some of the onlookers a curious sense of resemblance between him and another French champion of old, Joan of Arc."

On July 2, 1921, the modern-day Joan of Arc, with a sympathetic audience watching, lasted only four rounds. In the second round Carpentier landed a powerful right-hand punch on Dempsey's chin that rattled the champ, but broke the challenger's thumb. It was the only serious blow the Frenchman was able to inflict on his opponent. In the fourth round, Dempsey attacked fiercely, knocking Carpentier down with a series of blows. When he came up from the floor, Dempsey struck him with a right to the ribs and followed with a right to the jaw that finished the gallant contender.

The amazing $1,789,233 gate inaugurated boxing's golden age. But Tex Rickard couldn't milk the new popularity of the sport. The problem was a lack of real contenders in the heavyweight division. As a result, Dempsey didn't have one title fight in 1922.

Rickard was haunted by the success of the Dempsey-Carpentier match. In this brash post-World War I era, patriotism in America had given way to jingoism. The fans loved to see a foreigner beat up by the heavyweight boxing champion of the world, who, of course, was American. Rickard understood this but there was only one heavyweight who could possibly fill the house, and he would have to be built up. Rickard duly wired Luis Angel Firpo to come back to New York. He offered Firpo a guarantee of $20,000 to fight Bill Brennan, who had gone 12 tough rounds with Dempsey in 1920, to be the main attraction of the last boxing card at the old Madison Square Garden. Firpo counted the zeroes and wired back an economical reply: "Okay."

Brennan got things started early. In the third round he clipped Firpo over his left eye, leaving what would be a permanent scar. The Wild Bull of the Pampas was bleeding profusely, and the referee kept saying something that he didn't understand. Firpo spoke the only two words of English he could think of: "All right, all right." The referee allowed the fight to continue. In the 12th round Brennan, who had said scornfully of Firpo that "he punches like a guy throwing rocks," was hit on the head by a Firpo rock, and was counted out.

Two months later, Firpo knocked out Jack McAuliffe in the third round. Then he traveled to Havana and knocked out his old friend, Italian Jack Herman, in the second round. He went on to Mexico City for a second-round knockout of Jim Hibbard.

On July 12, 1923, Rickard devised a showcase for Firpo. He would fight the old champ, Jess Willard, now 42 years old but willing to expose the foreigner's shortcomings. A crowd of 80,000 gathered at Boyle's Thirty Acres. They came not for Luis Angel Firpo, but hoping to witness the miracle of rejuvenation by an *American* fighter.

Alas, it was not to be. Firpo wore down his ancient opponent through seven rounds. Then, in the Willard tradition, down on one knee in his corner, he allowed the towels to be flung into the ring one last time for old Jess.

Rickard was happy. He thought of the fans' reactions to Firpo at the fight. The women, especially, seemed taken by his darkly handsome face, his demeanor in the ring, his stoicism in the face of pain, his way of flinging those fists around. Rickard knew that in Latin America Firpo was a hero wherever he went, the Muhammad Ali of his day. Cigars were named after him, and toothpaste, too, and even "Firpo Form-Fitting Evening Suits." Rickard made his move.

He went to Doc Kearns, who, earlier in the year, had on his own promoted a heavyweight championship in Shelby, Montana. Dempsey beat a local misfit, Tom Gibbons, in an uninspiring 15-round decision. Only 8,000 fans showed up. Kearns needed a redemptive fight for his man, and redemptive money. Rickard gave it to him—a $300,000 guarantee and 37½ percent of the gross gate. For Firpo it would be his biggest ever payday—a $50,000 guarantee and 12½ percent of the gate.

When the fight was announced, sportswriters laughed it off. "Firpo is the clumsiest looking oaf ever proposed as a challenger to a heavyweight champion," one New York columnist wrote. "Has Rickard run out of common sense as well as competitors?" But the writers discovered that Firpo, because of his parsimonious ways, would make good copy. It wasn't so much that he was cheap out of the ring—that he bought shirts in bargain basements and would never tip a waiter. It was his cheapness as a professional boxer. He wouldn't tip gym attendants, he hated to pay sparring partners, he refused to shell out one third of his purses for a manager. He also didn't believe in spending money on training camps. He would keep in shape and learn more—and get paid—by fighting real fights. So he signed up for a series of pre-Dempsey matches that gave Rickard indigestion. "What if he should get knocked out?" the promoter moaned.

The Wild Bull of the Pampas came close. Between July 14 and August 17, he fought four times—in Battle Creek, Omaha, Philadelphia, and Indianapolis. He knocked out two of his opponents, but the two other bouts went the ten-round limit and were called "no-decisions." Was this the way to draw a crowd for what Rickard hoped would be his second million-dollar gate?

Finally, on August 18, less than a month before the meeting with Dempsey, Firpo gave in. He went to Atlantic City to train for the fight that the press would later call the most dramatic sports event of the first half of the century.

Each heavyweight champion in the first years of the 20th century, from Jim Jeffries to Jack Dempsey, reflected the clamor of American life It was a restless and raucous era, an era of hope and of change: immigrants flocking into the country to escape the poverty and oppression of their homelands; gutty citizens moving towards the Pacific to conquer the West; African-Americans bolting the rural south for the big cities of the north, seeking jobs and dignity for their race. In this oddly mixed cauldron, boxing flourished.

In 1899, James J. Jeffries, the 6-foot-2, 206-pound "California Grizzly," knocked out Bob Fitzsimmons in the 11th round to win the heavyweight title. Jeffries was a hard, no-nonsense kind of guy who defended his championship in style, knocking out Fitzsimmons once more, and another ex-champ, James J. "Gentlemen Jim" Corbett. But when in 1905 he found himself without any worthy opponents, he retired from the ring. There was, however, one worthy opponent around, but no one would fight him: Jack Johnson, who was African-American.

It was John L. Sullivan himself who had drawn the color line back in 1892s, when he issued a challenge to fight any and all challengers—"first come, first served," he had announced, "who are white. I will not fight a negro. I never have and I never shall."

By 1908, Tommy Burns, a French Canadian, was the champ, and he avoided Jack Johnson as long as he could. The challenger followed Burns everywhere, finally catching up with him in Sydney, Australia. A local promoter guaranteed Burns $30,000 if he would fight Johnson. Money, once more, talked. The fight was held on December 26, 1908, and in the 14th round, police jumped into the ring to save Burns further punishment. Johnson was the heavyweight champion of the world.

The American sporting public was not happy, nor were many of its representatives in the press. "Jeffries must emerge from the alfalfa farm," Jack London wrote in the *New York Herald,* "and remove the smile from Johnson's face." At first Jeffries resisted. He was 35 years old, had ballooned to 250 pounds, was content in his retirement. But when Tex Rickard, the co-promoter, who would also be the referee, guaranteed Jeffries $101,000, the old champ one more took up the profession.

Jim Corbett was in Jeffries' corner when the fight began in Reno, Nevada, on July 4, 1910 (matchmakers saved Independence Day for their most patriotic events). "Stand up and fight, you coward," Corbett hollered at Johnson early on as the fit 192-pound challenger was feeling out his opponent. But in the 15th round, when Jeffries was battered to the canvas, Corbett ran towards the ropes crying, "Oh, don't, Jack, don't hit him." Johnson did strike his opponent once more; Jeffries fell again, and could not get up.

One great white hope had been dismantled, and the black American was still champion of the world. And that night, in the large cities of America, race riots broke out and at least eight people lost their lives.

It wasn't until 1915 that a new white hope was found: Jess Willard, a six-foot-six, 230-pound giant from Pottawatomie, Kansas, always accommodating. By this time Johnson was in exile. He had been convicted of transporting an underage white woman across state lines "for immoral purposes," a violation of the Mann Act. He married the woman, but it didn't matter. The fight was held in the brilliant sunshine of Havana, Cuba, on April 5, 1915. Willard knocked out Johnson in the 26th round. Lying on his back, Johnson had his arms up around his head. Some said he was shielding his eyes from the sun, feigning that he was out cold. There was no questioning the propriety of the fight by the *New York Times,* which noted that Jess Willard had "restored pugilistic supremacy to the white race." It wasn't until the mid-1930s—the time of Joe Louis—that the color line disappeared from the heavyweight division.

Dempsey trained for the Firpo fight at Crying Uncle Tom Luther's Hotel, a few miles from Saratoga Springs, New York. Paul Gallico, who was then a cub reporter for the *New York Daily News,* was captivated by the scene. He described "sparring partners with bent noses and twisted ears, Negroes and white fighters, boxing writers, handsome state troopers in their gray and purple uniforms, doubtful blondes who wandered in and out of the layout of the wooden hotel and lake-front bungalows, and blondes about whom there was no doubt at all. There was nothing either high hat or sinister about the plant. It was gay, low, vulgar, Rabelaisian, and rather marvelous."

The Firpo camp at Atlantic City was no Saratoga Springs. The challenger wouldn't talk to reporters or let anyone take his pictures unless they paid him for the privilege. When Firpo remained aloof, reporters began looking for the offbeat, and they didn't have far to look. One major Firpo preoccupation was his consumption of food. Day and night the press watched in wonder as Firpo sat down for various meals, stuffed himself to the breaking point, then dropped off to sleep.

But it was his behavior with accounting ledgers that set him apart from the other fighters On the night before the fight, sportswriter W. O. McGeehan of the *New York Herald Tribune* chanced upon Firpo in his hotel room. The Wild Bull was sitting at a table "stark naked with a pencil in his hand." Firpo wasn't disconcerted by the sportswriter's visit. He explained that he was merely calculating how much income tax he would have to pay to the United States government for fighting Dempsey. Then, a beseeching look on his face, he asked the sportswriter if he could win the fight. McGeehan just shrugged.

The truth was, none of the sportswriters gave him a chance to beat Dempsey. Firpo, one of them said, was "just a right hand swinger who telegraphed his punches from the next county— collect—and hoped they would find the right address."

On September 14, 1923, a festive crowd jammed the Polo Grounds, weaving into the stadium as mounted police maintained order. All the seats, including those that, except for the ring, filled the playing field, were taken. Everyone who was everyone was there: the Vanderbilts, the Biddles, the Rothschilds, the Whitneys, along such athletic heroes as two ex-heavyweight champions, Gentleman Jim Corbett and Jess Willard, plus John McGraw, and Babe Ruth. The official attendance figure was 82,000, and 25,000 more were turned away. Most of the crowd were in their seats two hours before the fight, watching the preliminary bouts.

Just before 9 P.M. a cheer rose from one corner of the grandstand. A file of policemen was moving towards the ring. In their midst strode Luis Angel Firpo. "He looked fierce and dangerous as he approached the ring," Elmer Davis reported. "But he was frowning with a faraway, nervous, almost wistful look—the sort of look that comes over the face of even the least wistful of men as he prepares to get in the ring with Jack Dempsey." Firpo was attired in splendor. He wore a long, priestly robe covered with large black-and-yellow checks, with purple cuffs and collar. He climbed into the ring, looked around at the crowd, possibly counting the gate, then sat back, impassive, on his stool.

Next, a joyous roar from the crowd announced that Jack Dempsey had arrived and was climbing into the ring. The champion wore white satin trunks, with a white cardigan draped over his shoulders. The first thing he did was to stride over to Firpo, a slight smile on his face, and move his hand glove to glove with Firpo's. The challenger, surprised by the gesture, simply bowed his head.

Now Joe Humphries, the famous ring announcer of the period, came into the ring. Dempsey, who had been sitting on his stool, rose as Humphries intoned, "The champion of champions, our own champion, Jack Dempsey!" The crowd roared. Then Firpo stood as Humphries introduced "the pugilistic marvel of Argentina, the recognized champion of all South America, Luis Angel Firpo!" The roar was not as loud, but it was warm.

The two fighters, Firpo dwarfing Dempsey, stood in the center of the ring with their trainers, as well as a translator for Firpo, as referee Johnny Gallagher talked to the fighters, presumably explaining the rules, though not all those rules would be honored this night. When the words ended, the two were alone with each other.

At the clang of the bell, Firpo moved cautiously towards Dempsey. The champion skipped from his corner, flailing both arms at the challenger. Exactly what happened next is not certain. I have repeatedly studied the old movie of the fight. Years later, Firpo claimed that the official film had been doctored—that 142 frames had been removed. If the film I watched is the same "official" film, Firpo was right.

On the screen in those opening seconds, Dempsey is seen rushing at Firpo and then skidding to his left knee. Then, in a blink, he's back up, clinching with Firpo, his arms held securely around Firpo's back as the challenger leans on the ropes. But one newspaper account of that moment had "Firpo's ponderous right clipping Dempsey on the jaw, dropping Jack to his knees." Another said that "Firpo's powerful right hand whistled through the night and struck Dempsey full and solid upon the point of the chin…the knees of a world's champion buckled under him…He was toppling face forward, to dethronement." Those could have been the 142 frames that are mysteriously missing from the film Firpo and I saw.

"Dempsey was up again before they could more than start counting," Elmer Davis wrote, "and as he got up on his feet 90,000 people got up on their feet, too, and not one of them sat down before the round was over. Ninety thousand people realized in one breath that they were about to see one of the classic fights of all history."

Dempsey immediately took charge, bobbing up and down like a cork in the water, raining punches at Firpo, making the challenger look helpless. One left hook struck Firpo on the jaw. The giant buckled and went down on both knees. But he bounced back up without a count.

Firpo connected with a right to the body, but Dempsey countered with a right to the jaw, and Firpo hit the canvas again.

Once more he rose without a count. The third knockdown came from a short, crisp left to Firpo's jaw.

This time the challenger rose at the count of four.

Sensing the kill, Dempsey moved in, but instead received a searing right hand in his ribs from Firpo, followed by a second lightning-like smash, again in the ribs. The challenger had never thrown punches with such speed in his training camp, and it surprised the champ. Dempsey was hurting.

The two fighters closed in, Dempsey hammering away with chopping rights and lefts to the body. This time Firpo fell on his back, but, showing immense fortitude, he rolled over and, using his gloves as crutches, regained his feet. Before he could set himself, Dempsey was on him. The champion had not retired to a neutral corner, as he should have; the referee let him stay in the middle of the ring.

As soon as Firpo got up, he was struck again, and for the fifth time he fell down. This time he rose swiftly, enraged, swinging like a wild bull, rushing at Dempsey, hammering him with a right to the heart, and Dempsey's legs danced by themselves before he could regain control over them. When he did, he smashed Firpo in the face, and the Wild Bull went down for the sixth time. He got right up, but Dempsey was over him, driving Firpo into a corner, where he fell backward. Knockdown number 7.

Dempsey now looked like a lion toying with his prey. He stood close to his fallen opponent—still no neutral corner for him—his right arm resting arrogantly on the ropes, as if waiting for room service. The referee started counting over Firpo, peeking occasionally at Dempsey but never stopping the count to wave the champion to a neutral corner—the utter fury of the fight seemed to have hypnotized Johnny Gallagher.

As Firpo started to rise, Dempsey dropped his right hand straight down to his hip, palm side up. The movie clearly shows that he was about to fire a right-hand uppercut that would have ended the fight with a splatter. But, sensing the impropriety of it, he pulled back, allowing Firpo to stand tall.

With renewed strength from some primeval impulse, Firpo now rushed Dempsey, repeatedly throwing lefts and rights, forcing the champion to backpedal, his arms covering his face, until he felt the security of the ropes behind his back. Then came the blow that instantly turned the fight into myth.

On the film, which shows those surreal seconds in slow motion, it's clear what happened. Firpo connected with one of his patented rocks, a smashing right to Dempsey's face as the champ was leaning against the ropes. Its impact was quick and savage, but Firpo refused to let go, keeping his glove on the champion's face, following through, pushing, pushing, pushing, until suddenly, Dempsey flew out of the ring backwards, his legs flapping high in the air. He landed in the press seats.

There is a memorable painting of that moment that hangs today in a place of honor at the Whitney Museum of American Art in New York City. The artist, George Bellows, was at ringside. He was 43 years old, growing in reputation as one of the Ashcan school, artists who searched the underside of urban America seeking their inspiration. It is the artist's impression of the moment, and thus lacks fidelity. But the painting on the canvas creates a startling, almost chilling effect.

It shows a spotlessly clean Firpo (there is not a drop of blood or sweat anywhere on the canvas), his black locks hanging over his forehead, a dark, vindictive look on his face, following through on a left-handed swing; the referee, spotlessly clothed, is crouched—one hand holding a strand of ring rope, the other inclined, a finger pointing down. The champion, in the center, face unseen, is falling backwards, the left leg in the air, the right leg bent, the left arm up, the right arm back, seemingly searching for something to break the fall. Those in the front row of the press corps are stirring in their seats, mouths agape, a look of panic on their faces. The painting is Bellows's vision of boxing, the cruel sport, at its idealized essence.

For years afterwards people argued about how much help Dempsey got from the press that night, enabling him to beat the count of ten. The most authoritative account came from a young Western Union telegraph operator named Perry Grogan.

"As I saw Dempsey coming," he said, "I instinctively put up my left hand to protect my sending set, which I was working with my right hand. Dempsey's sweaty back skidded off my left hand and he landed on the typewriter of Jack Lawrence of the *New York Herald Tribune*, wrecking his typewriter. I stopped sending, grabbed Dempsey under his back and shoulders, and pushed him up. Jack Lawrence helped."

Luis Firpo, still standing close to the ropes, slowly began to step back towards mid-ring. He saw Dempsey still down there, sprawled among the reporters, almost bent backwards, the referee counting. Then he saw Dempsey getting up, parting the strands of rope, and standing upright inside the ring. ("A champion gets up when he can't see," he once said.) Firpo rushed at him, looking for the kill. But he was overexcited. Dempsey wrapped his arms around the Wild Bull, holding on, the fighters stuck together in a corner of the ring, trying to unlock their arms, each throwing ineffectual jabs. At last, mercifully for both gladiators, the round ended.

Firpo, in his corner, was dazed, wobbly, and sore. His seconds poured water over his head and massaged his arms and legs and torso. His huge head hung down, as if in prayer.

Smelling salts were being pressed under Dempsey's nose by a second known as Jerry the Greek. But Dempsey just sat in his corner, dreaming, dreaming that he had been fighting for hours and had struck thousands of blows. Then he opened his eyes. "What round is it?" he asked Doc Kearns. "The first round," Kearns said. Dempsey couldn't believe him.

The champ spat in the bucket and went out to meet his opponent, who was moving slowly towards him. The champion opened with two short-arm bursts. The second one was countered by a Firpo right to the champ's body that staggered him for a second. All the Firpo punches that landed, Dempsey would say later, had staggered him. Wounded, he began to move Firpo around. He knew he was now the stronger of the two. He broke free from Firpo's arms, leaving just enough space between them to pound Firpo with two crunches to the face. Firpo fell to his knees. He was breathing hard, but he could hear the count, and he rose to his feet at two.

He should have rested a little longer. Dempsey closed with him again, ripping a right to the body and a left to the jaw. Firpo sank down again, but, still a wild bull, rose once more, at the count of five. Reeling, he tried to hold Dempsey tight. But the champ pushed his opponent back and struck a left uppercut that caught Firpo at the point of the jaw. A follow-through right smashed into Firpo's face. For the tenth time the Argentinean toppled to the canvas, and he lay there on his back.

By an overwhelming force of will, he managed to turn himself over. He tried desperately to rise from the floor, but, his strength spent, his body aflame in pain, he fell back.

It was over.

As soon as Johnny Gallagher counted Firpo out, Dempsey bent over his opponent and, along with Firpo's seconds, helped him to his feet. When Firpo got to his stool and recovered his senses, the champion of the world came over and shook hands with this most persistent and gallant of challengers.

The fight—the ten knockdowns of Firpo, the two knockdowns of Dempsey and his wild flight out of the ring—took three minutes and 57 seconds. To the two fighters it felt as if they had been throwing punches forever. Everyone else—those who were there, those who read about it the next day, those who saw the film, and the multitudes who lied about being there—said essentially the same thing: that both Dempsey and Firpo were better men than anybody knew. The legendary columnist Grantland Rice called it "the biggest sports thrill of all times."

The next morning Jack Dempsey discovered that he was the idol of a nation. As details of that "battle of the century" splashed across the front pages of every newspaper—of Dempsey's courage and animal will to survive even when he was thrown from the ring (most newspapers carried a photo of that flight into the seats)—he became champion of champions. The ghostly figures of John L. Sullivan, Gentleman Jim Corbett, Jim Jeffries, Jack Johnson, and Jess Willard passed through the night, leaving Jack Dempsey out front for the ages.

Luis Angel Firpo came back to Argentina from his near-death experience as the best-known loser in the world and a hero of *his* nation. He had a few more inconsequential fights and then, true to his instincts, settled down to become a millionaire.

Jack Dempsey and Luis Firpo didn't see much of each other in the years that were left to them, but they remained good friends. Once, Dempsey called Firpo in Buenos Aires and asked him if he would give permission for an actor to impersonate the Wild Bull in a proposed movie of Dempsey's life. Firpo said that was fine with him.

"Now," Dempsey almost whispered, fearing the worst, "how much money do you want?"

"One dollar," Firpo said, "because you are good friends of me."

On August 7, 1976, Firpo, age 65, died of a heart attack. Jack Dempsey, who had always said that the greatest thing next to being the heavyweight champion of the world was to be the ex-champion, went to his grave in 1983 at the age of 87 with that conviction locked in place, and no one ever contradicted him.

3

1937
A SUPREME DAY
FOR TENNIS
Don Budge vs.
Gottfried von Cramm

I'm looking at a photograph in *Don Budge, a Tennis Memoir*, published in 1969. The caption says: "Gottfried von Cramm and I at Wimbledon in July 1937, that incredible month."

The two men, von Cramm half a head shorter, are standing close together in fashionable street clothes. Both are wearing double-breasted suits, white shirts, and conservative striped ties, with a flash of white tucked into the breast pocket of their jackets. Both are smiling. Von Cramm's smile is broader, but somehow it seems reserved, almost melancholy. Budge's smile is tight, slightly calculating, but there is mirth in his crinkled eyes, and his famous flaring ears add to the country-boy effect. The black-and-white photograph doesn't show his equally famous red hair. It's hard to imagine two men so different—one handsome and sophisticated; the other as down home as a bowl of porridge. Yet they are beaming in mutual affection.

The event that made that month incredible was perhaps the most dramatic tennis match ever played. The two young friends, Baron Gottfried von Cramm, 28 years old, representing Germany, and J. Donald Budge, 22 years old, representing the United States—each the best his country had to offer—battled it out for the supreme prize in tennis, the Davis Cup. The date was July 20, 1937.

The players would be escorted onto Wimbledon's sacred center court by another young man. In later life Teddy Tinling would be remembered for designing lace panties for the sexy young tennis player, Gertrude "Gussy" Moran, in 1949. Tinling's creation shook the hermetic tennis world into the twentieth century and hurtled Gussy to universal fame somewhat beyond her talents. But now, serving as a gofer at Wimbledon, Tinling's duty was to get the contestants to the church on time.

As they were about to leave the gentlemen's dressing room, an attendant ran up to von Cramm. "Long distance for you, sir," he said, pointing to the telephone. Von Cramm turned to Budge and Tinling, shrugging in embarrassment. "Quickly, please," Tinling said, "the queen is in her box."

Von Cramm, a man who could speak in six languages, answered the phone in English but quickly switched to German. "Ja, mein Führer," he said. When he hung up, his face was pale. Through tight lips he told Budge and Tinling, "He called to wish me luck."

It was more than that. What Adolf Hitler left unsaid, its undertone detected by Germany's greatest tennis player, was a sinister insistence that he beat Budge. Hitler's neurotic preoccupation with the match went back to the previous year. He had been humiliated at his own Olympic Games when an American Negro, Jesse Owens, won four gold medals, thus refuting the Nazi claim of Aryan superiority. A German victory in a sporting event of comparable world renown, the Davis Cup, would restore honor to Nazi Germany. And Baron Gottfried von Cramm, a slim six-footer with blond hair, flashing blue eyes, and an aristocratic demeanor, embodied the ideal of the Aryan race. Except that he had refused to join the Nazi party.

Hitler would deal with that if he had to. Now von Cramm was his ace to help erase the stigma of the 1936 Olympic Games. For International Davis Cup play had become a touchstone throughout the world, contested every year. The country that won this afternoon's match would play the country that had won the Davis Cup the last four years, Great Britain, in the "Challenge Round." And because England had lost its all-time star, Fred Perry, who disqualified himself from Cup play by turning professional, it was generally agreed that the winner of this day's match would take the Davis Cup back home. With Perry gone, von Cramm was ranked the number one amateur player in the world, and Budge was ranked number two.

The contest between the United States and Germany had followed the original format set by the Davis Cup founders in 1900: two singles matches the first day, a doubles match the second day, and reverse singles the third. On the first day, von Cramm beat America's Ellsworth "Bitsy" Grant in straight sets. In the other singles match Budge played Germany's Henner Henkel and, in the words of *The New Yorker's* courtside reporter, who called himself "Foot Fault," "swept Henkel practically up into the stands in the greatest exhibition of undiminished power and accuracy I had ever seen."

On the second day von Cramm and Henkel faced Budge and Gene Mako, a Californian whose specialty was doubles. It was a tough match, and Budge wasn't at his best, but, thanks to Mako, the United States pulled it out, 4-6, 7-5, 8-6, 6-4. That made it 2-1, United States. But in the first match on this final day, Henkel swept Grant up into the stands in four sets.

Two-two. The moment of decision had arrived. Von Cramm turned from the phone, and the two white-clad warriors, wearing white short-sleeved shirts, white flannels, and white tennis shoes, moved into the corridor leading out to center court. Applause rose from the 14,000 spectators who filled every seat. The applause was particularly heavy for von Cramm, the charmer, the sweet-natured underdog. Two weeks earlier, on this same court, Don Budge had won his first British Singles title by beating von Cramm in straight sets.

Now the young American, a Norman Rockwell portrait come to life, and the smiling, composed German turned toward Queen Mary in the royal box. The queen's hands were folded on her lap, and a flicker of a smile crossed her face. She remembered the first time she had seen Budge at Wimbledon, in 1935. He had just turned 20 and had been a bit of a hayseed. As the queen had entered her box that day, for the quarterfinal between Budge and England's Bunny Austin, the band had struck up "God Save The King," and the crowd had risen to its feet. Austin turned towards the queen and bowed. Meanwhile, Budge, unaware of the protocol, had been mopping his brow with his right forearm, his racket raised to his head. It had looked as if he were waving his racket in salute to the queen. One of the London newspapers had then reported, falsely, that Budge had shouted, "Hi, Queen."

Now, as Queen Mary chatted with von Cramm and Budge, she told the young American, "Actually, I didn't see what you did, Mr. Budge. But if you had waved at me, I would have waved right back at you." This time Budge bowed in tandem with von Cramm, Then both men went to their seats on opposite sides of the court, unsheathed their rackets, and walked on to the court.

Budge looked at the lower stands where the German team was sitting and noticed their coach, sitting a few rows down, a small smile on his long oval face. That coach was Bill Tilden, the player who had led the United States to seven straight Davis Cup championships, from 1920 to 1926. Now he was working for the Germans. Odd, Budge thought—Tilden always loved Germany, had said that Berlin was his favorite city, and now he had turned his back on his own country. It was something Budge found hard to understand. But he stood up ready to hit with Gottfried von Cramm. The players would have four minutes to warm up.

One day in June, 1999, I drove to Dingman's Ferry, Pennsylvania, to meet the 84-year-old Don Budge. I had made the appointment a week earlier over the phone with his wife, Loriel. I asked her how her husband was doing. "He's feebly," she said, "but his mind is fine."

Dingman's Ferry is about 100 miles from New York City, near the Delaware Water Gap. The country was beautiful. Emerging from a forest of evergreens, I suddenly realized that I was lost. But I spotted a sign that said "post office," and I drove up to what seemed like a loading platform. A man was just getting out of his car—the first live person I had seen in Dingman's Ferry. I told him I was looking for Mary's Road.

"Is there someone you're looking for?" he asked politely.

"Yes," I said, "the Budges."

"Are you a fan of Don's?"

"Well, sure," I said, "I have been for years, but I'm a writer and I'm doing a story on him."

"You be sure to ask Don about him and Joe DiMaggio."

What did he mean? "I will," I said. "And who are you?"

"I'm the postmaster."

The postmaster's directions were perfect, and I found the

Budges' home, a large gray ranch house sitting across the road from a lake. But no one answered the bell. The garage door was open, and I figured that the Budges were out. Maybe they forgot I was coming.

Ten minutes later a red car drove slowly up the road. As it neared the driveway the car paused, its occupants obviously wondering who this guy lurking on their property was. The driver, a middle-aged woman, parked in the driveway and got out of the car slowly. Then she went around and opened the other front door and helped her husband out of the car.

Don Budge was wearing a red warmup suit. His once-red hair was a dusty gray-white, cropped short. His face was mottled with sun spots and he seemed very thin. As he stood there, trying to figure out who I was, he looked like Dr. Seuss's "long-legged Kwong, with legs so terribly, terribly long." Except that Budge's long legs, which had skipped and run and jumped thousands of miles on the tennis court, were now hurting and unsteady. He had to be helped to a chair on his flagstone patio.

His pale blue eyes were red-rimmed but alert, and the aged warrior treated me—a stranger whom he and Loriel had apparently forgotten about—with grave courtesy as she propped him on the chair. In 1997, Budge told me, he had been operated on to remove an aneurysm on his aorta. The operation, he thought, was a success. But the recuperation gave him too little time to exercise properly, and it had atrophied his legs. So it was difficult for him to walk. But his voice was clear and strong.

I told him what the postmaster had said about DiMaggio. Budge grinned, the smile softening the inroads of age on his face. "We both came from the same area out of California," he said, "and over the years, whenever we bumped into each other, Joe would say, 'Don, I always wanted to be a great tennis player like you.' And I'd say, 'Joe, I always wanted to be a great baseball player like you.'"

Don Budge was born in Oakland on June 13, 1915, the youngest of three children. He had a sister, Helen, two years older, and a brother, Lloyd, who was six years older. Their father, Jack Budge, had come from Scotland where, as a young man, he had played soccer for the Glasgow Rangers. "I met Pele in Paris last year," Don told me as we chatted on that afternoon in Dingman's Ferry, "and I said to him, 'My father used to play soccer for the Glasgow Rangers.' 'Oh, he did?' Pele said. 'He must have been a helluva player, because the Glasgow Rangers were a great team.'"

But one snowy day, Don told me, Jack Budge was knocked out and lay on the field unattended. He caught bronchitis and pneumonia, and his lungs never fully recovered. So he came to America for his health. Jack Budge found the mild climate of Oakland agreeable. He also found a flaming Irish redhead named Kate. They married, and Jack Budge went to work driving a laundry truck.

As a boy Don played all sports, but loved baseball most. He had to be coaxed into tennis by Lloyd. "Lloyd was always grabbing me by the collar and the seat of the pants and pushing me onto the court," Don recalled. Bushrod Park was near the Budge house. It had several gravel courts, and that's where Don began to learn the game from Lloyd, who later became a notable teaching pro. Thanks to baseball, Don had a natural tennis backhand. Don was a righthanded thrower who batted lefthanded. For a lefthanded batter, the right arm does most of the work, guiding the stroke and the release itself. That tennis backhand, when Budge perfected it, would became celebrated as the most immaculate the game has ever seen.

In 1930, when Don was 15, Lloyd suggested to his kid brother that he enter the California State 15-and-under championship. Budge was then about 5-foot-5 and weighed maybe 125 pounds. He had the beginnings of a backhand, plus speed and tenaciousness. But he couldn't serve properly, lacked a real forehand, had no net game, and didn't know what an overhead meant. He was reluctant to enter the tournament but his parents told him they would give him a proper tennis outfit if he got by the first round. Wearing heavy corduroy pants and dirty sneakers, and using an old racket of Lloyd's that was too heavy for him, he got by the first round.

The next time he went on the court he had a new white tennis shirt and white ducks, plus his old speed and tenaciousness, and he went on to win the tournament.

Flush with victory, Budge reluctantly decided that he might go farther in tennis than in baseball. It also helped that California at that time was spilling out great tennis players. Budge's first idol was Maurice McLoughlin, another redhead from a working-class background. McLoughlin had also learned the game on public courts, and by 1914, with one of the strongest serves ever seen, had become "the California Comet." Some other champs from the area were "Little Bill" Johnston, Ellsworth Vines, Alice Marble, Helen Jacobs, and the incomparable Helen Wills.

"I met Helen Wills at the Berkeley Tennis Club about 1932," Budge remembered, "and I thought that if I ever wanted to become a champion I'd want to behave just like her." Whenever Wills was in town he would bike over to the Berkeley Club "to watch her hit topspin shots off both forehand and backhand, keeping them low over the net." That's how he had wanted to do it.

In 1932, however, Budge was still raw material. But he was learning. That summer he won the Pacific Coast Junior Championship, and a year later he won both the California State Juniors *and* the Seniors state championship. That caught the attention of the elders of the northern California Tennis Association, and in 1933 they sent Budge to the Culver Military Academy in Indiana to play in the 18-and-under national juniors tournament. It was the same summer that his future friend Joe DiMaggio was lighting up the Pacific Coast League, hitting safely in 61 straight games for the San Francisco Seals. His future doubles partner, Gene Mako, was No. 1 seed at Culver. Budge was unseeded and unranked, but he played himself into the finals against Mako. He took the first two sets, but he could win only one game in the next two sets. In the fifth set he fell behind 3-5, with Mako serving for the match. It seemed all over, but Budge was turning out to be a player who was most dangerous when cornered. With tremendous all-court coverage and that burgeoning baseball backhand, he went on to win the set, 8-6.

"I came back home by train," Budge told me, "and when we pulled into Oakland I looked out the window and saw a high school marching band out there. I couldn't believe it. Was this for me? But when I got off the train, my trophy in my hand, nothing happened— the band didn't play. But they did strike up when the man behind me got off. Later I found out it was the famous novelist Sinclair

Lewis. I never did find out what he was doing in town. My mother hugged me and said, 'They shouldn't have done this to my Don.'"

Don Budge had made an important new friend at Culver. "Gene Mako now wanted to play doubles with me," Budge remembered. But Perry Jones, the iron-handed developer of southern California junior talent, told Mako, "You don't want to play doubles with Budge. He doesn't play doubles." Gene said, "I think he can." Jones was adamant. He told Mako, "I can see him in singles but not doubles." Mako said, "Well, I can see him in doubles."

So Jones set up a practice match for the two in Los Angeles, fully expecting Budge to flunk the test. "The first thing Gene did," Budge remembered, "was put me in the deuce court, and he said, 'I want you to play over here and I don't want you to miss a ball.' I was so scared I didn't miss a ball."

The pivotal year for Don Budge was 1934. That was when his name first came up in the top ten rankings of American male tennis players, at number nine. He had also caught the eye of the influential tennis official Walter Pate. "Watching Don in 1934," Pate said many years later, "I realized this boy had all the makings of a future champion. I knew his forehand would need correcting, but I told friends he was the fellow who would win back the Davis Cup for us." And when Don Budge made the Davis Cup team for 1935, the person who placed him there was Walter Pate himself, the new captain of the United States team. He was looking for a winning combination after a decade of lean times for the United States.

In his classic book, *Match Play and Spin of the Ball,* Bill Tilden said it all about the kind of struggle that would be waged on that July afternoon in 1937: "When two players start a match it is always a battle to see who will dominate and who will be pushed around. One player or the other will ultimately impress his tennis upon the other."

Tilden had taught von Cramm how to improve his backhand grip, and now he looked on approvingly as his star student won the toss, elected to serve and did so in crushing manner. But Budge won his own service, and the two moved on that way, each holding service through the first four games. In the fifth game von Cramm had Budge

40-0 on his service, but the American fought back to deuce. In the ninth game the two exchanged shot after shot, the German firing his gorgeous first service, Budge's backhand pulling back balls that seemed to have already whizzed by him. Finally, Budge broke von Cramm in what would become the next-to-the-longest game of the match—16 points exchanged. The only longer game would be the last one.

Budge, at 5-4, about to serve for the first set, was feeling good. Von Cramm hadn't been able to take more than two points off his service in any game. Hold my serve, he thought, take the set 6-4, and "I'm winging." Budge hoisted his heavy 15-ounce racket. Players who competed against Budge and Tilden when both were at their peak, felt that Budge's serve was much heavier and had more drag than Tilden's—that Budge could hit bombs that exploded on contact, sometimes even ripping the racket from the receiver's hand.

Budge's first serve exploded at von Cramm. But, wait... the German fired it back, a return Budge couldn't handle. Budge hit another booming serve. Von Cramm fired it back again, and Budge's forehand let him down. Two more huge Budge serves were converted by von Cramm into magnificent placements. He had saved the set. The next three games went with service, two aces keeping Budge alive in the 12th game. But in the 14th game, von Cramm broke Budge, and the set was his, 8-6.

William Tatum Tilden II was enjoying the play of his protégé, the baron. Part of it had to do with his feelings about Don Budge. No new Bill Tilden had come along in American tennis, and he was chafing about the rise of the redheaded terror. Tilden, a complex personality—Alice Marble once referred to him as "that strange, temperamental man who nobody really knows"—had been one of the giants of the golden age of sports. With an extravagant ego, he was a perfect fit in the company of Babe Ruth, Jack Dempsey, Red Grange, Helen Wills, and Bobby Jones. "He strode the court like a confident conquerer," wrote the erudite sports columnist John Kieran. "He carved up his opponents as a royal chef would carve meat to the king's taste. He had a fine flair for the dramatic, and with his vast height and reach and boundless energy he was the most striking and commanding figure the game of tennis has ever put on the court."

Tilden's peak seemed to last forever, not only as a singles champion but as a stalwart of the United States. It started in 1920, when he and Little Bill Johnston finally wrested the Davis Cup away from Australasia (Australia and New Zealand were then a single entity) and took the cup back home for the first time since 1913. And kept it, and kept it, and kept it. In 1921, Japan made it to the Challenge Round but Tilden and Johnston routed them, 5-0. In 1922, 1923, and 1924, Tilden and Johnston continued to dominate Australasia, and then they turned their firepower on the amazing tennis nation of France—the France of the "Four Musketeers": Rene Lacoste, Henri Cochet, Jean Borotra, and Jacques Brugnon— beating France in 1925 and 1926, though they were all close matches.

The splendor ended for the United States in 1927, in Germantown, Pennsylvania. The 34-year-old Tilden and the 33-year-old Johnston lost to the spirited Musketeers, led by Lacoste, known as "the Crocodile." What the Crocodile did, wrote one writer, was to get "Tilden between his jaws and never let go." France thus became the first non-English-speaking nation to capture the Davis Cup. The bulky Shreve, Crump & Lowe silver bowl went into the Louvre for safekeeping and didn't come out for six years. Lacoste would later grow rich on his nickname, designing the crocodile shirt that we all still wear.

In the second set, von Cramm continued to dominate Budge. Both men were playing almost flawless tennis, but von Cramm was driving ground strokes into Budge's backhand corner, then rushing to the net and volleying out of reach of Budge's forehand. Budge was rushing to the net on his first serve, and when he faulted he had to go back for his second serve. Too many unneeded steps, he reasoned. He decided to fire his first serve even harder, stay back, take von Cramm's returns on the rise, and then come into the net.

Each player kept winning his serve, and in the 12th game, with von Cramm leading by 6-5, it was 40-0 for Budge. Von Cramm, with bold net play, took the next three points. The two men battled it out through two Budge advantages, and von Cramm got his advantage and set point. He went for it. He swept in on Budge's service, took the return at the net with a stunning volley that flew past the American, the ball raising chalk off the back line. It was von Cramm's game, and von Cramm's set. He was one set away from bringing Germany into the Challenge Round.

Gottfried von Cramm was born on July 7, 1909, at Nettlingen, near Hanover, one of seven sons in a German family of nobility and wealth that extended back six centuries. The neighboring estate was owned by the equally aristocratic Dobenecks, and it was on their tennis court that Gottfried was taught the game by Roman Najuch, a German star of the early 1920s. He began playing in tournaments in 1929 and also made the Davis Cup team that year, two years after Germany was allowed back in Cup play after the first World War.

In 1932, the British team and its two stars, Fred Perry and Bunny Austin, came to Germany for the inter-zone finals. Hitler, who hadn't yet seized power, was there to watch. What he saw on the final day was, first, von Cramm defeating Austin, and then Daniel Prenn, Germany's top singles player, upsetting Perry. Hitler came down to shake hands with the victorious Germans. By 1933 Hitler was chancellor, and Prenn, who was Jewish, was removed from the team; Hitler had approved a rule barring non-Aryans from representing Germany.

In the 1998 book, *The Davis Cup*, written by Richard Evans, there is a heartbreaking photograph of von Cramm from 1933 that captures his agony at being caught between the old and the new Germany. Dressed in tennis sweater and flannels, bending from the waist, almost cowering, von Cramm has his eyes focused on the ground as he gives his hand to Hitler. The Führer, flanked by his lackeys, is smiling down at von Cramm—a disdainful smile. The caption says: "Germany's greatest player prior to Boris Becker is forced into humiliating supplication." It adds that the picture "was taken before the Führer had him imprisoned."

Don Budge would organize a letter to the German government, signed by 25 leading athletes, protesting von Cramm's arrest by the Gestapo in 1938, and his three-year jail sentence on a homosexuality charge. "No country could have wished for a finer representative," the letter said, characterizing von Cramm as "the ideal sportsman, a perfect gentleman and decency personified."

That sportsmanship had long been a legend in international tennis. The story is still told of the inter-zone Davis Cup final between the United States and Germany in 1935, held at Wimbledon. With the teams tied at one victory each, the doubles match on the second day was crucial, and it turned into a hard-fought five-setter. Finally, the Germans—von Cramm and Kay Lund—brought it to match point against the Americans, Wilmer Allison and John van Ryn. Don Budge was on the sidelines that day, having won his singles match on the previous day, and when I visited him at Dingman's Ferry, he recalled the famous incident.

"Von Cramm returned the service," Budge said, "and ran in and tried to make a volley on the next shot. But he apparently missed the ball, and his partner put it away. 'Game, match, to Germany,' the umpire announced. But von Cramm held up his hand and said, 'Mr. Umpire, the point should go to America because the ball touched my racket when I swung at it.'" The revived American team rallied to win the match. Budge said it was the greatest act of sportsmanship he had ever seen.

Before the third set, Budge stood near the umpire's chair, towelling himself. He was also angry with himself, thinking he was about to let his country down in an event that meant so much to so many people. Sports was becoming all-involving in the United States—a release for people sucked in by the Depression, hurting for jobs, not knowing when or whether their economic misery would ever end. It was a particular joy to attach oneself to a great sporting event, where national pride was at stake. After 11 years, Americans wanted to see the Davis Cup returned to their country. Budge, back on court, waited for von Cramm's first service, vowing to himself to turn the match around.

And he immediately broke von Cramm. But in the fourth game, on his own service, Budge unraveled again—four straight cannonading returns by von Cramm streaked past him. By now, however, Budge's game was at a higher level. He broke von Cramm's serve at love and finished out the set at 6-4.

In those years, Davis Cup play allowed for a locker room break after three sets. It was still sunny and humid on the court, and Budge hurried off to take a shower and change into fresh clothes. He returned to the court refreshed and feeling better about his chances.

Von Cramm came out in a different mood. It was as if the rest had turned him lethargic, or perhaps it was the impact of Budge's elevated play in the third set. Now Budge, hitting almost every serve back to the far corners of the court, broke von Cramm at love in the first game, held his service, and then broke the German again. He won the first four games in five minutes of play, losing only four points. So von Cramm gave in to the inevitable and conserved his strength. Budge took the fourth set, 6-2.

Everything now came down to the fifth set, and Budge knew it wouldn't be easy. He would later recall his feelings at that pivotal moment in an article in the *Saturday Evening Post*:

"Gottfried felt that if he got anyone into the fifth set his chances of winning were 3 to 1. He was regarded as the greatest fifth-set player in the game. He made his opponents run so much farther than he did that the other fellow could not last it out. I said to myself, Here we go. I have never played him five sets before. Will I have a chance, or is he superhuman?"

A hush fell over a crowd that had been full of exuberance. It was a low-velocity buzz rather than a roar, prehaps reflecting the esthetic pleasure of being witness to such glorious tennis in a make-or-break international match. In retrospect, Don Budge saw it that way, too. "The players, winners and losers alike, were only one part of the whole scene," he would write in his memoir. "It was, simply, a supreme day for tennis and a triumph for all that the sport can mean."

In the first game von Cramm, looking steely calm, held his serve, allowing Budge two points. But on Budge's smoking serves in the second game, the German took only one point. In the third game, his serves kicking deep, von Cramm allowed Budge one point. Exchanging sides, von Cramm walked with head high, full of energy.

The long-legged Budge loped to the service line, his face impassive, got ready to serve for the fourth game.

Alistair Cooke, describing the match on the radio, told what happened next:

"Von Cramm, for that one game, looked the best player in the world, and to the women spectators the handsomest man there has ever been. He crept in and in to Budge's serve, with perfect timing dared to half-volley the Budge cannonball. When Budge strained himself for the hardest serve he had ever delivered, von Cramm lifted it back for a forehand that pounded the Budge bullet back for an ace. It looked all over, von Cramm leading 3-1."

Now the handsomest man stood on the baseline to serve, waiting for Budge to indicate that he was ready. Budge nodded, and von Cramm served a low sizzler to the American's forehand that he couldn't handle. 15-love. Von Cramm served another sizzler, rushed to the net and powered the ball past Budge. 30-love. On the next point Budge managed to get his racket on von Cramm's serve, smashing back a trademark Budge backhand. But von Cramm left him standing, mouth agape, with a tremendous stop volley from the center of the court.

"Oh, Baby!" Budge hollered in wonder. The crowd roared, applauding the American. The next day the English newspapers entered his "Oh, Baby!" in the lexicon of sportsmanship.

At 40-love, von Cramm's serve streaked by Don Budge, an Oh, Baby ace. Now von Cramm had him 4-1, and the match was within his grasp—and within the grasp of Hitler's Third Reich. Bill Tilden was seen to turn his head towards the stand where Germany's other star, Henner Henkel, was sitting. A smile crossed Tilden's face and he formed a circle with his thumb and forefinger, the universal symbol for "we've got it made."

Don Budge didn't see any of that. He was standing in a corner of the court, a faraway look on his face. Walter Pate offered him a towel. "Don't worry, Cap," Budge said, "I'm not out of this yet. I'm not tired. So don't give up the ship."

Aside from a forehand that had occasionally misbehaved, Budge thought he finally knew what was wrong. Von Cramm, his length so good, was outhitting him from the back of the court. He couldn't find any openings to get in, Budge told me on that afternoon in Dingman's Ferry, 62 years later. As he recalled what he decided to do, his cheeks turned pink and his voice took on a fervor, as if the game had been played only yesterday.

"I did realize I had to do something different from the baseline on his serve, because he was getting the best of me," Budge recalled. "So I said to myself, If Gottfried misses the first serve I'm going to attack the second serve and go in behind it."

But first he had to hold his serve in the sixth game, or it would really be all over. He did, at love, his forehand beginning to work better than at any time in the match. Now all he had to do was to break von Cramm twice and not lose his serve again.

"Fortunately for me, Gottfried missed the first serve," Budge told me, "and I made a good volley on his second serve and won the point. He missed the next serve, so I attacked his second serve again, made a good approach shot, and made a winning volley. So, I thought, he can't be that unlucky to miss another first serve; after all, he was only missing by an inch. He did miss it. He missed four of his five first serves, and I broke his serve."

Now it was 3-4.

The next game, the battle for Budge's service, was fierce and prolonged. Von Cramm, chagrined, decided that he had to be more aggressive than ever, to try to regain control of the match, and he was. Twice in a row, von Cramm stood at advantage. On the first advantage, he hit a shot to Budge's forehand as deep as it could go, hitting the chalk. But Budge blasted it back, straight down von Cramm's backhand line; it couldn't be touched. On von Cramm's second advantage, he smashed another marvelous backhand, but it went out by inches. So instead of von Cramm serving at 5-3, the match was tied, 4-4.

The battle had raged for more than two hours, and it was almost 7:30, the sun low on the horizon. Von Cramm held his serve and so did Budge, losing only a point. 5-5.

Von Cramm served magnificently, winning his game at love. 6-5. Budge held serve. 6-6.

In the 13th game, von Cramm served bravely, no one-inch

misses. But Budge had raised his game to new heights. Von Cramm continued to hit to Budge's shaky forehand that was shaky no longer. He could win only one point on his serve, and for the first time in the match the United States moved ahead of Germany. 7-6.

Both men sat in their chairs between the changeover, neither one in a hurry to get up. Von Cramm seemed exhausted, but Budge also looked tired. Who would be the one fittest to survive? The umpire politely asked the players to move out, and they walked slowly to their positions for the 14th game.

Budge took up the balls to serve, hesitated, dropped his arm, and took a deep breath. At last, he struck the first ball. His first serve wilted at the bottom of the net. Was the 22-year-old wilting, too? He managed to get the second serve in and win the point. Von Cramm fought back, tying it at 15-15. Budge took it to 30-15. Von Cramm came right back, 30-30, but he overhit the next shot. It was 40-30 and, for the first time, match point—for the United States.

Von Cramm fought back again, outlasting Budge in a long rally and scoring a placement to deuce the game. Budge came back with a placement of his own. Second match point. Once more, von Cramm took the net away from Budge and tied the game. Then, at the net again, he won the next point. For the first time in the game it was *his* advantage. But Budge fired back to deuce. Von Cramm came in tenaciously, picked off a Budge return and volleyed it out of reach. Von Cramm's second advantage of the game, Budge hit a serve with that old feeling on it, and von Cramm slammed it into the net. But once more Budge lost the advantage on von Cramm's placement to the American's forehand. Then, his face full of strain, the German ended a long rally with an out.

Now, on the 18th point of the game, Budge's fifth match point, he glared over at his opponent, his eyes the eyes of a hungry tiger. He flung himself at the first service—his 175th first serve of the match. It was so deep that von Cramm couldn't charge the net. Yet this amazing competitor made a long return that kept Budge back. They traded ground strokes.

"We were both on the same side of the court," Budge told me, picking up the story. He had been talking a lot that afternoon, and he was tired, but his manner still had a nervous excitement. "Gottfried is in the right-hand corner, and I'm in the left-hand corner. He made a good forehand crosscourt."

A *good* forehand crosscourt? It was more than good; it was beautifully hit, and von Cramm followed it in towards the net.

Budge instantly saw what was happening; tennis aficionados always said that Budge saw the ball better and quicker than anyone else. He began to run—it was all he could do. He ran to his right towards the ball, running at full speed, fully extended, his body outstretched, and finally leaving his feet and falling because the ball seemed to be beyond his reach. As he fell he took one desperate swipe at the ball and somehow made contact.

"I crashed on the grass," Budge told me. He paused a moment to catch his breath. "They said my shot hit six inches inside the corner and six inches inside the baseline. So that's how I won the match." He'd won it 6-8, 5-7, 6-4, 6-2, 8-6.

After that shot, Budge got up and brushed off the grass and ran to shake hands with von Cramm. The German was waiting for him with a smile. "Don, now that you have won the match, I'm very happy for you," he said. "You deserved to win because you pulled it out from a very difficult situation. That was the best match I have ever played." They threw their arms around each other.

The match ended at 8:45. It was still light when Budge and von Cramm went into the dressing room. The first one the victor found waiting for him was Bill Tilden, who had swallowed his disappointment. He clasped Budge's hand and said, "Don, this was the greatest tennis match ever played." Throughout his life Don Budge would hear echoes of Tilden's remark from people all over the world. Long after it was over, his captain, Walter Pate, summed it up this way: "No man, living or dead, could have beaten either man that day."

Finally, the dressing room cleared and Budge was able to take a long shower and then walk out into the night. He was amazed to see a large portion of the crowd still there—in semi-darkness—and they were cheering him and cheering him, until Budge, smiling shyly, got into a car. For many nights after his victory he had the same recurring dream. He was standing alone, behind 1-4 in the fifth set, with Gottfried von Cramm staring at him across the net.

A week later, still at Wimbledon, Budge and company routed England, 4-1, and carried back the Davis Cup. The team was treated to a ticker tape parade in New York City, "just like Lindbergh had," Budge remembered with a smile. The whole country was smiling over the kid. "Budge," Alstair Cooke said, "rates next to Mark Twain as the most popular redhead in American history."

A year later, he extended his reputation by winning the first tennis Grand Slam—Australia, France, Wimbledon, and the United States' championships. And he became the first tennis player to win the coveted Sullivan Award as the greatest amateur athlete in the country.

Gottfried von Cramm, who had been imprisoned by the Gestapo in 1938, was released to become a soldier in the Herman Goering Division of the German army. He survived the war and returned to international tennis, playing into the early 1950s. On November 8, 1976, at age 67, von Cramm died in an auhomobile accident near Cairo, Egypt.

In December of 1999, Budge, with his ruined legs, somehow was able to get into his car at Dingman's Ferry, and drive into the night until he lost control. He was critically injured and died in a nursing home on January 26, 2000. I read about his death with sadness, but felt a little better when I remembered what he had said to me that dreamy afternoon in Dingman's Ferry. We were just rehashing 1937 and 1938, those two most glorious years of his life, and I couldn't help complimenting him on his beautiful career. With a combination of pride, modesty, and wistfulness, Don mused, "Well, not everyone can wind up being the best in the world at something."

4

1951
THE MOST THEATRICAL
HOME RUN
Bobby Thomson and Ralph Branca at the Polo Grounds

On the afternoon of October 3, 1951, the two bitterest rivals in baseball—the New York Giants and the Brooklyn Dodgers—took the field for the deciding game of a three-game playoff that would finally end a season so unbelievable that even today it's almost impossible to believe.

Consider the arithmetic. On August 11, the Giants were in last place in the National League, 13½ games behind the first-place Dodgers and 16 behind in the lost column. From that day on they won 37 of their last 44 games, steadily closing the gap on the faltering Dodgers and ending the season dead-even, both teams at 96-58. How does it feel, a reporter asked Giants' manager Leo Durocher on that last day, to be a miracle-maker? "To hell with that," Durocher said. "It's a brand new season—for cash money."

So these old enemies—the two had been at each other's throat since the 1880s—went at each other again in the playoff, and still neither could score a one-two knockout punch. At Ebbets Field, the Giants won the opener, 4-1, on home runs by Whitey Lockman and Monte Irvin. The Dodgers' starter Ralph Branca later ruefully said, "I scattered four hits—two inside the park and two outside." But the Dodgers got revenge the next day at the Polo Grounds; Gil Hodges, Andy Pafko, Rube Walker, and Jackie Robinson all hit home runs in a 10-0 rout.

The Polo Grounds, described at that time as "the raddled, gray, pigeon-speckled old rookery," would host the make-or-break game. And why not? The worn cathedral was the rookery of John McGraw, Christy Mathewson, Bill Terry, Carl Hubbell, Mel Ott, and other Giants immortals. Their descendants on the present team included pitcher Sal Maglie, known as "the Barber" for the close shaves he inflicted on batters, and a rookie centerfielder who was already a candidate for future sainthood, Willie Mays. The rest of the team was somewhat unsettled, except at shortstop and second base, the scrappy veterans Al Dark and Ed Stanky anchoring the infield. The other ace of the pitching staff was the stylish Larry Jansen. Both he and Maglie had won their last starts—crucial clutch performances—on the last two days of the regular season.

The Dodgers players were probably the most talented group ever to wear a Brooklyn uniform at the same time: the vacuum-cleaner infield of Gil Hodges, Jackie Robinson, Pee Wee Reese, and Billy Cox; the solid outfield of Andy Pafko, Duke Snider, and Carl Furillo, and two extraordinary pitchers, Preacher Roe and Don Newcombe, who together had won 42 games. Only catcher Roy Campanella, the league's most valuable player in 1951, would be missing from the lineup because of an injury.

The extraordinary rivalry between the Giants and the Dodgers was reflected through each borough's odd personalities. Murray Kempton, a New York newspaper columnist who wrote beguiling pieces about American concerns, including sports, once observed this difference between the fans of Brooklyn and the Bronx: "Dodgers fans had every vulgarity but the vulgarity of wealth. Giants fans had no vulgarity at all." Let's try that on Bob and Lila Green of Ann Arbor, Michigan. Bob Green was raised in Brooklyn and Lila in the Bronx. Remembering that he was always a nervous Dodgers fan, I asked to interview him. But his wife insisted on being interviewed, too, although I had never heard her express any obligations to the Giants or to baseball itself. She waved her credentials at me by belting out:

COME ON YOU BALL FANS, ALL YOU GIANT BALL FANS
COME WATCH THE HOME TEAM GOING PLACES,
 ROUND THE BASES
WE'RE FOR YOU GIANTS, OUT AT COOGAN'S BLUFF
COME WATCH THOSE GIANT PLAYERS DO THEIR STUFF

Astounded not only by her vocal prowess, I said, "Lila, I never knew you were a Giants fan." "I wasn't," she said. "I had a boyfriend from the Bronx, Al Heller. He made me learn the song. Only reason I didn't marry him is that if we had a daughter I didn't want her to be named Melvin Ott Heller."

The Giants players were now striding onto their field, and were promptly greeted by the Dodgers' ambassadress-at-large, Hilda Chester. For years Chester had been tramping up and down Ebbets Field's aisles jangling her frying pan, ladle, and cowbell. Here she was, in enemy territory, scouting Giants players to bedevil—and spotted one she felt required her attention. In that boom-box voice of hers she screamed, "Look at me, Bobby! Look at me when I talk to you!" And Bobby Thomson, the tall, handsome Scotsman by birth, knowing that if he didn't look at her she'd holler him to death, fed Hilda a friendly wave.

On this climactic afternoon there were 22,000 empty seats in a park that could seat 56,000. Odd, some said, but it was a weekday afternoon and tickets had gone on sale hurriedly, the best seats going to VIPs. One such was General Douglas MacArthur, the ex-supreme commander of United Nations' forces in Korea, a longtime Giants fan who had had the summer pretty much off after being fired for disobeying the orders of his own commander-in-chief, President Harry Truman. Another celebrities' box held an unlikely quartet: the saloon owner Toots Shor, the comedian Jackie Gleason, the singer Frank Sinatra, and the FBI director J. Edgar Hoover. The distaff side was notably represented by the actress Laraine Day, wife of Leo Durocher, and Mrs. John McGraw, the most fervent Giants fan of all. Sitting behind third base were a group of Yankee players, ready to take on the winner but rooting for the Giants because the cash money from the World Series would be bigger if played in this stadium rather than tiny Ebbets Field.

Whitey Lockman, the soft-spoken Giants' first baseman, was looking up at Mrs. McGraw's box, flashing her a smile. Lockman watched the crowd file in, smelled the honey from the freshly mown grass. Looking around, he suddenly felt small in the expanse of this field that swept back 500 feet in its center. "This park gets bigger the farther you hit the ball, ever think of that, Rig?" he asked his teammate Bill Rigney, who stood beside him. Rigney grinned. "Chip a nice easy shot down the foul line—a homer. Slug one out 450 feet—that's an out, son."

While there were only 34,000 eyewitnesses to the event that would make history, in New York's five boroughs the people were at work but not working. Millions were listening to the radio. The bars were overflowing, loyalists of both teams watching the first baseball game ever televised nationwide. In the schools, children implored their teachers to keep them up to date on the score. At 1:30 P.M., when the umpire said "Play Ball!" fans old and young fell quiet and said their silent prayers. The long, nail-biting season had drained almost the last drop of collective emotion. In a few hours, one way or other, it would be over.

Except for the fatigue factor, the pitching match-up was made in heaven. Sal Maglie and Don Newcombe had won 43 games between them, each pitcher also winning five games from the team he was now facing. Maglie pawed around the mound, scuffing dirt and smoothing it down, trying to get comfortable. He was then a 33-year-old who looked older, a menacing figure once described by a sportswriter as "the most savage pitcher I've ever seen." Maglie stared down at the Dodgers' leadoff hitter, Carl Furillo. Furillo stared right back. He had once been heard to say, "If that son of a bitch throws at my head again I'll break my bat against his fucking dago head." Maglie struck him out.

But then he walked Reese and Snider, and the Barber was not pleased with himself, because now he had to face the clean-up hitter, Jackie Robinson. The two men, to put it simply, loathed each other. The feud had begun a year earlier when Durocher made Maglie a starting pitcher and watched with satisfaction at the way he handled Robinson, pitching him high and tight, brushing him back, knocking him down, shaving him close, setting him up for his wicked curve down low and outside. The enmity deepened during a game that was played in the first week of the 1951 season. Maglie threw one high and tight, a hair from Robinson's head, and Robinson hit the dirt. He picked himself up, settled back into the batter's box, and hit a home run.

On his next time at bat, Robinson laid a bunt down the first base line. As he hoped, Maglie fielded it and tried to step on first. Robinson, running at full speed, crashed into the pitcher, sending him on his back, and the two had to be pried apart. The next day baseball commissioner Ford Frick warned both men—Maglie about throwing dusters, Robinson about "popping off." The feud continued all season long.

Now, in the most crucial game of the year, Maglie had to face his enemy in an early showdown. He wasn't quite up to it. Robinson hit the first pitch into left field for a single, driving in the first run of the game. Durocher called to the bullpen for his other ace, Larry Jansen, to get ready; he would try to use only his best men today. Then he walked out to the mound. Durocher told Maglie not to be upset about Robinson's hit, although Durocher himself was always upset when Robinson struck against his team—which was all too often. The conversation seemed to steady Maglie; he got Pafko on a groundout and Hodges on a pop foul to Bobby Thomson. But he left the mound still seething over his pitch to Robinson that had allowed the run to come in.

Newcombe shut down the Giants in the bottom half of the first inning, and Maglie settled down and stopped the Dodgers in the top of the second. In the bottom of the second Whitey Lockman got the Giants' first hit, and the Polo Grounds began to grow noisy. Bobby Thomson came up, thinking he hadn't had much luck with Newcombe this year. He wasn't sure what to expect—the 95-mile-an-hour fastball or the sneaky slider meant to break way down. It was the fastball, and Thomson, who could hit fastballs, lined a shot down the left field line. The usually non-demonstrative Scotsman had psyched himself up for this game, and he was determined to make it to second base. He did, but as he slid into second he saw that Lockman was there, too. Pafko had picked up the screamer in left field and gunned it into third base. Because Lockman knew the strength of Pafko's arm he had held up at second—which Thomson hadn't figured on—and he was tagged out. He was angry at himself; he had cost the Giants a run, maybe two. But it had happened and it was over; he hoped he could get it out of his mind. Willie Mays flied out to end the inning. Still 1-0, Dodgers.

At 2:02, in the top of the third, with clouds thickening over the stadium, the lights were turned on. But there were no revelations, except for the way third baseman Billy Cox swept up Ed Stanky's hot grounder and turned it into a double play.

And so it went—both Maglie and Newcombe rolling along—until the fifth inning, when Thomson hit another scorcher to left center. This time he made it into second base alone. But he never got any farther—Newcombe was hot. But so was Maglie; he had silenced the Dodger bats, allowing only three hits through seven innings, and was feeling only mild fatigue. And in the bottom half of the seventh his team came to life.

Monte Irvin, the first black player to make the Giants, who had led the league in runs batted in with 121, doubled off the fence in leftfield to start things off. Lockman, with orders to bunt Irvin to third, dropped the ball in front of the plate. Rube Walker, who was catching for Campanella, fired to third, but Irvin slid in under the throw. Bobby Thomson hit a high fly to deep center that was caught by Duke Snider; Irvin tagged up and scored easily, tying the game. It was the first run allowed by Newcombe in 21 innings.

I've never forgotten the only time I visited the New York Giants' clubhouse during the reign of Leo Durocher as manager. It was that same summer of 1951, and I was a junior editor for *Sport* magazine, a vintage year for baseball. It was the year of Joe DiMaggio's last hurrah and of Mickey Mantle's first hurrah, It was Bob Feller pitching another no-hitter and the Yankees' Allie Reynolds pitching *two*. I had gone to the Polo Grounds to interview Durocher about a story I was ghosting for the magazine with Charlie Fox, who was about to start his career as a manager in the Giants' farm system for the Class C team in Wellsville, New York. I wanted to ask Durocher what it would be like for Fox down in the minors, and whether he thought Fox would ever be able to pull himself up to the biggies—which, in fact, he did, enjoying a seven-year major league career in the 1970s, mostly as manager of the San Francisco Giants.

When I entered his office, Durocher was sitting at his desk in his undershirt, wearing his game pants, his stockinged feet up on his desk, a cigar in his mouth. He was then 45 years old and bore the face of a stand-up comedian: thinning dark hair slicked back like patent leather, fishy blue eyes, a bulbous nose rich in capillaries, and thick lips that verified his nickname, "Lip," though the word had more to do with his carefree use of the English language. He was gabbing away with a couple of beat reporters in his deep-throated voice, almost a bellow, until he saw me. He stopped cold, his eyes narrowing into slits. Finally he acknowledged my presence.

"What the fuck do you want, kid?"

I mumbled something about the story I was doing—that I had been told to see him at *this* time, just wanted him to answer a few questions "when it's convenient for you."

"Well," he muttered, "it ain't convenient now."

I tried to pin him to a time. He grunted something about calling him back and indicated that the interview was over. My Charlie Fox story ran in the magazine without a Durocher quote— and I never talked to the man again. That was Leo Durocher—a guy who all his life liked to put people in their place, no matter the consequences. As his patron saint Branch Rickey once put it, "Durocher had an infinite capacity for immediately making a bad case worse."

Rickey would know. Back when Durocher was starting his playing career, first with the Yankees and then with the Cincinnati Reds, Rickey was aware that Durocher was a pool-hustler, a horse player, and a woman chaser (especially other men's women); that he liked to hit people, teammates as well as enemy players and paying customers. But Rickey, then general manager of the St. Louis Cardinals, also knew that Durocher was the best shortstop of his time. So in 1933, this man of religious scruples set aside his Bible and scruples and hired Durocher to play for St. Louis.

Those were happy days for Durocher, to be a part of the legendary "Gas House Gang" of 1934 that won everything there was to win in baseball—"the roughest, rowdiest, most colorful team of them all," the Lip once said. The Cardinals were led by the fireball player-manager Frankie Frisch at second base and featured such other freewheeling extroverts as Pepper Martin, Joe Medwick, and the pitching brothers Dizzy and Daffy Dean. But, in 1938, Durocher, fading as a player, was traded to Brooklyn by Rickey. A year later, Durocher became the Dodgers' player-manager, a perfect fit for a team on the rise that needed his type of swagger. He managed the Dodgers the next nine years—missing 1947 because he had been suspended a year for, among other things, consorting with gamblers—and drove them to a pennant in 1941. In midseason of 1948, Durocher suddenly was traded from the Dodgers to the Giants, causing Brooklyn fans to react with their usual vigor: "Leoooooo! You bum you! You no good stinkin' traitor you!"

Now it was July of 1951, and Charlie Dressen's Dodgers had just swept a three-game Fourth of July weekend series with Durocher's Giants. The gap between the teams was wider than the Mississippi River. "We knocked 'em out," Dressen crowed. "They'll never bother us again."

Counting those three games, the Giants had lost 11 in a row and plunged into the National League cellar, and Durocher decided to make some moves. Monte Irvin wasn't happy playing first base; he wasn't playing it well and that affected his hitting. It was Durocher who had converted Gil Hodges from a catcher to a first baseman when he managed the Dodgers. Now he went to leftfielder Whitey Lockman and told him he wanted him to switch positions with Irvin. Lockman said sure, settled in at first, and felt comfortable. Irvin's comfort level was also raised when he went to leftfield, and both players came on in the second half.

Durocher's second major move was to call up Willie Mays to play centerfield. It wasn't a daring move—Mays was hitting .477 for the Giants' Triple-A team, the Minneapolis Millers. Still, it caused some unrest. Bobby Thomson was unhappy at being evicted from centerfield; Alvin Dark, the team captain, called a meeting with Durocher and told him, at least put the kid in leftfield. Durocher refused. Mays went 0 for his first 12 at bats, but then got his first major league hit, off Warren Spahn, a towering home run. After that, he never looked back. He was like a mascot to his teammates that summer, a chatterbox who whinnied and whined, and helped keep the veterans loose.

Durocher's biggest reclamation job was with Thomson, who wasn't hitting. On the Giants' second western swing the manager platooned him; Thomson would hit against lefties but not righties. Sitting on the bench on those days, feeling that he had let his team down, he thought of himself as "the lowliest and saddest man in baseball." One day in June, Durocher said to Thomson, "You aren't having the kind of year you should have." Thomson thought, oh-oh, he's going to send me down. "Tomorrow," Durocher said, "take infield practice at third base—from now on you're my third baseman." Hank Thompson had been playing third but, dogged with injuries, had become erratic. Durocher also insisted that his new third baseman give up his wide-open, stand-up batting stance, which Thomson had copied from Joe DiMaggio. "Move closer to the plate! Shorten your stride!" Durocher growled. Thomson had trouble adjusting, but began to feel looser. In early July he hit four home runs in four straight games. In the last 47 games of the year—that greatest of stretch drives—he hit .357. The makeover was complete.

Durocher always said that the night of August 9, at Ebbets Field, was the turnaround moment for his team. The Dodgers had just completed another three-game sweep and, after the game, they celebrated raucously in their dressing room, which was back-to-back with the Giants' dressing room. Through the wall the Giants players could hear Charlie Dressen hollering that it was all over for the Giants; they could hear the players and their manager singing "Roll out the barrel, we got the Giants on the run" and players pounding bats into the wall. Durocher and his guys were incensed. "The incident struck a chord with the whole team," Monte Irvin said years later. "It was like, right then and there, every man made some private decision that we were going to take it to them and make a run of it, no matter how hopeless it looked."

Five days later, the two teams met again in a three-game series at the Polo Grounds, and the Giants took all those games. From there they went on to win 16 games in a row. The gap was closing.

Throughout Durocher's managerial career, when his team began to over-achieve, as his Giants were doing now, he became a driven man. "With a chance to win," said the Giants' broadcaster

Russ Hodges, "he was hard to live with." From his third base coaching box he began screaming at his players, needling umpires mercilessly, spewing obscenities at the opposing players. Some of them wouldn't take it. One day Durocher's dog urinated on the cleats of back-up catcher Sal Yvars, and Yvars belted Durocher on the jaw. Yvars figured he'd be sent down the next day. But Durocher kept him; he had special plans for Yvars.

Mostly it was Dodger blood that Durocher was smelling. "When Leo left home for each game against the Dodgers," said Laraine Day, "he could have been a man taking off for the Crusades." The one player he really wanted to take on was Jackie Robinson, whom he had previously managed on the Dodgers. The two men shared the one characteristic that had to ruin their relationship once Durocher moved to the Giants and became his enemy: each man's need to win, whatever the cost. As Durocher once explained that compulsion to *New York Times* writer Gilbert Millstein, "Look, I'm playing third base. My mother's on second. The ball's hit out to short center. As she goes by me I'll accidentally trip her up. I'll help her up, brush her off, tell her I'm sorry. But she doesn't go to third. Anybody can finish second, I want to finish first. After that I've done my job. Otherwise, I haven't." Of Jackie Robinson, years later when all the bitterness was over between them, Durocher wrote in his autobiography, *Nice Guys Finish Last*, "He beat me a thousand times in a thousand ways. Getting a base hit, making the double play, hitting the home run, stealing a base, stealing home, upsetting my pitchers with his antics on the bases. I kept trying to find some way to upset him, anything to take his mind off the game."

The Dodgers wouldn't even be facing the Giants in this play-off—they would have been eliminated in their final game of the 1951 season, against the Phillies—except for a pair of last-minute feats by Robinson that were perhaps the most brilliant ornaments of that miracle year. It was 3:55 P.M. at Shibe Park in Philadelphia when the Dodgers learned that the Giants had clinched first place in Boston by defeating the Braves in their own final game. In the Giants' dressing room someone spread the word that the Dodgers had lost. "We're the champs, Bobby, we're the champs!" Larry Jansen hollered at Bobby Thomson. But when they got on the train that would carry them home they found that the Dodgers hadn't yet lost. The game was still going.

Early in the game the Dodgers had trailed the Phillies, 6-1; going to the top of the eighth they still trailed the Phillies by 8-5, and they could almost hear their death rattle. But Gil Hodges and Billy Cox singled, and Rube Walker doubled them both in. The Phillies' manager, Eddie Sawyer, summoned Robin Roberts, his peerless 21-game winner, who had pitched less than 24 hours earlier. The first man he faced, Carl Furillo, singled in the tying run. It would be the only hit off Roberts for the next five innings.

Charlie Dressen brought in Don Newcombe, who had beaten Roberts the day before. Newcombe pitched a scoreless ninth, tenth, and 11th inning. But in the bottom of the 12th he walked the pitcher. He got the next two men but Eddie Pellagrini, the veteran second baseman, bunted Roberts to second and beat out the throw. Willie Jones was walked intentionally to load the bases. And it was up to first baseman Eddie Waitkus.

What happened next was vividly described by Red Smith in the *New York Herald Tribune*:

"Waitkus smashes a low, malevolent drive toward centerfield. The ball is a blur, passing second base, difficult to follow in the half-light, impossible to catch. Jackie Robinson catches it. He flings himself headlong at right angles to the flight of the ball; for an instant his body is suspended in midair, then somehow the outstretched glove inteceps the ball inches off the ground. He falls heavily, the crash drives an elbow into his side, he collapses. But the Phillies are out, the score is still tied."

Doc Wendler, the Dodgers trainer, rushed onto the field, not sure what was wrong because Robinson couldn't talk. He could only point to his stomach; his elbow had jammed in there on the fall, knocking the wind out of him. Up in the stands, rumors circulated that Robinson had had a heart attack. After five minutes he rose unsteadily and his teammates helped him to the dugout, where he slumped in his seat. "Push him out here, Doc," Pee Wee Reese said.

"He'll be all right once he gets on the field." Wendler heaved Robinson to his feet and the second baseman walked to his position.

In the bottom of the 13th, Newcombe got two men out, then walked two. Charlie Dressen came to the mound to ask his pitcher how he was feeling. "I'm not as good as I was," he said. Dressen called on reliever Bud Podbelian, who got the third out. It was still 8-8.

In the top of the 14th, the stadium had begun to darken and the umpires hurried the players to their positions. The first two Dodgers, Reese and Snider, fouled out. Robin Roberts seemed to be as strong as ever. Now facing Jackie Robinson, who had kept the game alive, he took a little extra time, then pitched with extra care. Robinson looked at a ball and looked at a strike. The next pitch, a fastball up and in, zoomed towards him and Robinson jumped on it, swinging with all the strength left in his exhausted body. The ball flew out in a high arc and landed in the upper left field stands.

In the bottom of the 14th, as night fell over the ballpark, the Phillies went down one-two-three. Robinson had done it. Milton Gross, one of the tough, muckraking sportswriters of the era, underrated in his time, sat with Jackie and Rachel Robinson on the train ride back to New York, husband and wife bound together in complete happiness because they had won. "The game was done and they could kid each other, but their voices still shook," Gross wrote. What that game confirmed in Gross's mind about Robinson was that this was no ordinary man, but "one who must forever remain unique in the sports and social history of our land."

Bobby Tomson's RBI in the bottom of the seventh that tied the game, 1-1, quickly became a memory. After Carl Furillo lined out to Maglie to start the eighth Pee Wee Reese singled over Stanky's head into right center. Then Duke Snider pulled one past Stanky, who wasn't what he had once been at second base; and there were men on first and third, with Robinson up, and Durocher probably thinking, is he going to find a new way to beat me? Maglie may have felt the same way because he fired the first pitch into the dirt. It broke through catcher Wes Westrum's legs, and in came Reese with the tie-breaking run: Dodgers 2, Giants 1.

In 1950, Maglie's first year as a major league pitcher after a stint with the outlaw Mexican League and a three-year suspension, he won 18 games and lost only four. He pitched five shutouts and beat the Dodgers four times, but it was never easy, and Robinson was always at his throat. One time, with Robinson up and the count 2-2, Maglie became enraged at Robinson's stalling tactics and refused to throw the curveball to Robinson that his catcher, Sal Yvars, was calling for. Yvars ran out to the mound. "What's the matter with you?" he hollered. "Throw your goddam curveball." Maglie's overhand curve was wicked, a pitch "from the hand of God," someone once said. "Forget it," the Barber told Yvars, "I feel like kicking him on his ass."

Now, with Snider on second base, the count went to 3-1 on Robinson. Durocher came out to talk with Maglie. In effect he told his pitcher not to kick No. 42 on his ass, but to walk Robinson intentionally. He also asked Westrum whether Maglie still had his stuff; Jansen and, the Giants No. 3 pitcher, Jim Hearn were bearing down in the bullpen. Westrum said Maglie was throwing strong.

What happened next put Bobby Thomson—who had gotten two hits, driven in the Giants' only run but messed up on the bases—on the downside once again. Andy Pafko drove a bouncing ball towards third that took a short hop. Thomson's job was to go over and backhand it; it was a do-or-don't play. Thomson could make those plays, but not as consistently as Billy Cox. This time he didn't, and Snider scored. Thomson did catch Gil Hodges' pop-up for the second out, but then up came Billy Cox himself, who was having a virtuoso day in the field. Not only had he started that nifty double play in the third; in the seventh he took a hit away from Dark with a breathtaking stop to his left. Now, against Maglie, Cox hit a line shot that skidded off the grass—*shewoo!*—towards Thomson, who knew he couldn't get there with his glove. He had to block it with his body, even if the thing killed him. But the ball sliced by him into leftfield, and Robinson scored the third Dodgers run of the inning.

Sal Maglie finally got the third out and walked slowly off the mound to the cheers and applause of Giants fans. They knew that was the end for him, because he was scheduled to bat second in the ninth, and a pinch-hitter would be used. He deserved better. So thought the depressed Giant fans. Their team was now down 4-1 and in need of a ninth-inning miracle.

This was Bobby Thomson's fifth year in the majors, in a career that was peculiar for its up-and-down quality—up one year, and down the next. Born in Glasgow, Scotland, in 1923, Thomson was brought to the United States as a boy, and settled with his family on Staten Island. His older brother, Jim, taught Bobby how to play baseball and he became a star shortstop in high school. The day after he graduated, with Jim's guidance he signed with the Giants for $100. The following spring, in 1942, he played 15 games with the Giants' farm team at Bristol, Virginia, in the Appalachian League. Then he went into the Air Force, for the next three wartime years.

In February of 1946, the Giants took all their returning servicemen to Jacksonville, Florida, where their Triple-A Jersey City Giants trained, to see who among them had grown up. They thought Thomson had. He could run, he could throw, he could handle balls in the infield or outfield, and he could hit with power. On opening day in Jersey City, Thomson was in the starting lineup. He played so well that the parent club brought him up late in the season, and he stuck.

The next year, playing leftfield, Thomson batted .283, with 29 home runs and 85 RBIs. But in 1948 he slumped to .248 and had only 16 home runs. Halfway into that season Leo Durocher became manager, and when it was over he told Thomson, "You got all the tools of the trade but you're a little unstable." The Giants cut Thomson's salary from $14,000 a year to $10,000. Thomson was unhappy. "If I have a good year," he aked Durocher, "how about giving me my money back?" Durocher said O.K.

Thomson got his cut back after the 1949 season—he hit .309 with 27 home runs and 109 runs batted in. Durocher needed Thomson's power because he had begun to build his own kind of team. First, he got rid of the slow-moving slugger, Johnny Mize. Then he told owner Horace Stoneham, his sometime drinking companion, to "back up a truck" to relieve him of the slow-fielding, slow-running power hitters he had inherited: Walker Cooper, Sid Gordon, and Willard Marshall. Durocher had history on his side because, in 1902, John McGraw, the Giants' new manager, had done the same thing, turning over the team he had taken over. He wanted "McGraw types" on the diamond. Those would also be Durocher types—players with speed and versatility and swashbuckling aggressiveness. So the three sluggers went to Boston in exchange for two swashbucklers, Dark and Stanky, who had helped the Braves win a pennant in 1948.

But Thomson's career pattern reasserted itself in 1950. He hit only .257, and he started out the same way in 1951, until Leo set him right.

When the Dodgers came into the dugout for the bottom of the eighth, leading 4-1, flush with the three runs they had just scored, Pee Wee Reese and Jackie Robinson came over to Newcombe.

"How you feeling, Newk?" Reese asked.

"I can't make it," Newcombe told him.

Robinson, intense and emotional, wouldn't have it. "Goddammit, get in there and pitch," he said. So Newcombe went out and pitched. Hank Thompson came up first, to bat for the catcher, Wes Westrum, and Newcombe blazed his fastball past him for the strikeout.

Ralph Branca had been the only Dodger in the bullpen in the early stages of the game, but he hadn't started throwing until the sixth inning. If Newcombe had been knocked out in the first or second inning, Branca would have come in. He started throwing on his own in the sixth.

He knew that his arm would be tight because he had pitched two innings on Sunday in the final game of the season, and eight innings Monday, and here it was Wednesday. So he started and found he could throw the ball maybe 50 feet, not any farther. But by the eighth inning his arm was loose and he was throwing 60 feet; it was O.K., and he started to throw hard. By now he had company in the bullpen—Carl Erskine and Clem Labine were also throwing, and pitching coach Clyde Sukeforth was looking them over closely.

Charlie Dressen had been on the phone frequently during those middle innings, asking, "Who's ready, Sukey?" By this time Sukeforth was thinking, well, not Erskine, his arm's been sore and he isn't showing his best fastball or curve.

With one out in the eighth, Bill Rigney, a contact hitter, came up to bat for Maglie. Stanky in the on-deck circle, told him that Newcombe was losing it. But first baseman Gil Hodges speared a hard groundball, and Rigney was gone. The third batter, Stanky, found out for himself: Newcombe struck him out.

In the Giants' dugout, Bobby Thomson threw his glove down. He was in total depression, thinking, I guess we aren't good enough to take that last step, just good enough to get this far. He was also thinking he would be the fifth hitter in the ninth inning, and he wouldn't even get a chance to hit.

As the Giants' 23-game winner, Larry Jansen, came to the mound to pitch the top of the ninth, he was mocked by Dodgers players standing on the edge of the dugout. "Jansen, you can go home now!" Jansen pitched a perfect inning, first disposing of the leadoff man, Newcombe; Dressen wouldn't pinch-hit for Newk because he needed the big bear to get three more outs. Then Jansen got Furillo and Reese. But it was 4-1, and Dodgers fans were on their feet cheering; Hilda Chester was jangling her bells and working her voodoo.

In the press box, Gary Schumacher, a Dodgers publicist, announced over the microphone: "The Dodgers will hold a victory party tonight at the Hotel Bossert, beginning at 6 p.m., and all members of the working press are invited."

As Leo Durocher started out to take his place on the third-base coaching line, he saw Laraine Day standing in her box near the dugout. His wife was crying. Then he saw her, in supplication, shaking her fist at her husband. Nearby, Mrs. John McGraw was sitting placidly; her husband had gone through all that stuff over the years and had won his share of games that seemed lost. On an impulse, Durocher went back to the dugout and gathered his players around him.

"Fellas," said the normally gruff Lip, "you've done just a hell of a job all year long. I'm proud of every one of you. We've got three whacks at them! It's not over yet. Let's give them all we've got. Let's leave the ballfield, win or lose, with our heads in the air." His team screamed back at the manager as he walked out to the coach's box.

Branca, in the bullpen, throwing alongside Clem Labine, both men warming up easily, stopped to watch what the leadoff hitter, Al Dark, would do. What he saw was Dark scratch a hit off Hodges' glove. Then Don Mueller was at the plate, the 23-year-old right fielder, who'd had a big year and won some big games with his bat and his defense. For some reason, Hodges was holding the runner on first. Branca couldn't understand why—that's not the run you should worry about with a three-run lead. Sure enough, Hodges was out of position when Mueller stroked one past him into right field. Oh, Branca stewed, if Gilly had been positioned right, he would have caught the ball and thrown to second and gotten Dark and maybe the double play, and the Giants would be dead. But now the situation was man on first, man on third, and no outs.

Newcombe, really laboring, took a visit from Dressen, who looked the big guy in the eye and left him in. Newk threw Monte Irvin a fastball high and outside; Irvin swung and lifted a pop foul that Hodges gobbled up. Whitey Lockman, the lefthander, came to the plate, and Thomson moved to the on-deck circle.

The first thing Lockman did was sneak a look a look at the rightfield wall. If I hit one out there, he thought, the score is tied. He remembered his conversation with Bill Rigney, Rig saying, "Chip a nice easy shot down the foul line—a homer. Slug one out 450 feet— that's an out, son."

Lockman took the first pitch from Newcombe, a strike. Then, as he told a reporter later, "muscle memory took over." He lined a double to left scoring Dark, and Don Mueller slid into third.

But something had happened over there by third. Mueller was on the ground, crying out in pain. While Dressen was walking slowly to the mound, Durocher was leaning over his ballplayer; Mueller's ankle was horribly twisted. They carried him off on a stretcher and Durocher called in Clint Hartung, the 6-foot-5 "Hondo Hurricane," to run for him. Hartung had come out of World War II with a legend as a pitcher and a hitter, as maybe the next Babe Ruth, but he never quite rose to hurricane force as a major leaguer. Durocher later realized he had picked Hartung to run for psychological reasons, because he was the only Giant bigger than Newcombe; throughout the game the Lip had been riding Newcombe mercilessly, hoping the pitcher would punch him and get him thrown out of the game. But Newk refused to bite.

Now the Dodgers' question was what to do with the valiant pitcher. Gathered around Dressen were the catcher, Rube Walker, and the infielders. "How do you feel?" the manager asked Newcombe.

"Talk to Pee Wee and Jackie," Newk said. "They've been watching my stuff. They know how much I've pitched in the last week."

Jackie Robinson said, "C'mon, big fellow, how do you feel?"

"I'm tired," Newcombe said, "but I'll give it all I can."

Pee Wee turned to Charlie Dressen. "Charlie, get a fresh man out here," he said.

Dressen told the guys that Clyde Sukeforth had phoned him from the bullpen and that, between Branca and Labine, Branca was throwing harder. Dressen called him in.

Ralph Branca, 6-foot-3, 220 pounds, with a massive chest and lightning fastball, had been a Dodger for five years and was still only 25 years old, the next to the last child in a family of 17. Like Bobby Thomson, Ralph was pampered by his older brother, John, who was a star pitcher for his Mount Vernon, New York, high school team. But young Ralph, taller and stronger, became the pitcher of record in the extended Branca family. In 1943, John took his kid brother to tryout camps with the Giants, the Yankees, and the Dodgers. Only the Dodgers were interested. They signed him and sent him to their Pony League team in Olean, New York. Three years later, in 1946, culminating a roller coaster rise to the majors that brought him to the Dodgers, Branca had the honor of starting the first baseball playoff in history against the St. Louis Cardinals.

The baseball year of his life was 1947, when, at the age of 21, he won 21 games. A workhorse on the Dodgers staff, he led the league in starts, was third in ERAs, second in strikeouts, made the All-Star team, and started the World Series against the Yankees, retiring the first 12 men in a row, five on strikeouts. "The kid's got golden muscles in his right arm," said Branch Rickey. But after that, baseball was never quite the same for Branca. In 1948, he was 12-5 at the All-Star break, but a badly infected leg laid him low and he only won two more. In 1949, he had a sore arm and spent some time on the disabled list; when he came back he knew he had lost something off his fastball. So he began to throw more breaking balls, and ended up with 13 victories against five losses.

White-haired Burt Shotton, who became the Dodgers' manager when Durocher left in 1948, lost confidence in Branca and, in midsummer of 1950, he removed him as a starter and stuck him in the bullpen. That 7-9 season was a mystery to Branca because he felt his arm was getting stronger, and he had perfected a slider. A year later, when Charlie Dressen replaced Shotton, Branca thought he would be back in the starting rotation; Dressen had been a Dodgers coach under Durocher in 1946 and had always treated Branca with respect. Yet Branca opened the 1951 season in the bullpen. He worked impressively. And on May 28, Dressen rewarded him with a start. Branca won that one, 4-1, and followed it with three more tight, low-scoring, one-run wins. He was a starter once more.

In mid-August, while the Giants began piling up wins and the Dodgers were slipping, Branca became the stopper, pitching his best games of the year. He beat the Braves, 8-1, striking out ten. Then he shut out the Chicago Cubs, 1-0, and, at Pittsburgh, with two days' rest, he had a no-hitter going into the ninth. He didn't get the no-hitter, but he did get the win. Soon after that he felt a strain in his right shoulder. It never completely went away, and that was when No. 13 lost some of his effectiveness.

Now, as he trudged out of the bullpen, Branca was met by Andy Pafko, who patted him on the back. "Go get 'em, Ralph," Pafko said. He'd watched Branca and and noticed that Ralph had a great curve. Recalling the moment for Roger Kahn in his classic *The Boys of Summer*," Pafko said, "Thomson couldn't hit it with a fan."

Thomson didn't even know that the Dodgers had changed pitchers. He was watching Mueller, in pain down there at third base.

Curiously, the accident had taken Thomson's mind off the game; he was feeling real loose, and it wasn't until they carried Mueller off that it went through his mind, hey, back to baseball. The tension was broken.

Just before he stepped into the batter's box, Durocher called time and ran up to him and said, "Be ready for it, Bobby! Go to ripping at it! Get me a base hit here! Bobby, if you ever hit one, hit one now." Thomson thought, Leo, you're out of your mind. He never even looked at his manager, but just headed to home plate.

Thomson felt as if he was the only guy in the park. And he began doing something he had never done before—talking to himself. Do a good job. Give yourself a chance to hit. Do a good job. Wait and watch, wait and watch, you son of a bitch. He called himself a son of a bitch several times. He knew where that came from—from hanging around Dark and Stanky, the aggressive guys. Finally he settled himself in, swinging the bat loosely, looking out and seeing that it was Branca on the mound, a different pitcher. Didn't matter. Crouched in the batter's box, knees bent, he was in a world by himself. Wait and watch…wait and watch…wait and watch.

Branca reared back and threw a fastball right through the heart of the plate. Thomson took it. His guys told him later they wanted to kill him for taking that pitch, a ball that could be driven. Reese and Robinson looked at each other, both thinking that Bobby could have creamed it. But it was just strike one.

Thomson stepped away from the plate, bent down and spread a little dirt in his hands. The home run he had hit off Branca two days earlier had been a slider. Today's strategy between Branca and his catcher, Rube Walker, was first to get a strike (which they now had), then move Thomson back with an inside fastball, and then throw him a curve low and away.

Thomson was uttering his mantra before the second pitch was thrown: wait and watch, wait and watch. The pitch came in and Thomson caught a glimpse of it, coming up towards his right shoulder. I'm seeing the ball! I'm seeing the ball! And he swung; he was always quick with his hands. The pitch was a little inside, but not so much that Thomson couldn't get out in front of it. And, at the point of impact, he knew he had hit it well. But then he saw the damn thing start to sink and thought, Jeez, I must have gotten a little bit on top of it to create that overspin, and he wondered if he had seen it right.

Branca had tried to get it up and in, but he saw that it just wasn't in enough when Thomson had hit it. But the ball was sinking; Branca swore it was sinking, and he was yelling, *Sink!* hoping it would hit the top of the wall.

Durocher knew it was going to hit the wall, but it didn't occur to him that it was going over the wall. Very few home runs were hit into the lower deck because of the 29-foot overhang from the upper deck. This line drive was far too low to hit the overhang, and it was sinking.

But now Thomson knew. He saw it. He thought upper deck, because he had really hit it well. Then, he thought, it's not a home run, it's just a base hit. The next thing, the ball disappeared.

Then Branca also knew. He saw it go over the wall and disappear. It skimmed over the wall by no more than the width of the baseball, and landed in an empty chair just vacated by a fan.

The photograph I'm looking at must have been snapped just after the ball disappeared. The leftfield scoreboard, located between the upper and lower stands, says: "Bklyn 100000030-NY 00000010." Confetti has begun to fall from the upper deck but the spectators look dazed, still unsure, wondering. The confetti is floating down towards the leftfielder, Andy Pafko, who is slumping, his arms akimbo, like a toy soldier dangling from a wire, a blank look on the toy soldier's face.

Of all the photos taken of the shot, which Red Smith called "the most theatrical home run in baseball history," the most telling one shows Thomson, theatrically inclined, dashing into home plate, hyperventilating—A-huh! A-huh! A-heh! E-hha!—and laughing at his last exhale, seeing home plate and all the players waiting for him, taking that last orgiastic leap onto home plate and jumping into their arms.

Two umpires watch Thomson closely to make sure he has touched the plate; no Fred Merkle boner here. Behind the second base bag one other person, Jackie Robinson, dying inside, is watching intently, and in the far right-hand corner is the pitcher, walking away from the scene, his head down, his glove dangling from his right hand, his shoulders slouched, a figure of exhaustion and despair.

It had ended at 3:58 P.M. in the half light, and now everybody knew. Now they knew. They began pouring out of the stands from all directions, like fountains of water all turned on at once, cascading down onto the field. They all seemed headed in the same direction, toward home plate. Thomson was locked in the hysterical embrace of his teammates; they had formed a circle around him that nobody could penetrate, not even Durocher. The manager had been jumped on by Eddie Stanky at third base, the two sprawled on the ground, whirling around in joy. Now Durocher was trying to push into the circle around Thomson, looking like a monk with his tonsured head; his cap had been swiped. Thomson felt somebody playing around with his legs. It was Whitey Lockman, who somehow managed to lift the new hero up on his shoulders. Thomson felt like a bucking bronco. But then the crowd started to surge towards them, and the players decided to make a run for the clubhouse, out beyond centerfield.

Thomson was in front of them, sprinting, bareheaded, his cap gone, too, a smile plastered on his face that seemed to be asking, Am I dreaming this? He felt strange when he entered the clubhouse. It was empty. He looked at a table that had several whiskey bottles on top, probably booze from the owner, Mr. Stoneham, to console the losers and, of course, himself. Thomson figured that everyone was over on the Dodgers' side, thinking they'd be sucking up to the winners. He looked again at the table and felt nauseated. But then the room began to fill up, until it was wall to wall with people.

He stood there, trying to answer all the questions the reporters were asking him while accepting congratulations from well wishers. One of them was Carl Hubbell, one of the greatest of Giants, who now worked in the front office. Hubbell was sure it was a miracle. Several times Thomson had to get up and go outside to make curtain calls to the crowd. He waved down at them like a monarch; now the Giants had two kings, Hubbell and Thomson.

Even Durocher was intimidated by the predatory reporters, who were suffocating him in a corner. But they gave way when Pee Wee Reese came over from the Dodgers' clubhouse to congratulate his old manager; after all, it was Durocher, back in 1940 when Reese came up to the Dodgers as a rookie, who took the No. 1 off his own back and gave it to Reese because he knew that Pee Wee would become the shortstop of his dreams. The Dodgers' captain had had to drag himself over there to hug Durocher. In the Dodgers' clubhouse after the game he had just sat on his stool, unable to move, saying over and over to himself, It's not so; they just called time for a minute.

The second Dodger to come in to congratulate Durocher was Jackie Robinson. "I know Jackie was bleeding inside," Durocher would write in his autobiography. "I know he'd rather have been congratulating anybody in the world but me. And he had come in *smiling*." Even Rachel Robinson found it hard to understand how her husband was able to smile. "After the excitement of that final game in Philadelphia," she told me, "our hopes were at the highest level, and then to have that letdown was tremendous, and we were just sick. I mean really really sick. We didn't talk. There was nothing we could say, and the mood was just like a mourning. But Jackie knew the game was winning and losing, and the next day he shrugged it off. Wait till next year wasn't just a phrase with Jackie. It was a motto."

With Branca there would be no shrugging it off—then or ever. Somehow, he had made his way to the clubhouse where he sought refuge on a staircase. He sat on the top step, his face buried in his hands, his head between his knees, his eyes staring at the cement floor. A reporter found him and asked quietly, "What kind of pitch did he hit?"

"Fastball, sinking a little," Branca said. The writer couldn't ask him any more and left, but others came after him, wanting to know. All Branca could say was. You know what happened, leave me alone.

Outside, in the great city, it was bedlam, as if World War II had just ended. Times Square was full of commotion and joy, people kissing each other and waving hastily constructed banners that said THOMSON FOR PRESIDENT. MAGLIE FOR MAYOR. The switchboard at the *New York Herald Tribune*, whose writers had predicted a Dodgers victory, was swamped by incoming calls from people who wanted to say, I told you so. And everyone who cared—who couldn't care?—was sealing the moment in their memory: This is where I was when Bobby Thomson hit the shot heard round the world.

If you were a Dodgers fan, it was a slightly different story, you just wanted to kill yourself. Up at the VA hospital in the Bronx, Bob Green, a resident physician, was allegedly on duty. "They had a lounge upstairs, in which there was something called a television set," Green remembered. "There was a guy named Joe Dubinsky, a resident in pathology, whom I hated—he was a *Giants* fan. The only other guy in that room was Joe Dubinsky. And there's the Polo Grounds, a longtitudinal field, and there's the cheapest home run ever hit. When it happened I went into total depression. To this very day," Bob Green said, "I still can't believe it happened."

Ralph Branca was the last Dodger to leave the clubhouse. He had his car in the parking lot, and he and his fiancee, Anne Mulvey, whose father was a part owner of the Dodgers, were going to dinner; they would be married in two weeks. They went out with Rube Walker and his wife. Branca then dropped Anne at her home in Brooklyn, returned to his home in Mount Vernon, and resolved "that I wouldn't let the thought of Thomson's hit haunt me." Sure.

For Bobby Thomson it was different. He was signed to appear that night on the *Perry Como Show*, one of the most popular television programs of the time. They paid him $1,000, which was big walking-around money for a ballplayer in 1951. Afterward, back home in New Dorp on Staten Island, his mother told him that she had turned off the radio when the Dodgers got those three runs in the eighth inning; she was too nervous to listen anymore. Then she heard her neighbors pounding on the door, hollering, "Bobby hit a home run!"

Almost a half-century later, in 2000, I caught up with Thomson and Branca. Both of them seemed to have survived the years with reasonable grace. In fact, when Thomson opened the door of his home in Watchung, New Jersey, he looked exactly as I remembered him when he was the boy of that summer of 1951. Though slightly stooped, he didn't seem to have lost height. Except for a head of white hair, he looked much younger than his 77 years; his face was barely lined. He was alone in the big house where he and his wife, Elaine, who had died seven years earlier, had raised their two children. We pulled up two chairs in the living room, and then Thomson started interviewing me. Who was I and what was I doing?

When I explained that this would be a chapter in a book about some of the most dramatic sports events of the twentieth century, he relaxed and we talked for a long time. He seemed happy to speak about things that he had surely repeated over and over again, but he made it all sound fresh.

"You know, it's taken me years to realize that the effect of that home run hasn't gone away," he said, "and I'm still amazed. Just last week I had three different things to do in New York, and people were still coming up to me. They've done it all my life, but more so in the last ten or 15 years. I think it's increasing."

I asked him, "What would your life have been if this hadn't happened?" He said politely that it was a good question, but I knew that everyone had asked him the same thing over the years. He said it didn't transform his life. After 1951 he continued to play major league baseball, and had a solid 15-year career, mostly playing the outfield, where he was always more comfortable, and hitting 264 home runs. After baseball he became a salesman for a paper company and was still doing some consulting for the firm. He doesn't deny that the home run helped him. "I always referred to myself as Bob Thomson, but people knew who I was. After I left baseball I got out of bed every morning with a sense of responsibility for myself, my wife, and my family. I just wanted to push my past out of my way and go on my own."

But the past won't go away for either man. Ralph Branca lives today with his wife in the manor house on the grounds of the Westchester Country Club in Harrison, New York, and that's where we met. It was a cool Sunday morning in late fall, and Branca was in a windbreaker. At 74, he looked like an aging stevedore, tall, with a thick torso, maybe 20 pounds heavier than he was in his playing days. He said he had never been able to shake off the burden. "I've taken all the BS," Branca said, the bitterness still alive in his voice. "I was never going to hide. I lost the pennant, in case you didn't know that. Singly. To this day nobody has ever said, 'Don't blame Ralph. We lost it.'" He told me he was once at a Sports Illustrated dinner and was seated next to Sal Maglie. "Sal pats me on the thigh and says, 'Hey, dago, if you wanted him to hit the curve, why the hell didn't you throw him a curve?' Basically, he's got a point. The pennant was on the line and I was only 25 years old and still trying to learn how to pitch." Then the pain returns. "The Polo Grounds," he sighed. "It wasn't one of those monster shots."

Branca has new knees, which have helped his golf game, and he closely follows the adventures of his son-in-law Bobby Valentine, manager of the Mets. But he has also stayed involved with baseball himself. He helped found BAT, Baseball Assistance to Players, and was its first president and is now chairman of the board. Since 1970, BAT has raised a ton of money to help old, needy ballplayers and their families. It's an honorable charity in a sport not known for its charitable impulses.

They're the odd couple, Branca and Thomson, not exactly enamored of each other, but still doing major gigs together: card shows, special baseball events, anniversary celebrations. But when the gig is over they go their own ways, as they always have, glad to be apart.

A year after I saw them, came the 50th anniversary celebration of The Shot, something that baseball fans looked forward to, but the occasion was sullied by revelations of a sign-stealing operation that Leo Durocher had activated in July of 1951. In January of the golden anniversary year, a Wall Street Journal *reporter, Joshua Harris Prager, cracked open the story. The sting worked this way: one of the Giants was stationed at a clubhouse window of the Polo Grounds, 500 feet away, with a telescope, picking off the catcher's signs. He would then send an electric buzz to the bullpen where Giants' reserve catcher Sal Yvars—that's probably why Durocher forgave Yvars for slugging him—was waiting. One buzz meant a fastball; do nothing. Two buzzes meant a breaking ball; Yvars would throw a ball in the air.*

Almost all the Giants of that time admitted to Prager that such a system had been in place, but half of them said they never used it. Monte Irvin was one of them. In the Negro leagues, where sign-stealing went on all the time, he'd seen too many get hurt. It is interesting to note Bobby Thomson's home run stats from August 11, the start of the Giants run, to the end of the season—three home runs in the Polo Grounds and seven on the road, where the buzzer could not be used. "Not one New York regular showed a substantial improvement over the last third of the season that could be linked to stolen signs," wrote Stan Jacoby, a member of the Society for American Baseball Research (SABRE) in the New York Times.

But the allegations marred the anniversary and affected relations between Branca and Thomson. In some interviews Branca indicated that the fatal home run was helped by the sign-stealing. But to one New York Times *reporter, Chuck Slater, he said, "Bobby told me he was too focused to take a sign, and I believe him." Thomson, who admitted that he used the signs a few times, swore that he was on his own when he lifted that 0-1 fastball into the seats. "We've come apart a bit, and that hurts me," he said about the revelations. "We're just too damned old for this."*

A year earlier, as Branca and I wound up our conversation, I threw the expected question at him: What would your life had been if you never got to pitch in the ninth inning of that game? Branca's answer surprised me. "I really think it would have helped my baseball career," he said. "Because after that happened to me I pressed to make good. I pitched with a sore arm." His career ended in 1956, when he was only 30 years old.

"But in the long run, Ralph," I said, "if it hadn't happened nobody would have known you."

"That's true," Branca said, but his voice wavered. "Hey, you can't change it. You can't change the fact that I threw a home run. So what am I supposed to do, go in a closet and hide? I've nothing to be ashamed of. You get dealt a hand and you play that hand."

There aren't many Giant and Dodger players left from that thrilling summer, but the two leading actors are still on stage, reminding us of a game, and a moment, that will never be forgotten.

5

1958
SUDDEN DEATH
The Colts vs. the Giants

For John Steadman

On that Saturday morning of December 27, 1958, the Baltimore Colts flew to New York and settled in at the famous Concourse Plaza Hotel in the Bronx, a glide down from Yankee Stadium where, the next day, they would meet the New York Giants to decide who would be champions of the National Football League. One player who was delighted to be staying at the Concourse Plaza, which had long been home to many New York baseballers and New York Giants footballers, was Arthur Donovan, Jr., a defensive tackle for Baltimore who came to camp each year weighing 300 pounds and usually melted it down to 275. Donovan was the son of the Arthur Donovan who had been the great boxing referee of the Joe Louis era. Young Arthur grew up on the Grand Concourse, 40 blocks from the hotel. "I used to steal beer from American Legion dances when I was a teenager," he told me. When the Colts players strolled to Yankee Stadium for a light practice session on that Saturday afternoon, Donovan recalled, "All the Jewish fellas with baby carriages were down there with their kids, yelling at us: 'You guys are going to get it tomorrow!' I yelled back that we were going to shove that title you know where."

Now tomorrow had come. CBS would cover the game nationally on television for the third time. CBS was particularly happy about one development; NFL Commissioner Bert Bell had just decreed that all championship games tied after 60 minutes of regulation play would be decided by a sudden-death overtime period. The first team to score any points would be the winner.

Neither the Giants nor the Colts had prepared their players for such an eventuality.

With the temperature in the mid-40s—"Mara weather" they called weather that was good for the Giants and the Mara family that had always owned the team—62,500 spectators streamed into the stadium, most of them Giants fans. But not all. Three trainloads of Baltimoreans had arrived, toting blue-and-white Colts pennants and a hunger for sports glory that had been denied their city throughout the twentieth century. Twelve thousand Baltimore fans felt sure they would be witness to a new day dawning.

The two teams had already played each other once—in mid-season—before the largest crowd ever to watch a pro football game in New York, 71,123. The Colts came into that game undefeated but with a major handicap: their great quarterback John Unitas couldn't play; in their previous game, against Green Bay, he had taken a hit that resulted in three broken ribs and a punctured lung. The word was that he was out for the season. The Giants won the game on a late field goal by Pat Summerall.

Now, down in the catacombs of the stadium, both teams were making their final preparations. In the Giant clubhouse, the offensive and defensive units were huddling with their brilliant assistant coaches—Tom Landry for the defense and Vince Lombardi for the offense, who would one day become legendary coaches in their own right. The head coach, Jim Lee Howell, a 6-foot-6 former combat Marine in World War II, shuttled between them. Howell considered himself more a chairman of the board than a head coach. "After we got Landry and Lombardi, all I had to do was blow up the footballs," he explained. For this game Lombardi had created 15 new variations, hoping they might confuse the Colts' defense. But it was the Colts' offense, the best in the league, that the Giants feared; and the guys Tom Landry feared the most were Unitas—his ribs and lung healed—and his extraordinary running back, Lenny Moore. Landry told his defense that they should always assume the Colts were leading by 7-0 because either Unitas or Moore was bound to score at least one touchdown. Still, the Giants had been the best defensive team in the NFL during the regular season, and Landry counted on the muscle and agility of his interior line—those thick-legged Rockettes named Andy Robustelli, Jim Katcavage, Dick Modzelewski, and Roosevelt Grier.

There was more emotional clamor in the Colts' locker room, fueled partly because this team had never tasted success the way the Giants had, and partly because 14 members of the squad had been failures elsewhere. That was the topic of head coach Weeb Ewbank's emancipation proclamation to his charges. It was the pre-game speech of his life, directed towards almost every player in the locker room.

First he pointed to Unitas: "Pittsburgh didn't want you, but we picked you off the sandlots." Then he went over to defensive back Carl Taseff: "Cleveland didn't want you. If there are any more around like you I'll take them." To Bert Rechichar, the place-kicker: "I cut you last year to make a man out of you, and you are a man today." To Lenny Moore: "You can be as good as you want to be; that's what they said when we drafted you, and look what you've done." To Gene "Big Daddy" Lipscomb: "The Rams didn't want you. You have come a long way." To Jim Parker: "They said you couldn't play offense and were so-so on defense. But we sure used you." To Raymond Berry: "Nobody wanted you in the draft; you are a self-made end." To Gino Marchetti: "They said you are the greatest end in the league and you just couldn't get any better, but you continued to get better every week, and you will today."

Ewbank ended with Art Donovan: "They got rid of you, you were too fat and slow. Then I got you back. I'm awfully glad you're here today." At this point Donovan ran to the bathroom and threw up. It wasn't the speech that did it; it was his tradition—he had been throwing up before every game in his life. Spurred by their coach's address, and feeling that this was to be the game of their life, the players streamed onto the field. Weeb Ewbank, wearing a top coat and a fedora, clutched two sheets of paper that held his compressed plan for this game. Murray Olderman, a writer-cartoonist for NEA, later asked Ewbank if he could have the game plan. Subsequently, Ewbank gave it to him, and many years later Olderman let me have a copy. What I found most interesting was Ewbank's comments about the strengths and weaknesses of the opposition. It read like

Chairman Mao's *Little Red Book*: "One of the keys to our winning this week will be predicated on how well we pass-protect, pass the ball, and how well we catch it. Run good patterns—study your opponent—make him wrong."

The Giants won the toss and chose to receive. The Colts' Bert Rechichar boomed the kickoff nine yards into the end zone—today he was a man. Don Heinrich was starting at quarterback for the Giants, while Charlie Conerly stood on the sidelines with Howell and Lombardi. It was Howell's custom to open a game with his No. 2 quarterback so that his 37-year-old quarterback could save some energy, watch the Colts with his coaches, and note any tendencies. The downside of this odd strategy was that Heinrich wasn't a first-rate quarterback. But there he was, stepping back and trying to throw a spiral to Kyle Rote, who was out on the flank, only to have Gino Marchetti storm in, leap, and bat the pass down. Two more times Heinrich smelled the hot tar of the Marchetti steamroller, and Don Chandler, one of the league's best punters, did his job. The Colts took over on their own 30.

John Unitas's first play was a handoff to Lenny Moore, but Moore was stopped for a three-yard loss. On the next play, Alan Ameche, the fullback with the straight-on, head-bobbing style that had earned him a nickname, "the Horse," galloped up the middle for seven yards. Unitas dropped back as if to pass, and then started to run with the ball, but the Giants' all-pro middle linebacker Sam Huff met him head-on, and Unitas lost the ball. Another all-pro, Giant safety Jim Patton, recovered on Baltimore's 37-yard line. Suddenly, the Giants had the first opportunity to score.

Heinrich was still at quarterback, and he handed off to his right halfback Alex Webster for a quick slant. But middle linebacker Don Shinnick stopped Webster for a one-yard loss. On the next play, Heinrich fumbled the handoff, and Marchetti recovered for the Colts at midfield. Unitas threw a swing pass to halfback L. G. Dupre for a four-yard pickup. Then, Dupre carried the ball and gained one yard. Third and five. Unitas dropped back to pass and tried to hit his tight end Jim Mutscheller on the sidelines, but the pass was picked off by safety Lindon Crow. In his first two series, Unitas had caused two turnovers. What was going on? The cowbells stopped ringing in the Baltimore stands. But the Giants were impotent, too. On their next series they managed only seven yards, and Chandler had to kick it away. The Colts took over on their own 10.

Unitas was thinking, time to shake things up. His first call was a long pass to Moore, and he let fly. Moore, with one-man coverage, had flown behind Patton, and that's where the ball was coming. He made a leaping catch at the Giant 45 and raced 20 more yards before Patton caught him from behind at the 25. It was the first first down of the game. Unitas handed off to Ameche, and the Horse picked up five yards. But Dupre was stopped for a one-yard loss; the Giants defense was stiffening. Unitas peered out, didn't like what he saw, tried to change the call. and was nailed with a delay-of-game penalty. On third and 11, Moore could pick up only two yards, and Steve Myhra came in to try a 31-yard field goal. The ball sailed wide of the goal posts but the Giants were offside, and the ball was moved to the Giants' 19, where Myhra tried again. This time Sam Huff blasted through and blocked the kick. The Giants had willed their way out of trouble. Throughout the vast stadium, the approving cry was raised: "Dee-fense! Dee-fense."

Finally, Heinrich was replaced by the much maligned Charlie Conerly. Later on, that lean and leathery face of his propelled him to fame when they sat him on a horse, with a cigarette dangling from his mouth, as the first "Marlboro Man." Conerly had come to the Giants in 1948, fresh out of an All-America career at the University of Mississippi. Those were not good years for the Giants because they didn't have the material, and it was always the quarterback's fault. Fans would tramp into the park waving placards with such epithets as GO BACK TO MISSISSIPPI, YOU CREEP. But Conerly endured. The novelist Robert Daley was publicity director for the Giants in those years, and he was full of admiration for Conerly. "He was a fantastically wonderful football player," Daley says today. "He should be in the Hall of Fame and he isn't."

Conerly's first call was a slant to Webster, but Donovan mauled him to the turf. Mel Triplett, the fullback, did better on second down, swinging wide and picking up nine yards. Third and first, and Frank Gifford, who had yet to be heard from, swept left. "There were about eight of us one inch from bringing him down," Don Shinnick later recalled, "and if someone had just gotten in his way for a split-second he would have been buried. But the defensive flow just couldn't catch him." Blocks by Roosevelt Brown and Kyle Rote helped spring Gifford free, and he raced down the sideline to the Colts' 31—a 38-yard gain. The crowd was on its feet for the first time. On third and eight, Alex Webster faked a block and ran down the middle. Conerly saw that he was all by himself at the Baltimore 15, and his pass was true, but Webster lost his footing and the ball fell to the ground. With three minutes left in the quarter, Pat Summerall came in for the field goal and split the goal posts, and the Giants had a 3-0 lead. The Colts took over but could do nothing and punted. The quarter ended with the Giants in possession on their 18-yard line and Giants fans dancing in the aisles.

The Giants' 1958 season ultimately rested on the right foot of Pat Summerall. It was Jim Lee Howell who had wanted the 28-year-old Summerall for the Giants. Although had a poor field-goal average—45 percent—with the Chicago Cardinals, he was versatile. He could play tight end, he could catch passes and block like a tight end, and he also played defensive end, and sometimes even returned kicks. An off-season trade brought Summerall to the Giants.

At his first team meeting at training camp, Summerall quickly learned what it was to play New York Giants football. "I was sitting next to Don Heinrich and the room was kind of loud and raucous," he told me. "In came Lombardi. He just cleared his throat and the room instantly became quiet. I whispered to Heinrich, 'What the hell was that?' Heinrich said, 'You'll find out soon enough.'"

Until his midseason field goal that upset the Colts, Summerall had been conspicuously ineffective, managing only three field goals in ten attempts and blowing two extra points. He knew he had been playing badly, confessing to a teammate, "The pressure's killing me." But he came out of that Colts' game with his confidence renewed. Considering his background, it was amazing that Summerall was kicking at all. He was born with his right foot turned backwards—the doctors had to break the baby's foot to turn it around—and they told his parents that he would be able to walk but would never be able to play on it. And here he was, coming up to the Giants' biggest game of the year.

With one game left, the Giants trailed the Cleveland Browns by a game. They would play the Browns on December 14 at Yankee Stadium. They had to win just to get into a playoff. A tie wouldn't help. A crowd of 63,192 braved the 25-degree temperature and a snow-covered field and almost immediately wished they had stayed home. On Cleveland's first play from scrimmage, on their own 35-yard line, Jim Brown, the second-year running back who had already broken the NFL's season rushing record with 1,379 yards, burst over right tackle and raced 65 yards for his record-breaking 17th touchdown of the season. Suddenly there was nothing but silence from the stands, a silence that matched that of the snow falling on the turf.

The Giants then mounted a fitful drive that stalled on the Cleveland 38, and Pat Summerall was sent in to try to kick a field goal. He wasn't supposed to be in there at all. The previous week, it had been Summerall's last minute-field goal that beat Detroit, 19-17. Then, after kicking off to Detroit, a Lions' blocker hit him flush on his right thigh. The thigh was bruised, and the swelling spread to his kicking knee. All week long, preparing for the Browns, Summerall was unable to kick a ball. Before the Cleveland game he tried a few practice kicks in the snow. He told Tom Landry he was sure he couldn't kick off, but he might be able to try to hit an extra point, maybe even a short field goal. So Don Chandler handled the kick-offs and Summerall came in to attempt a 45-yard field goal, and he failed. With four minutes left, the score was tied at 10-10 and Summerall came in again, for a 33-yard field goal attempt, and missed again. He was devastated. When he came back to the bench a teammate, Cliff Livingston, said, "Don't worry. We're going to get the ball back."

And they did. With 2:16 left and the ball on the Cleveland 41, coach Howell went over to Summerall. Trying to loosen him up, Howell said, "Break your leg if you have to, Pat, but kick the hell out of the ball." By now the snow was coming down heavily. The

Giants' co-owner, Wellington Mara, was up in the press box, snapping Polaroids of the Browns' defense, which he would lower to the coaches on the field in a weighted sock; it was the pre-technology age. When Mara looked down there, he could just make out the figure of Pat Summerall through the swirling snowflakes. "He can't kick it that far. What are we doing?" he said to an assistant coach sitting next to him.

The kneeling Conerly brushed away the snow; the center, Ray Wietecha, spun the ball back, and Conerly took the snap and placed the ball down. As soon as he hit it, Summerall knew it had the distance, but he wasn't sure whether it was going to be accurate. Sometimes, if you hit a ball too close to the center, it behaves like a knuckleball, breaking from side to side. He saw the ball weaving out, but when it got to the ten-yard-line it started breaking back to the middle. A photograph of that moment made the front page of many sports sections the next day. It shows snow covering the ground, with only clods of dirt like chocolate chips offsetting the white frosting. Conerly, No. 42, is in the kneeling position and Pat Summerall's right leg is fully extended, the foot that was backwards at birth, pointing straight up in the air.

When Summerall returned joyfully to the sidelines after his clutch 49-yard field goal, the first person to grab him was Vince Lombardi, all his gigantic teeth showing ("teeth," one writer suggested, "that resembled a tank trap on the Maginot line") as he cried out: "You know, you son of a bitch, you can't hit that far." Some years later Kyle Rote said that Summerall's kick was "the single most clutch play he had ever seen in any sports."

Thanks to Summerall, the Giants won the game they had to win. A week later, in the playoff, they faced the Browns again, and shut them out 10-0, to put them in the game that would determine the world championship of professional football.

Opening the second quarter of the championship game, Conerly took the snap and passed to Gifford, who was out on the sideline, hoping to take off. But as soon as the ball reached him, he was smashed by Art Donovan and Big Daddy Lipscomb, and as he went down he lost the ball. Donovan remembers picking Gifford off the ground—"and I didn't even know he had lost the ball." Lipscomb did; he recovered the fumble.

On the next three plays, Unitas kept the ball on the ground: Moore for 4 yards, Ameche for 5, Ameche for 1 and the first down. Unitas then faked to Ameche, spun around, and handed the ball to Moore. He got major help from Jim Parker, the Colts' 6-foot-3, 273-pound human avalanche at guard. As Jim Lee Howell once said, "When you look at films of Baltimore games you usually see the defensive end hung up on Parker's shoulders with his feet spinning." That was the fate of Andy Robustelli, the Giants' defensive end; Parker's crushing block on Robustelli allowed Moore to break clear. Patton saved the touchdown as he had in the first period, with an ankle tackle at the two-yard line. But on the next play, Ameche busted into the end zone. Now it was the Colts, 7-3, and the Giants were facing another come-from-behind situation.

Rechichar's kickoff was returned to the Giants' 33. Conerly immediately threw a 14-yard pass to Kyle Rote, still a super-clutch player even with bad knees, for a first down at midfield. But then the offensive line sagged, allowing two Colts in to blitz the quarterback—a nine-yard loss. for Conerly. Webster took a reverse but was cut down after three yards. On third and 15, Conerly faded back, was knocked sidewise by Marchetti but somehow kept his feet. He saw Gifford free down the middle and hit him belt-high. The ball was on the 14-yard line when Gifford caught it and then, inexplicably, lost the ball. Don Joyce recovered for the Colts.

The Gifford takeaway lit a fire under the Colts. From their own 14, Unitas directed a 15-play drive, mainly, as Tex Maule wrote in *Sports Illustrated,* with "the backs following the quick, vicious thrusts of the big line, going five and six yards at a time, the plays ending on a quick-settling swirl of dust." One of the plays was a 16-yard scramble by Unitas after he found all his receivers covered. Then three pin-point passes to Raymond Berry, the first completions of the day for Unitas's favorite receiver, took the ball to the Giants' 15.

Now Unitas called two consecutive running plays. The first was an off-tackle slant by Ameche. The Horse drove through the line for six yards and was stopped by safety Jim Patton, who had come up from his secondary position to make the tackle. Unitas had set up his pigeon. The next play was run off in the same pattern, but this time Unitas faked to Ameche, who went cracking into the line without the ball. Patton was misled just enough to take one step in. That enabled Raymond Berry to break behind Patton into the left corner of the end zone, where Unitas hit him with a perfect pass. Now the Colts led by 14-3, and there was not time for the Giants to retaliate. The half was over.

In the stands, the buzzing among Giants fans was laced with uncertainty: Could their team, 11 points behind, come back? The surprise—the chagrin, really—was that Baltimore's defense was showing more class than the Giants, which was supposedly the best in the league, while the Colts were also maintaining their superiority on offense. Baltimore's total yardage in the first half was 198 to the Giants' 86. Unitas, despite an interception and a fumble, had completed 8 of 12 passes for 115 yards; Conerly and Heinrich together had made only 39. So it was the Baltimore crowd that was doing all the backslapping and singing and dancing as the Colts' band and majorettes entertained them at halftime.

Opening the second half, the Colts couldn't move the ball and punted. The Giants also failed to move and had to punt back, giving Baltimore the ball on their own 41—good field position if Unitas could take advantage of it. On the first play, he found his tight end Jim Mutscheller on single coverage and hit him, a 32-yard strike to the Giants' 27-yard line. On third down, it was Unitas to Raymond Berry to the Giants' 11. Berry was shoved out of bounds by Sam Huff, and Huff, wanting to make sure, put an extra hit on the receiver. Coach Weeb Ewbank, all 5-feet-5 of him, was so enraged that he ran onto the field and took a wild swing at Huff. Huff swung back half-heartedly, and players and officials separated them. Unitas, unbothered by the amateur fisticuffs, completed a pass to Moore at the Giants' 3-yard line.

Desperately facing a goal-line stand, the Giants defenders were heartened, as always, by the presence of Roosevelt Brown— a 6-foot-3, 255-pound all-pro offensive tackle—who loved to come in and play defense under these tough conditions. Brown was to the Giants what Jim Parker was to the Colts. Like Parker, Brown was known as a "quick hitter"—he could knock a defender off the line before the guy knew what was happening. He was so fast that he was one of the first pro tackles used to pull on sweeps, roar out from the line in front of the runner who was heading wide. And when he was inserted on defense he gave that unit an emotional as well as a physical lift. On the first play, the Colts' Ameche bulled his way up the middle for two yards, the ball placed down three feet from a score. On second down, Unitas tried to sneak it in, but Rosey Brown, among others, stopped him cold. On third down Ameche tried the middle. No gain.

Fourth down. A field goal would have been a chip shot and put the Colts ahead by 17-3. But Ewbank would have none of that. "I wanted to bury them right there with a touchdown," he said later. He told Unitas to go for it.

In the huddle Unitas barked out the call: "flow 28," a quick pitchout to the halfback who would then throw the option pass. Alan Ameche was in the halfback spot because Lenny Moore was out wide, where he would draw double coverage. But Ameche failed to hear the rest of the call from Unitas, the number after 28, which required him to throw the option pass. Jim Mutscheller was the "inside" or tight end on the right, and he found himself in the end zone all by himself, waiting for the pass. "It was supposed to work," Mutscheller explained later, "because Ameche hadn't thrown all year and it would surprise the heck out of them." "Throw the goddam ball!" Marchetti screamed at Ameche from the sidelines. Instead Ameche drove wide right, and before he could cut in he was leveled by linebacker Cliff Livingston for a loss at the 5. The Giants had held; they were breathing again. Yells of relief thundered through the stands.

On first down, Conerly slipped the ball to Gifford who made five yards. Second down, Webster for three; third and two on their own 13. Then Conerly decided to use a play that Vince Lombardi had drawn up at halftime. He faked a pitchout to Gifford, who was running right, drawing defenders to him, while Kyle Rote was gunning down the left sideline. When Rote reached midfield he cut sharply to his right, and Conerly lofted a deep spiral towards him. Rote made a brilliant diving catch, picked himself up, and started juking downfield, eluding tackles until he was run down at the 25 by Andy Nelson, who flung Rote to the ground, causing the ball to squirt loose. But Alex Webster, trailing Rote, picked up the ball and lumbered towards the goal line, almost making it; Carl Taseff nailed him at the one-yard line. A photograph of the next play shows full-back Mel Triplett banging in for the score, his head butting the padded goal post, with Donovan and several other Colts draped over him like stuffed sacks. Summerall made the extra point. The Giants had closed the gap to a four-point deficit: 14-10.

After the kickoff, the Colts could do nothing, and the ball was punted back to the Giants' 19. Conerly completed passes to Rote and Gifford, and on the last play of the third period, he faked to Gifford and whipped the ball to wide receiver Bob Schnelker for a 17-yard gain. On the first play of the fourth quarter, Conerly faked two handoffs, made a complete turn and fired down the middle to Schnelker, a 46-yard gain. First down on Baltimore's 15. With the Colt defense concentrating on Schnelker on the left side, Gifford moved to the right, and Conerly found him in the right corner of the end zone. Fifty-three seconds into the fourth quarter, the Giants led by 17-14. And Yankee Stadium was pitching and yawing. A mist had reduced the visibility, and the lights were turned on.

The Colts took the kickoff and moved the ball down to the Giants' 39, where they stalled. Rechicher's try for a 46-yard field goal sailed short. The Giants took over on their 20. Rookie Phil King gained four yards. A Conerly pass to veteran halfback Ken MacAfee went to the 39. Gifford lost seven yards, Triplett gained seven, and Gifford gained ten more, to the Baltimore 46. The Giants were moving again. Then Phil King fumbled and the ball was kicked backwards and was picked up by the Colts' Ordell Braase on the New York 44.

Unitas decided to startle his opponents and he bombed one down to the four-yard line, where Lenny Moore, with both Emlen Tunnell and Lindon Crow in his face, made a spectacular catch. But an official ruled that he had caught the ball out of bounds. So Unitas loped back and hit Berry for 11 yards and a first down. Dupre slammed off right guard for another first down on the Giants' 27; now it was the Colts who were moving. Unitas went back to pass. Defensive end Andy Robustelli, who had previously been outmuscled by big Jim Parker, used finesse to beat Parker off the ball and slammed Unitas down for an 11-yard loss. Unitas went back again, and again he was blitzed; this time it was Dick Modzelewski coming through the middle to drop him for a nine-yard loss. The Colts had to punt; Jim Patton took it on the five and brought it back to the 19.

The Giants moved the ball to their own 40-yard line, and the clock showed 2:22 left to play. It was third down with four to go for the first down that might enable them to run out the clock. The 11 Giants' players stood together in the grainy mist, pawing the ground, knowing what they faced. A roar of expectancy thundered through the stadium from Giants fans, almost all of them on their feet. They, too, knew what was at stake.

Charlie Conerly took the call from the bench. It would be a sweep right to the strong side—the power play created by Vince Lombardi, which, during his glory years as coach of the Green Bay Packers, would be celebrated as "the run to daylight." The ball would go to Frank Gifford, the shifty and versatile 190-pound left halfback, who often moved to flanker to catch passes and stir up other mischief when the Giants were on the attack. The ball was snapped. Conerly faked to fullback Mel Triplett, who drove up the middle as if it was he carrying the package. But the ball was tucked into Gifford's hands and he was sweeping right, with Alex Webster in front of him. Webster blocked Colt cornerback Taseff outside, and Gifford cut back in. But the 240-pound Gino Marchetti grabbed Gifford around the ankles; linebackers Don Shinnick and Bill Pellington hurtled over Marchetti and smashed into Gifford, and they all fell to the ground in a wild pile, close to the first-down marker. Pursuing from the other side came "Big Daddy" Lipscomb, who once described his art as "just reaching out and grabbing an armful of players from the other team and peeling them off until I find the one with the ball. I keep him." On this play he simply threw his 6-foot-7, 290-pound body onto the mess, falling on Marchetti's right ankle. Somewhere in that human tangle you could hear the snap of bone. Between Gifford's screaming "I made that first down!" and Marchetti's screams of pain, the officials had trouble pulling people off the pile. Referee Ron Gibbs called time to have Marchetti moved so a measurement could be made. Gibbs bent over the ball. Then he rose and held up his hands; they were six or seven inches apart. "Fourth down!" Gibbs hollered.

Almost everybody on the Giants wanted to go for it. "With Marchetti gone," Jack Stroud, the Giants' all-pro guard, told a sportswriter some years later, "I figured a quick dive with Webster over that same spot would have gotten us the first down; it would have been a lot easier with Gino out of there. Besides, at that point we would have run through a brick wall." But Jim Lee Howell called for his punting unit to get the hell on the field.

Don Chandler boomed one high up into the swirling mist. To kick-returner Carl Taseff it must have seemed like hours before the ball came down, and he called for a fair catch on the Colts' 14-yard line. Now Baltimore, with one time-out left, had 1:56 to go 86 yards. As end Raymond Berry sprinted out with the offensive unit he couldn't help feeling apprehension. So little time left, said this paragon among pass receivers, who had tied for the league lead with 56 receptions. He looked downfield through the gloom and saw the distant goal posts. They looked a million miles away.

The perfect headline on the state of the Union in 1958 ran on the date of the game: "Ike Deserts Bridge To View Football Game." In those days the President of the United States had time for bridge and football and, in President Eisenhower's case, golf, too. It was also a time when professional football was stumbling to gain a toehold with the American sporting public. Traditionally, in the words of the old Giants' coach, Steve Owen, pro football was "the game that is played in the dirt and always would be"—a blue-collar sport played for blue-collar fans by blue-collar athletes. Art Donovan once described these athletes as "oversized coal miners and West Texas psychopaths." But the quintessential blue-collar football player of the time was neither a coal miner nor a psychopath; John Unitas looked as distinctively American as one of those itinerant farm workers in a

Walker Evans photograph. With his rough, creased face, he was not a pretty boy. His smile seemed to come tentatively, out of the corner of his mouth. It was a face that seemed in conflict with itself, reflecting self-assurance, but also reflecting the effects of a tough life. "Nobody ever gave John anything," John Steadman, sports editor of the Baltimore *News-Post* in 1958, told me. "He worked for everything."

Unitas was born and raised in Pittsburgh. His father, who delivered coal all over the city, died when John was five. His mother, with four children to feed, worked days and nights to support the family. By the time he got to St. Justin's High School, where he was a star quarterback, Unitas thought, This is what I want to do with my life. He hoped Notre Dame would take him, but he wasn't yet big enough, and he wound up at the University of Louisville. The Pittsburgh Steelers made him their ninth pick in the 1955 college draft, but they released him during the exhibition season, and he went to work with Bethlehem Steel, operating a pile driver. But football was still his life, and he signed up with a semi-pro team, the Bloomfield Rams, for $6 a game. "I don't think they ever understood that what mattered most to me was not the six dollars, but the fact that there was a football team that wanted me," Unitas once said.

In 1954, the diminutive 46-year-old Weeb Ewbank became head coach of the Baltimore Colts, one of the hangdog teams of professional football, a team which, the year before, had been the Dallas Texans. But it was unwanted in Texas, so the franchise moved to Baltimore. Ewbank kept only 13 players from the Texans, the two most notable being Arthur Donovan and Gino Marchetti. "Nobody handed me a football team," Ewbank said, but he had a talent for recognizing ability. In his first draft, on the 20th round, Ewbank picked as a "future" choice a skinny pass receiver from Southern Methodist University, Raymond Berry, who wore contact lenses and a canvas support for a chronic lower-back weakness. What Berry did have was a tremendous work ethic. As Donovan once recalled, "Me and Marchetti would have a dozen beers after practice, and Raymond would still be out on the field catching passes."

In 1955, Ewbank drafted quarterback George Shaw, the All-America from the University of Oregon, but he was looking for a backup. Herman Ball, who had joined the Colts as backfield coach, remembered a kid he had seen when Ball was working for the Steelers. He thought John Unitas might be worth a look. Ewbank told Ball to call Unitas. Ball liked to tell reporters he got the quarterback for 80 cents. It wasn't quite that simple. John Steadman, who was then assistant general manager of the Colts, told me what happened.

"We had a collection of free agents, maybe 60 of them, including Unitas. The idea was to bring them all in and just take them up the road for a workout to see if they had any speed and agility. The Johns Hopkins field wasn't available, so we wound up using a grass plot that was alongside the public swimming pool. It was a Saturday afternoon in May, and a few coaches went out to look. On Monday morning when I came to work, I asked how the session had gone. 'There was a kid named Unitas that looked pretty good,' one of the coaches said. They weren't giving him an endorsement for the Hall of Fame, just that he looked good enough to bring to training camp. He was the only one of the bunch they invited. He went to the camp, made a good impression, and stayed. The Colts signed Unitas to a $7,000 contract for the 1956 season, but even that sum wasn't guaranteed; if he got cut, he would only receive a piece of the money."

In the Colts' fourth game of the season, against the Chicago Bears, George Shaw was injured and Unitas came in. The first thing he did was throw an interception. Then he messed up the handoffs on a couple of running plays that resulted in fumbles. The Bears ended up slaughtering Baltimore, 58-27. "When we first saw this guy," Donovan said, "we all thought he was a bum who was never going to make it." At the end of the 1956 season, Shaw's record was 1-3 in the games he worked; and Unitas's record was 4-4. But Ewbank was happy with his performance. "The most important thing about him," he told me when I interviewed him in 1959, "is that he has a real hunger. This is a kid who has wanted success and hasn't had it too long to waste it now that it's come."

That hunger made him a fearless quarterback, too. One game when the Colts trailed the Chicago Bears by three points with 19 seconds left, Unitas was hammered face down to the ground. He got up slowly, bleeding from a split lip and a split nose. One of his team-mates, Alex Sandusky, tried to stuff the nose with mud to stop the bleeding. The Colts' trainer wanted to take Unitas out. "You take me out, I'll kill you," Unitas said. He got up, staggered into the huddle, called for Lenny Moore to fly down the right sideline. He hit Moore over his shoulder in the end zone, giving the Colts a last-second vic-tory. "That's no big deal," Unitas said later when asked how he did it, "I don't throw with my face."

In 1957, Unitas was the starting quarterback all season long, leading them to a 7-5-1 record, their first winning season ever.

In the current 1958 season, the key game for Baltimore had been a home affair against the San Francisco 49ers. The Colt players crept into the locker room at halftime, trailing by three touchdowns. Unitas, who was wearing a nine-pound steel and foam rubber corset that covered his chest and back to protect his mending ribs, hadn't had a good first half, throwing one interception that went for a touchdown. Ewbank just sat there, his face flushed, not saying a word. Then he rose and wrote on the blackboard: "WE NEED FOUR TD'S." The Colts, with Unitas leading the way, went out and scored the four touchdowns and held the 49ers scoreless, winning the game and the Western title. "When we came back for the second half," Lenny Moore said, "Unitas played maybe the greatest half of football I've ever seen."

With the Giants holding the 17-14 lead, and less than two minutes to go in the game, sportswriters in the press box were vot-ing for the Most Valuable Player of the game; the winner would receive a Corvette from *Sport* magazine. Charlie Conerly won the vote and the Giants' publicity director Robert Daley went to the bench to tell him the good news. Conerly mumbled that the game wasn't over yet.

Unitas came into the huddle knowing that there was so little time to catch the Giants. He took a quick glance at Gino Marchetti, who was on a stretcher in the end zone, his right ankle broken, refusing to be moved into the dressing room. "Okay, guys," he said to his players, "here we go."

His first play was a pass to Dupre. Incomplete. Second down, another pass incomplete. On third and ten, he hit Lenny Moore chest high. Moore was knocked down by two Giants on his own 24, but it was enough for the first down. Seventy-six yards to go, and now there was no more time to huddle. Unitas was calling audibles on every play, and noticing things about the Giants defense. "The thing I've found out about pro ball," he once told me, "is that no matter how good the defense is, you can always find a weakness somewhere. You find that gap and start hitting it. Then, when they close it up, you've got to find the next weakness." What Unitas noticed at this moment, with less than a minute to play, was that Berry seemed just to be covered by linebacker, Harland Svare. Unitas called "76-CL." L. G. Dupre would run a close flare out of the backfield, and Raymond Berry would run an L pattern, which was a ten-yard square-in.

"One of the things John and I practiced," Berry told *Newsweek* in 1999, "was that if the linebacker ever walked right up to me on the line on 76CL, we'd convert the play to a slant without saying a word. We rehearsed it for two or three years, but that situation never happened. Well, we come up to the line of scrimmage, and Harland Svare walks right up on my nose. So there we are: I look at John, he looks at me, and we know what we're going to do. I fake to the outside, Svare comes after me, and I duck underneath him. John drills me about five yards deep, and I run for 25 yards. The next play comes to me, too, and we pick up 15 yards. But the clock's running—no huddle. John calls a 10-yard hook pattern. He drills me. I catch the ball and fake inside, then spin, and break for another 10 or 15 yards, down inside the Giants' 20-yard line."

Three straight passes to Berry had gained 62 yards. "They were great calls," Vince Lombardi commented many years later. "Like everybody in the ballpark, we thought Unitas would shoot for the sidelines, but we didn't tell our secondary to leave the middle wide open."

With 19 seconds left, Steve Myhra headed in to try to tie the contest with a field goal. The field-goal team came on the field. Art Donovan always called it "the big ass team," for the massive guys up front: Donovan, 275 pounds; Jim Parker, 273 pounds; Sherman Plunkett, 300-plus pounds, on the right of Parker. Someone on the Giants side was hollering, "Stay onside! Stay onside!" Just then the ball was snapped.

Myhra had never been one of the elite field goal kickers; in 1958, he had made only four field goals in ten tries, and, in this game he had already missed one. As Unitas drove the team downfield, Myhra, who was said to be "a nervous type," was pacing back and forth, telling himself that he'd better not miss it or it would be a long cold winter back on the farm in Wahpeton, North Dakota.

The snap came fast and true from center Buzz Nutter. George Shaw adjusted the laces and stood the ball on point. Myhra rushed his foot into ball and thought he'd hit it squarely. He saw that the fat-assed squad had held off the Giants and that the ball was up in the air, but the visibility was so poor that he couldn't tell whether the trajectory was right. Neither could the players huddled on the sideline. Peering out through the mist, they agonized, would the game be tied up, or would they be heading home losers? George Shaw took one stride towards the bench, still looking back at the ball, Myhra right behind him. It was Shaw who clapped his hands together first. Then Myhra, his heart suddenly lightened, did the same. Both men had seen the official extending his arms in the air. Hallelujah! Myhra exulted, I didn't let the guys down. The Yankee Stadium scoreboard flashed the numbers 17 alongside each team. Beyond the confines of the stadium itself, an elevated train rumbled by; to some Giants worshippers in that congregation, it looked like a string of hearses.

The game was over.

Or was it? Nobody knew what to do next. "We had never discussed anything about an overtime," Unitas later recalled. "We were standing around scratching our heads, waiting for someone to make a decision."

Referee Ron Gibbs told the two coaches, Jim Lee Howell and Weeb Ewbank, that there would be a five-minute break and then a 15-minute sudden-death period. No matter how long it would take, the game would not end until someone scored.

The team captains, huddling under dark capes to keep out the chill that was enveloping the field, ran out for the coin toss; Unitas was subbing for the wounded captain Gino Marchetti who, when the field goal was made, finally allowed the stretcher bearers to carry him into the dressing room. "Yea, Gino!" the Baltimore fans cried as he left the field. Near the bench, the Colts formed a huddle, Ewbank in the middle. "When we get the ball," the coach told them, "we gotta hold it. Here's our chance to win it for Gino."

Ron Gibbs flipped a half-dollar up into the mist-thickened air and Unitas called "tails." It came up "heads"—the Giants would receive. If they could score, the game would be theirs without the Colts ever touching the ball again.

The Giants rookie, Don Maynard, took the kickoff at the eight-yard line and ran it back to the 20. Gifford swept right and gained four yards. Conerly threw to Schnelker, who was free and in first-down territory, but the pass was overthrown. On third and six, Conerly went back to pass, saw that his receivers were covered, tucked the ball under his arm and ran for his life; the Giants were short by a foot. The crowd yelled for them to go for it but that was too much of a risk in a sudden-death situation. Don Chandler boomed a 60-yard punt to the Colts' 18 and Taseff ran it to the 20. The first words Unitas said in the huddle were: "We're going to take the ball right down and score." "And we all believed him," Ameche later remembered.

Unitas's first call was to L. G. Dupre off tackle, and Dupre took it to the 31 for a first down. Now it was Lenny Moore's turn. Unitas let him loose and launched the ball down the sideline. Moore thought he had it, but Lindon Crow, on single coverage, just managed to tip the ball away. The near-reception scared the Giants enough to put back double coverage on Moore. Unitas knew they would; it was what he wanted. He saw that Huff was keying on Ameche and called a draw play for Dupre, hoping Huff would move off the middle. He didn't, and Dupre gained only a yard, but Unitas figured he had set something up. On the next play, he flipped a swing pass to Ameche in the left flat. Linebacker Harland Svare had left Ameche to cover Berry, and Ameche took it to the 41 before being hauled down late by Svare. The yardsticks came out: the Horse had made the first down by two inches.

After handing off to Dupre for two yards, Unitas went back to pass, but "Little Mo" Modzelewski (he had a brother who played pro football, who was known as "Big Mo") was on him, dropping the quarterback for an eight-yard loss. Third down—Unitas had to come up with something.

He brought the Colts out in a formation they hadn't yet shown, with Moore a slot back to the right and both ends spread. The play was meant to be a pass to Moore, but Unitas saw that Moore was covered. Raymond Berry, however, was downfield, with cornerback Carl Karilivacz trying to cover him. Just then Unitas saw Karilivacz slip, and, like an orchestra conductor, he flicked his left hand twice, urging Berry to run deeper. And then he cocked his arm back in the Unitas manner, as if flinging a shotput, and let the ball go. Berry caught it in his midsection, twisted away from one man and plowed forward to the Giants' 44, where it took five Giants to battle him down, dust exploding all around him. It was a 24-yard gain, and Unitas began to feel so fully in command that he thought he could do almost anything.

He remembered the hit that Modzelewski had put on him and figured that Little Mo would be blasting in again to keep him from throwing the ball. Good, let him try—maybe Sam Huff would drop back off the line to his left, looking for a pass. He had noticed that Huff was dropping back a little farther each time, trying to help linebacker Harland Svare, who was having trouble covering Berry. The trap worked. Little Mo charged across the scrimmage line, coming in so fast that he didn't see Art Spinney, the guard, who had taken one step back and exploded into Modzelewski from the side. Meanwhile, George Preas, the right tackle, cut off Huff. Ameche took a handoff from Unitas and streaked through the gap for 24 yards to the Giants' 20. Tom Landry remembered that play with regret. "We were looking for a pass," he later said, "and went into a special defense. Both linebackers, Svare and Livingston, were over on the strong side to double up on Moore. Patton and Karilivacz doubled Berry. Huff was playing pass, and they caught us."

Up in the CBS television booth, Chuck Thompson intoned: "Something historic that will be remembered forever is happening here today, ladies and gentlemen." On the next play Thompson said, "Berry makes a diving catch inside the 10. The ball is on about..." and the sound went off and the television screen went white; a cable had become disconnected. The officials called a time-out that lasted two and a half minutes before the screen lit up again. Unitas used the time to talk with his coach. "What do you want to do?" he asked. Ewbank said, "Keep the ball on the ground. Give it to the sure-handed carriers, Ameche and Dupre. Keep the ball in front of the goal posts. On fourth down we'll go for the field goal."

Television got its power back and Unitas tried a power surge with Ameche, but it only made a yard. Then Unitas disobeyed his coach. He called a pass play to Jim Mutscheller in the right flat. "Get the hell out there real quick," he told Mutscheller.

It was an unorthodox call, the riskiest of passes; if picked off, it could have been run back all the way. But Unitas had noticed—he noticed everything—that the Giants were overshifting and key-ing on Berry. Only Cliff Livingston was on the right side of the field for the Giants, and he was playing Mutscheller head-to-head. By running straight out to the corner, Mutscheller would have a stride or two on Livingston. He would also be giving Unitas a corner consisting of his own body and the sidelines. Afterwards, everyone said it was a foolhardy call. Unitas didn't think so. He reasoned (1) that there wasn't anybody out there who could intercept; (2) if the Giants changed their defense he would simply change the play; (3) if Livingston anticipated the call and hung on to Mutscheller he would throw the ball out of bounds.

Unitas took the handoff, pumped twice, and lofted the pass towards Mutscheller. The ball was thrown high and to the wrong side of Mutscheller, who had to turn around and then grab it high in the air with both hands. Losing control of his body, he fell back out of bounds inside the one-yard line. "That pass wasn't meant to get *close* to the goal line," Unitas said later. "It was meant to go for a touchdown."

Now it was third and one, and there would be no field goal. Unitas called "16 power"—Ameche off tackle. When Unitas slapped the ball into Ameche's belly and saw him take off, he knew nobody was going to stop him. With terrific blocking in front of him—Mutscheller blocked Livingston, Preas took Katcavage, and Moore knifed low into the veteran cornerback Emlen Tunnell—the Horse crashed between tackle and end.

The drive had taken eight minutes and 15 seconds. The clock on the scoreboard said 4:51 P.M. Night had fallen on the Giants.

Up in the press box, the writers erased Conerly's name as MVP and inserted the name of John Unitas. It was Unitas who had done it. He set a championship game record with 349 yards passing, and a record 17 first downs on passes. He also helped Raymond Berry to set a record—12 completions for 178 yards.

On the field it was chaos. After the call for "sudden death," hundreds of Colts fans, not knowing about the new rules, had left their seats and rushed onto the field. They were herded back behind the sidelines, where they were kneeling five deep. As soon as Ameche scored, some of the fans rushed him; the rest took down the goal posts, dismantling them in 18 seconds, what some wag said was a new pro record. Ameche had to fight his way back to his feet, stop the fans from trying to lift him on their shoulders and hustle to the dressing room. In the confusion he lost the football, but teammate Buzz Nutter saw the thief, gave chase, and recaptured it. He carried it into the dressing room, where Jim Parker, the first player in, took the ball, hugged Gino Marchetti, who was lying on the training table, his uniform pants cut away from his injured leg, and presented him with the game ball.

The atmosphere was much different in the Giants dressing room. The gray-faced players sat by their lockers in silence, cutting the tape off their bodies. "Nobody made a move to shower or dress," Alex Webster said later. "Nobody talked. It was the end of the season and we had no place to go."

Before he left the stadium that night, Weeb Ewbank pulled out his two-page game plan, the one he had clasped throughout it all. With a stubby pencil he wrote and underlined on top of the first page: "Won 23-17."

In the late spring of 2000, I went to see John Steadman in Baltimore. He was 73 years old, suffering from an incurable cancer. He had had a long and distinguished journalism career, becoming sports editor and columnist for both the Baltimore News-Post *and the* Baltimore Sun. *He was still writing a weekly column for the* Sun. *We had lunch together and he showed no concern about his condition. He wanted to talk about the old days, and so did I. He was held by the wonder of the past, particularly of Baltimore in late December 1958, that wonder still lighting up his face. He talked about the huge crowd that gathered at Friendship Airport late into the nigh to welcome back their World Champions. "There were 30,000 people," he said. "It was a crowd that was just temporarily insane. And our paper the next day sold 18,000 extra papers, the biggest sale since the end of World War II. We covered every line on page one with Colts. Even the weather said—'Not so Colt.'"*

He remembered one other thing. Just as the game ended, he was rushing down to the Colts' locker room, when he ran into the Commissioner of the National Football League. Misty-eyed, Bert Bell gripped Steadman's hand. "Johnny, old boy," he said, "I never thought I would live to see 'sudden death.'" Steadman thought, well who would manage to live long enough to see glory come to Baltimore?

6

1960
HEAD ON, THE
GENERATIONS COLLIDE
Hogan, Palmer, and
Nicklaus at the U.S. Open

The battle of past, future, and present at Cherry Hills made the 1960 U. S. Open the greatest golf tournament ever played.

—CURT SAMPSON

For three days in the middle of June 1960, the stars were in odd alignment in the mile-high Colorado air as the most important championship in American golf, the U.S. Open, got underway at the Cherry Hills Country Club, 20 miles from Denver. Any one of the brilliant golfers of the era had a chance to win this tournament of tournaments. But the oddest constellation, the one that would give the 1960 U. S. Open its emotion, was the intersection of three of the sport's all-time giants—Ben Hogan, Jack Nicklaus, and Arnold Palmer—at three dramatically different stages of their careers. Hogan, who was almost 48, represented golf's glorious recent past but, as was his way, refused to let go. Nicklaus, just 20, represented the future, but right now was considered the most talented of the 28 amateurs who would compete in the tournament. (However, *New York Times* golf writer Lincoln A. Werden defied convention and picked Nicklaus to win the tournament.) Palmer, at 30, seemed to be on the brink of greatness, but no one was quite sure whether he was for real. The generational battle wouldn't be decided until the last two holes.

In the practice rounds before the June 16 opening day, many of the contestants came off the course at Cherry Hills disparaging its challenge. "It has the easiest rough of any Open I've played in," said Billy Casper, Jr., the defending champion. Hogan told the press that the players were going to embarrass the United States' Golf Association with their low scores and, in fact, the golfers *were* blistering the course in those practice rounds, Hogan and Palmer shooting in the mid-60s. But the player who was really impressing the onlookers with his prodigious shotmaking was Nicklaus. Cherry Hills's 545-yard par-5 17th hole was officially described as "green on island protected by moat; trees border fairway." Nobody had been able to clear the moat on his second shot. Jack Nicklaus did.

Cherry Hills, however, proved deceptively difficult. Although the course played short, tournament officials counted on its narrow fairways, deep gullies, nine water holes, and plentiful out-of-bounds areas to keep the Open challenging. Another hazard was the altitude. Thirty-eight golfers in the practice rounds had taken oxygen every day, and portable tanks were set up around the course. Hogan had a severe headache three days before the opening round, which he blamed on the thin air. It had also been quite dry in Denver, and on the final practice day a wind storm hit the course that left the greens lightning fast. The only previous Open staged at Cherry Hills, in 1938, was tough on the contestants. Only one player broke 290—the winner, Ralph Guldahl, who shot 284. It was his second straight Open championship.

Arnold Palmer came to the tournament feeling ready. It didn't bother him that he was a 4-1 favorite to win (right behind him in the betting was Mike Souchak, the long-hitting, 6-foot-2, 220-pound former defensive end for Duke). Palmer had come off a stunning victory in the most popular American golf championship, the Masters, and was just establishing his persona. And what a persona it was. He was built like a light heavyweight fighter: 5-foot-11, 170 pounds, with thick thighs and negligible hips, with exceptional upper body strength and the bruising hands of a steamfitter. He was boyishly handsome, too, with the aura of a grown-up Huck Finn, a waterfall of hair spilling onto an almost perpetually furrowed forehead, the sweet, crooked grin that was a mixture of modesty and cockiness, the gritting of the teeth, the hitching up of the pants, his extravagant human emotions ranging from joy to pain hanging out for all to see.

It was the twilight of the Eisenhower era. There was almost nothing Ike liked more than playing golf, and in the eight years of his presidency he became the No. 1 ambassador for the sport. Arnold Palmer first met him at the 1960 Masters. They played a round together, ultimately forging a friendship that lasted for the rest of Eisenhower's life. Once, at a surprise birthday party for Palmer, arranged by his wife, Winnie, the biggest surprise came when Palmer answered the doorbell. Standing in the doorway clutching a small overnight bag, was a familiar figure with a familiar smile. "You wouldn't have room to put up an old man for the night, would you?" said Eisenhower.

Thursday, June 16, dawned warm and clear and sunny, Cherry Hills's cottonwood trees, evergreens, and Chinese elms tranquil in the light breezes that fanned the course. Large green tents flanked the rambling neo-Tudor clubhouse. A thin haze failed to spoil the view of the Rocky Mountains, massed in the distance. Mount Evans, Longs Peak, and Pike's Peak, all over 14,000 feet, were capped with snow.

Gene Neher was captain of the marshals on the first tee when Arnold Palmer came out to begin his crusade a little after 2 o'clock. His playing companions were Cary Middlecoff and Jack Fleck, former Open winners, two of the most deliberate ball strikers in the tournament, unlike Palmer, who was never one to let the bluegrass grow under his feet. It took almost five hours for the threesome to finish the 18 holes, about as long as a nine-inning baseball game today.

Neher was eager to see what Palmer would do on this 346-yard par-4 hole. Almost every one else had used a 3-wood, but Palmer, the longest hitter in the game, wanted to drive the green, felt he could and should at least try because—who knows?—you might end up with a hole-in-one.

"There's a little crick that runs down the right side of the green," Neher told me when I interviewed him 40 years later, "and Arnold hit the ball into that little crick." Palmer paid a penalty stroke and ended with a double bogey six. Steam was coming out of his ears. "I swung too fast," he said. His first round could have been worse; he birdied holes 2 and 5, took a bogey on 9, had two birdies and two bogeys on the second 9, and wound up with a one-over-par 72. Mike Souchak held a one-stroke lead with a 68. One stroke behind Souchak were two longshots, Jerry Barber and Henry Ransom. Eight players were tied at 70. Nicklaus shot a steady 71. But Ben Hogan couldn't buy a putt, and wound up with a 75.

In the press tent, Arnold Palmer, who had 18 players finishing ahead of him, was asked whether he thought he was still in contention. He gave a gritty smile. "I hope I'm this close Saturday afternoon."

He was born on September 10, 1929, in Latrobe, Pennsylvania, a working-class steel town east of Pittsburgh. His father, Milford "Deacon" Palmer, was 17 years old in 1921 when he was hired to work the grounds of the new 9-hole Latrobe Country Club golf course. He soon became head groundskeeper, and when the Depression arrived he doubled as the club pro. He was a big, strong man who could hit a ball a mile, but not heavenly-blessed like his son. "Hit the ball hard" is the way he told young Arnold to play. "Go find the ball, boy, and hit it hard again." The golf swing that he taught his son was a weird corkscrewing motion which, as Palmer once explained, "relied almost entirely on my great upper body strength."

The boy broke 100 for the first time when he was seven. Then he took his dad to the sixth green. "Watch me! Watch me, Pap!" he holler as he tried to hit the ball over a ditch with his sawed-off lady's driver. He did. Every Tuesday morning, which was ladies' day at Latrobe, he would hang around the sixth hole, waiting for one of the women golfers to ask him to please hit the ball across the ditch. There's a video documentary of Palmer's life, produced by the Golf Channel (I watched it over and over again), that shows a little boy, wearing shorts, his short blond hair flying in the air, banging a ball across that ditch and then receiving a kiss and a nickel from one of the women.

When he was 13, Palmer was thrilled by an exhibition match at Latrobe between his father and Babe Didrickson, probably the world's greatest all-around woman athlete. Palmer was captivated by Babe's personality and showmanship, but also by "how she hit a ball down the fairway, one of the sweetest, most compact swings you've ever seen." It occurred to him "how great it would be to make lots of people—complete strangers at that—ooh and aah over a golf shot." He began competing in junior golf tournaments; won a scholarship to Wake Forest and led the college's golf team; spent three years in the Coast Guard, and began to play serious golf in 1954.

That year, he won the U.S. Amateur championship, and his mother, Doris Palmer, ran up to her son and hugged him, her eyes filling with tears of joy. "Where's my father?" Palmer called out, looking around. Finally, his Pap showed up, with a rare proud smile on his face. "You did pretty good, boy," he said. Palmer remembers his heart swelling nearly to the breaking point, years later saying, "I don't know if I've ever felt as much happiness on a golf course."

Round 2 was the hottest day of the year in Denver—94 degrees—and Mike Souchak was sizzling. A masterful 67 gave him a three-stroke lead and a U.S. Open record two-round score of 135. But his 67 was matched by one other: Ben Hogan's.

It was Hogan's best round in a U.S. Open since his regal year of 1953, when he won the Masters, the U.S. Open, and the British Open. (It would be 47 years before another golfer, Tiger Woods, would match Hogan's three majors victories in one year.) Hogan birdied four of the first seven holes, finishing his first 9 in 32. Hogan's playing partner, Dow Finsterwald, who himself shot a 69 to put him in a tie for third place, called the Hogan round "one of the greatest rounds of golf I ever saw."

Jack Nicklaus played a steady round for another 71. He told people his swing was feeling great. "I was hitting my shots a little like Hogan," he said.

Arnold Palmer scrambled to stay with the pack. "I made several bold escapes from the rough and five birdies," he wrote in his 1999 autobiography, *A Golfer's Life,* "but I failed to convert several pars at crucial moments." He reached the halfway mark at 143. Ahead of him were Jerry Barber, Jack Fleck, and Dow Finsterwald, at 140; Sam Snead, Don Cherry, Bruce Crampton, and Ted Kroll, at 141; and Julius Boros, Ben Hogan, and Jack Nicklaus, at 142.

Originally, the United States Open was a 36-hole championship. But, in 1898, it was expanded to 72 holes, with the last two rounds played on the same day, a Saturday. That decision added an element of stamina to an event that had previously emphasized physical control. Playing 36 holes on the final day of the most important American golf championship would result in what one observer called "ten miles of fatigue wedded to eight or nine hours of mental stress." In 1965, television moved the grand finale from Saturday to Sunday afternoon, prime time for sports viewing. What television wanted, television usually got, even more so today in the new century.

Some experts felt that Ben Hogan would be the player most affected by a day-long effort to win his fifth Open because of his age and other infirmities. But Hogan himself wasn't worried. "Never in my life when I had to play 36 holes in one day," he said, "have I failed to play the second round in a lower score than I made on my first 18." Hogan felt this would be his make-or-break chance to win the record fifth Open that he coveted so desperately.

But at the 36-hole cut there were 54 other golfers left, and at least half of them had a chance to win.

Until 1960, in the whole long history of golf, the United States had produced only three supreme deities. The first was Francis Ouimet, who stunned the world at the age of 20, in 1913, by beating the supreme British golfer, Harry Vardon, and his next-to-supreme British partner, Ted Ray, in a playoff at the Country Club in Brookline, Massachusetts. Vardon had first come to the United States in 1900 and promptly won the U.S. Open. Against Ouimet 13 years later, he was amazed by the play of the local boy he had never heard of, who came from a family of modest means in a sport that was dominated by people of privilege. As Ouimet was being carted off on the shoulders of his new-found fans, the *New York Times* reported, a slight woman came up to the parade, on tiptoes, whispering something to the youngster. "Thank you, mother," her son said, "I'll be home soon." It was Ouimet's victory that began the democratization of golf in America. The middle class took up the game, and in ten years the golf-playing population rose from 350,000 to two million.

The next deity was Bobby Jones, who was born a gentleman yet who fitted perfectly with the rough-hewn superstars of the Golden Age of sports—Babe Ruth, Jack Dempsey, Red Grange, and Bill Tilden. From 1923 to 1930, Jones, who remained an amateur his entire life, played in 15 U.S. and British Opens and won seven of them. In 1930, his greatest year, he won a version of the grand slam of golf at that time: the British Amateur, the British Open, the U.S. Amateur, and the U.S. Open. Then, at age 28, Bobby Jones retired.

"The Hogan Age" flourished right after World War II. Ben was a dirt-poor Texan whose father killed himself when his son was nine years old. Growing up in Fort Worth, he caddied and scrabbled to perfect a game that would become his life. Those were hard years for ambitious young pros like Hogan, Byron Nelson, Ralph Guldhal, Sam Snead, and Lloyd Mangrum, who lived a nomadic life. "They drove from city to city in broken-down cars that were barely able to move," writes Robert Summers in his history of the U.S. Open. "They lived in the cheapest hotel, washed their own socks and underwear in their rooms, and lived on chicken salad sandwiches when they could afford them."

Hogan won his first U.S. Open in 1948. His character as a competitor was already forged. Will Grimsley, a golf writer of the time, described him as "a tight-lipped Texan with an iron rod of self-discipline, always protected by a hard crust."

He would need all of that for what happened to him in February of 1949. Driving back to Texas from a golf tournament in Arizona in an early-morning fog, his car collided head-on with a Greyhound bus. Hogan instinctively threw his body over that of his wife Valerie—a move that saved his life, because the shaft of the steering wheel rammed through the driver's seat. But he was critically hurt with a broken collarbone, broken pelvis, broken ankle, broken ribs and various internal injuries. Yet he somehow willed himself to come back. In 1950, pale, limping (a limp he never lost), both legs wrapped in rubber stockings, he endured an 18-hole play-off and won his second U.S. Open. His devastating injuries hadn't devastated his game. He won the Open again a year later, and won it again in 1953, the greatest of his years.

And here he was, in 1960, still feared by all those who were competing against him. He was a slight, 5-foot-7, weighed 140 pounds, always wore a flat-billed white cap, seldom smiled on the course, and seldom talked to his playing partners or to anyone else— "Hogan's trance," it was called. When he did say something, it was either a terse "you're away" to his playing partner, or a remark laced with contempt.

And then there was the kid.

Jack Nicklaus first saw Arnold Palmer in 1954, when he was 14, at the Ohio State Amateur tournament in Toledo. "It was pouring down rain," he remembered, "and I came off the golf course and there wasn't anybody playing." But Nicklaus did notice one person on the practice range who was banging balls one after another. "All I saw were these balls going out there quail high, hit with a 9-iron. And I thought, 'Boy, that guy hits a ball hard.' I asked someone, 'Who's the guy hitting golf balls in the rain?' And he said, 'Oh, that's Arnold Palmer.'" Palmer went on to win the tournament.

The two shook hands for the first time in 1956 at an exhibition match in Athens, Ohio, honoring the local boy, Dow Finsterwald. Palmer, who was then 26, had been hearing about this dude, 16 years old, who could already drive a ball higher, straighter, and farther than almost anybody else. "Just for fun," Palmer recalled, "we had a driving contest. I beat him by a hair." That afternoon, the older golfer played for the first time against the kid who would be joined at the hip with him for the rest of his life. He shot a 62. "I just worked as hard as I had in any tournament," Palmer said, "only because I wanted to impress this young guy. At the same time I was impressed by him."

Jack William Nicklaus, who was born on January 21, 1950, was also mated to a golf course early in life. When he was ten his father, Charlie Nicklaus, a prosperous owner of drugstores throughout Ohio, took his boy to the Scioto Country Club in Columbus to learn the game from a respected teaching pro, Jack Grout. Young Nicklaus also learned a thing or two about golf from the heritage of Scioto. In 1926 Scioto was the site of the U.S. Open, and Charlie Nicklaus had been there. He had been 13 and given a ticket to the storied event by the drugstore owner he'd worked for and also caddied for. Bobby Jones, who had just won the British Open and had been feted with a ticker-tape parade up Broadway, had hurried to Columbus a bit out of sorts after his long trip back across the Atlantic, but he had won the tournament and became the first man to hold the national Open championship of both the United States and Great Britain in the same year.

Charlie Nicklaus had been a golfer of promise, but when he had entered Ohio State's college of pharmacy, sports had taken a back seat to education, and he later put the sports focus on his only son. When that son was 13, playing with his dad at Scioto, he found himself on the 18th green with a chance to break 70 for the first time. All Jack had to do was to hole a 35-foot eagle putt. He desperately wanted to do it for his father. And he did—a 69 round he would never forget.

In 1959, Nicklaus made his national breakthrough. He was chosen for the Walker Cup team, the biannual rivalry between the United States and England in which only the best amateurs are selected. The Americans came to Muirfield, Scotland, and Nicklaus sparkled, winning his matches as his team breezed to a 9-3 victory. He came home brimming with confidence but wondering whether he should be just a golfer. He was a natural all-around athlete. In high school he had been a strong basketball, baseball, and football player and would have liked to have played them all at Ohio State, where he enrolled in 1957. He weighed 210 pounds, but the weight was not so evenly distributed; his future wife, Barbara, called him "Fat Boy."

The deciding event was the National Amateur championship in 1959. In four previous tries he had never gone beyond the fifth round. This time he wanted to do better; he wanted to make a statement about himself. The championship would be played at the Broadmoor Country Club, in Colorado Springs. It was a difficult course, 6,400 feet above sea level. But Nicklaus looked forward to playing a major tournament in rarefied air; he knew that next year's U.S. Open would also be held in Colorado. Playing what he later described as "steady but not spectacularly good golf," Nicklaus reached the final. His opponent in the match-play event was the 35-year-old captain of the recent Walker Cup team, Charlie Coe, who was also the defending Amateur champion, and when it ended the reporters all seemed to have one word for the Coe-Nicklaus duel: *classic.*

In the morning round Nicklaus shot a 71, but Coe outdid him with a 69. After the first three holes of afternoon play Nicklaus made up the deficit. The two then traded the lead all the way to the 36th, where it was dead-even. The home hole was a par 4, 430 yards long. Coe drove a deep, accurate shot onto the fairway, but Nicklaus hit his shot three yards farther. Coe struck his next shot, an 8-iron, a bit too hard, and it ran off the back of the green into a little hollow of rough. Nicklaus's 9-iron was truer, landing eight feet below the pin. With the pressure on him, Coe pulled out his sand wedge and hit a beautiful ball over the bank that rolled slowly down the incline dead on line for the cup and then stopped just short. Nicklaus and Coe exchanged smiles, a smile of sympathy on Nicklaus's part, a smile of regret in Coe's eyes, which also said, hey, that's life. But Nicklaus still needed the birdie. He read the 8-footer to break slightly from left to right. He bent over, hit it firmly, and the ball rattled into the center of the cup. With that putt he became the youngest amateur champion in 50 years.

The cherubic youngster was now gathering attention. Fans could see that inside a body that still carried baby fat was an athlete who seemed to be able to do anything with the ball and had a secure grasp of the complexities of the game. Even then, as Will Grimsley put it, he was "a cold and calculating competitor, poised and mature beyond his years."

Hogan started the third round at 9 A.M., and the golfer he would be playing with was Nicklaus. He liked Jack Nicklaus—felt that at 20 he already had a veteran's sense of the game. He was a quiet kid, too, who respected Hogan and was patient with the old man as he hung over the ball, hesitating to roll another putt. Putting was what was killing Hogan in the tournament. He had driven to the green in regulation on almost every hole, but it was so hard for him to get himself up for the putt, to get the club in motion. In that third round, however, putting didn't bother him much. He hit every green in regulation and made two birdies for a 69. Now if he could shoot a lower round in the finale, as he said he had always done, the title could be his. Meanwhile Nicklaus, drawing strength from his partner, also shot a 69.

Julius Boros and Gary Player went off next, and Boros had the best score of the third round, a 68. Gary Player shot a 71, which kept him in the competition.

Arnold Palmer was playing with Paul Harney, the pro from Massachusetts who was having a fine tournament, and Palmer's troubles started on hole one. Pulling out his driver, he tried once again to drive the green, missed again, ended up in the rough, and bogeyed the hole. He was topsy-turvy the rest of the way. Cherry Hills member Jim Stadler was in Palmer's mini-army, all 30 of them, that morning. "I followed him down to the 10th hole. He proceeded to knock his second into the right trap. The pin was down in a very easy location on the flat. He took a swing and left the ball in, and then took another and barely got it out. The ball sort of hung on the fringe and then rolled on the green about six feet. He had taken four strokes by now and most people figured he was going to wind up with a seven on the hole. But he ended making the putt for a bogey five."

Palmer shot five birdies over the 18, but there were three bogeys and one double bogey, and this young man of unfailing optimism, who always said, "I've never seen a hole that I didn't think I could birdie," stomped off the course with another 72.

Just off the 18th green at every U.S. Open is a small tent where the players go over their scores, hand them in, and seal their dreams. Joseph C. Dey, Jr., executive director of the USGA for many years, referred to it as the tent of broken dreams. "This is the seat of reckoning," Day once wrote. "Here the player comes face to face with his deeds, be they good or bad. Here his struggles of the last several hours—his moments of elation, his times of distress—are compressed into the cold capsules of figures on a little card."

Palmer walked into that tent heavy with foreboding: he was tied with six others at 215, 14 players were ahead of him, and he was seven strokes behind the leader, Mike Souchak. The coldest statistic of all was that no man trailing by more than five strokes after 54 holes had ever won the Open.

It wasn't supposed to be this way for Palmer. Almost from the beginning of his career he was like an eager young corporate trainee, on the slippery ladder, rising up almost to the highest rung, aiming to be the next CEO of golf—to succeed Ben Hogan. He first met Hogan in 1955 at Augusta, when he played in his first Masters. It was a moment he would never forget—as a teen-ager he had fantasized about beating Byron Nelson and Sam Snead and especially the one who was the best of them all, Ben Hogan, taking Hogan at Latrobe "on the perfect fairways of my vivid daydreams."

The meeting was not what he had expected. "Hogan was polite enough," Palmer says in his autobiography, "but I felt the cool, disturbing distance that others sensed when in his presence. I was surprised—and later angered—about the fact that he never in the years I knew him called me by my first name. He only called me 'fella.'"

But not everyone felt the same way about him. Paul Harney was once offered the opportunity to play with Hogan for six days in a row. Harney had just won the Egyptian match play championship, which earned him an invitation to compete in the Colonial Open at Fort Worth, Hogan's own dream course; he won the Colonial five times. Harney came to Fort Worth a week early to practice. On the first morning he and Hogan were by themselves at breakfast. As Harney recalled it, Hogan asked him if he would like to play. "I said sure. We went out there. I parred the first hole and didn't make another one. The next morning I went down to breakfast, and there was Hogan. He said, 'Would you like to try it again?' I said, 'Okay, if you're game, I am.' I was kind of annoyed, though; he hadn't said one word to me when we'd played the first time. This time I parred the first hole and I parred 18, and that was it." After it was over Hogan turned to Harney and said, "Son, you're improving."

"I could have hit him over the head," Harney told me, "but he was my idol, underneath it all, really a very congenial guy. And he'd completely mastered the game of hitting the ball. I played with him those six days straight and he never missed the center of the fairway; every ball he hit was going to hit the center. I just learned that I had to work harder."

Arnold Palmer came of age at the 1958 Masters. He had driven all night to get to Augusta, and when he went out on the course with Dow Finsterwald to play a pre-Masters practice round against Jack Burke, Jr., and Ben Hogan the next morning, he played badly. Afterwards, in the locker room, he heard Hogan say to Burke, "Tell me something, Jackie, how the hell did Palmer get an invitation to the Masters?" Palmer was livid. He wondered, what's that guy got against me? He vowed to show Hogan why he had been invited to the Masters.

He shot opening rounds of 70, 73, and 68 and in the final round had a one-stroke lead coming to the infamous 12th hole, generally agreed to be the toughest par 3 in tournament golf. Palmer's tee shot carried over the green and embedded itself in the soft turf between the putting surface and the green. Because of heavy rains earlier in the week, the tournament was being played under wet-weather rules. That meant that a "plugged" ball could be lifted, cleaned and dropped without a penalty. But an official at the scene told Palmer he had to play it as it lay. Furious, still stung by Hogan's words, he said he would play two balls and appeal his verdict to the rules committee. First he dug the ball out with his wedge and wound up with a double bogey 5. Then he placed a new ball at the same spot and ended with a par 3. After that, while Palmer waited to hear from officials, he went to the 475-yard hole 13 and made one of the most miraculous shots of his life.

On his tee shot, he creamed one that left him about 255 yards from the hole. He decided to go for the green on his second shot. He took a 3-wood, settled into his stance, and moved into his swing smoothly. The ball landed 18 feet to the left of the hole and straight above the cup. His putt, struck firmly and with confidence, slipped into the hole and Palmer had an eagle 3.

Bobby Jones saw it all from a hill above the fairway. Jones called that 3-wood shot one of the two greatest shots he ever saw, the other being Gene Sarazen's double eagle in 1935 on Augusta's par 5 15th hole.

Now, at that same 15th hole, Palmer was summoned to meet with officials who were gathered around Jones's green golf cart. After some heavy discussion, the rules committee chairman said, "Mr. Palmer, the committee has ruled in your favor. You will have a 3 at the 12th hole."

Palmer was so happy that he birdied the home hole for a final round 73 and a four-round 284. "Winning that first major as a professional," he said, "told me something about myself—that with the right kind of focus and hard work, and maybe a little luck, I could be the best player in the game." Financially, Palmer did end up as the best player in 1958, netting $42,608.

Two years later—again at the Masters—one of the most loyal legions of followers in the annals of sport was born. It was Sunday, April 10, 1960, and 40,000 people were streaming over the Masters course, with its backdrop of jasmine, dogwood, red bud, and azaleas in full bloom. Soldiers from nearby Camp Gordon had been recruited to man the scoreboards, along the course. One of those scoreboards, near the 11th green, flashed the message: "Go Arnie." Underneath the two words was the sign-off: "Arnie's Army."

"By the thousands, in a ragtag horde armed with binoculars and umbrellas and folding stools," Bud Shrake wrote in the Dallas Morning News, describing the new phenomenon, "they march with their leader. They grunt with him when he swings a golf club. They suffer with him. They worship him." Shrake went on to describe Arnie's Army as "smelling like grass, like beer, and a freshly mowed lawn, like mustard and damp laundry." Palmer was still only a hero-in-waiting, bunched with a pride of other thoroughbreds, waiting to break out of the pack like a great thoroughbred racehorse, but it was his promise and his persona that the army loved. It was the way he played the game, striding onto the first tee like a prizefighter about to climb into the ring; lighting his L&M's, sipping Cokes from a can, waving at spectators, smiling, grimacing, anxious, and excited, his nervous energy flowing over to his army.

Coming to the 15th green, Palmer looked at the scoreboard. Ken Venturi was already off the course, probably being measured for the 1960 green jacket; he'd finished with a two-under-par 70 and a four-round total of 283. With four holes to go, Palmer would need one birdie to tie, two to win. On 15, he missed a 15-foot birdie, and he could only par hole 16. "You've got it," a reporter said to Venturi, who was waiting in a cottage. "Nobody's going to play those last two holes in two under par." Venturi just shrugged; he understood that it was never over until it was over.

When Palmer birdied 17, he jumped in the air and punched the sky with his upraised fist. His new-found army, lining the fairway and swarming around the green, went mad.

On the 18th hole, a 420-yard par 4, he boomed a deep drive down the fairway into the wind, the ball gliding 120 yards from the green. Palmer took the last puff of a cigarette, tugged at his glove on his left hand, jerked at his trousers and yanked out a 6-iron. "The crowd began murmuring," Will Grimsley wrote, "the noise like an ocean swell." Palmer's punch shot skimmed low, stopping six feet from the cup. Playing for a break, he bent, stroked, and watched the ball curl into the hole: the first momentous charge of his career. The headline in *Life* magazine read: "At Masters, Palmer replaces Hogan, Snead."

Not quite yet.

Now, two months after the Masters, Palmer's quest for the 1960 Open title had come down to the final 18 holes of the Cherry Hills course, and his chances looked grim: 14 players ahead of him, Souchak out in front, seven strokes ahead of him. He sat in the locker room, having showered and changed his shirt after his third tepid round, ordered a cheeseburger and a Coke, and chatted with the writers Bob Drum and Dan Jenkins, both friends of his, and the golfers Ken Venturi and Bob Rosburg, who were both still in the running. The day had turned hot and Arnold Palmer was even hotter under the collar as he listened to the discussion of who would win the Open if Mike Souchak faltered. Nobody looked at Palmer.

Suddenly, Palmer said, "What would a 65 do?"

Bob Drum, who wrote golf for the *Pittsburgh Press,* replied: "Nothing for you."

"Sixty-five is 280," Palmer said. "Two-eighty always wins the Open."

"Yeah, when Hogan shoots it," Dan Jenkins said.

"Two-eighty won't do you one damn bit of good," Drum said.

"Oh, yeah? Watch and see," Palmer said, chucking his cheeseburger and stomping out of the room. At the practice tee, mad as hell, he slammed ball after ball until he heard his name being paged.

He marched out there with Paul Harney to the tee of the first hole—the tee that had defied him for too long. Once again, he pulled out the driver he had used three previous times. It was a Hogan driver, but Palmer had changed the sole plate, put in a Palmer shaft, and added an Arnold Palmer decal. Palmer was thinking eagle, not birdie. His swing was once described by a writer as not so much a swing but a slash: "He slashes violently at the ball with the same chopping motion lumberjacks use to fell a tree with an axe."

Gene Neher, the marshal on hole one, watched that Palmer slash, watched the ball soar through the air, watched it land on the green 346 yards away. No other golfer in the tournament had done that. Neher ran to where a loudspeaker was mounted on a pole and hollered to the announcer to tell everyone Arnold Palmer had *driven the green*. "I had the feeling," Neher told me, "that Palmer's drive was quite significant." Quite significant? It was one of the most meaningful drives in golf tournament history. The irony of the moment, however, was that Palmer's gallery still numbered only 30 people. His newly mobilized army, sworn in at the Masters, had fled to Hogan and Nicklaus and Souchak, the real leaders of the afternoon.

Palmer narrowly missed his eagle putt of 30 feet, but got his birdie. Now he felt the "inner glow" that had come to him at other special times out on the course. His caddie, Bobby Blair, knew what was going on. "He gets that smile," Blair said later, "He hitches up his pants and rubs his arms and begins to walk fast, excited like. You can feel the man is hot even before you see the way the ball is being hit." This is how the inner glow worked for the possessed one:

Hole 2, 410 yards, sinks a 35-foot putt from off the edge of the green. Birdie.

Hole 3, 348 yards, wedges his chip shot one foot from the cup. Birdie.

Hole 4, 426 yards, drops in an 18-footer. Birdie.

Hole 5, 538 yards, drives into the rough and settles for the par 5.

Hole 6, 174 yards, hits the center of the green with a 7-iron, nails a curving 25-foot sidehill putt. Birdie.

Hole 7, 411 yards, dogleg left, strokes a chip shot six feet from the hole, makes the putt. Birdie.

Six birdies in the first seven holes! Even with a bogey on 8 Palmer ended with a 30, tying an Open record for nine holes. The charge was on. Arnie's Army, shamed by their defection, hurried back to reinlist. Palmer had turned the tournament upside down.

After nine holes, Jack Nicklaus, with a spectacular eagle on 5, led the field. One stroke behind at the turn were Souchak and Jack Fleck;

two strokes back were Julius Boros, Ben Hogan, and Arnold Palmer; three strokes back were Jerry Barber, Don Cherry, and Dow Finsterwald.

Then, as Souchak put it later, "everything happened." On the first tee, playing right after Palmer and Harney, Souchak saw how Palmer crushed that ball onto the green and decided he would also drive the green. His ball landed in the creek, he failed to recover well, and he double bogeyed the hole. He also bogeyed the ninth, and that was when he lost his lead for the first time. "For four unbroken hours," Herbert Warren Wind would write in *Sports Illustrated,* "there were so many contenders performing such fantastic things that it was impossible to keep track of who was leading and who was falling back and who was coming on."

But by the final seven holes, the focus was pretty much on the generation gappers: Hogan, Nicklaus, Palmer.

On the 563-yard 11th, Palmer reached the green with a drive and a 4-iron. Two putts and he had his birdie 4, which would be his last birdie of the match.

On the 12th hole, a 212-yard par 3, Palmer had no trouble parring 12. But the hole finished Souchak; he dropped his tee shot into the water for a 5.

Hogan and Nicklaus, playing together, never wavered. Hogan took a 3-wood and lifted a high, soft draw that landed ten feet from the flag. Nicklaus took a 2-iron and hit it 20 feet past the flag. Hogan holed his putt, the birdie placing him three under par for the tournament. Nicklaus holed *his* putt, his birdie putting him five under par. As he approached the 13th tee, Nicklaus glanced at the scoreboard—he was still leading, a stroke ahead of Boros, Fleck, and Palmer.

The 13th is a straightaway 385-yard par-4 hole, and Hogan as usual reached the green in regulation and made par. Nicklaus also felt that he was in good position, driving his ball just where he wanted to, on the flat part of the fairway. Next he lofted a 9-iron approach 12 feet below the pin. Here, he thought, was a chance for a birdie that would put him two strokes ahead. But his ball slipped 18 inches past the cup. As he was getting ready to put away his short putt for par, Nicklaus noticed an indentation directly in his line, the remains of a ball mark that should have been repaired. He didn't know what to do. He thought it would be O.K. to fix the ball mark himself, but he wasn't sure. Should he ask an official? He could have asked his playing partner, but he didn't want to bother Hogan's concentration. He may also have been afraid that Hogan would turn cold on him—not say a word, or, worse, say something sarcastic, which he had done with others who played with him. Nicklaus was 20 years old, so he did nothing and his putt hit the ball mark, causing his ball to slightly alter course, enough to catch the left side of the cup and spin out. That error of judgment, born of immaturity, would be remembered.

On the 14th hole, rattled, Nicklaus couldn't get down a 7-foot putt and took his second bogey in a row. Hogan got his par.

On 15, a par 3, 196 yards, Hogan made a tremendous 20-foot putt to go four under.

On 16, both men had birdie opportunities, but Hogan missed a 7-foot putt and Nicklaus, still shaky, missed from 5 feet.

Meanwhile, to the rear, Arnold Palmer birdied the 11th hole, tying Hogan and Fleck for the lead and made consecutive pars on 12 through 16. He was playing smoothly, almost with a giddiness after his spectacular charge. When Hogan was told that he shared the lead with Palmer, he cried, "*He's* not a contender, is he?"

Approaching the 17th hole, it broke down this way: Hogan and Palmer were 4 under par; Nicklaus and Boros were 3 under.

Seventeen is a par 5 that measures 548 yards. It's set on a small island, the green protected by a moat—20 feet of water separating the end of the fairway from the front of the green. One had to be careful. The proper course was to go with an intelligent drive, a careful lay-up and a safe pitch to the green. A further danger was that the pin was positioned dangerously close to the front of the green, with a slope that could carry the ball back into the water.

Ben Hogan was probably more tired than any one of the leaders, though he had been playing superbly; he had hit 34 consecutive greens in regulation. Nicklaus knew what it was all about, and he wasn't going to try to get home on his second shot. He took a 4-iron, lobbed a little wedge that rolled 12 feet past the hole, and missed the birdie, but he was still three under par for the tournament. Hogan lay up in the center of the fairway, about 25 yards short of the water. Behind Nicklaus and Hogan on 17, Julius Boros and Gary Player waited to hit their second shots. Behind them, Palmer and Paul Harney stood back on the tee, watching.

Hogan figured that Palmer was still on his tail. What to do about that? All he knew was that he wanted that fifth Open so bad that it squeezed his heart, and Palmer stood in his way. Hogan couldn't understand how Palmer had come so far so quickly, his game was so odd. What he was thinking was once described by Dow Finsterwald: "Palmer took a whack at the thing, and sometimes it didn't go down the fairway, but he always had a vivid imagination as to how to play shots from areas that were not normally visited by many players." What Hogan didn't understand was that Palmer's emotions matched his own. He had the great players' faith that *anything is possible*."

About the decision that Hogan made on 17, Palmer would write in *A Golfer's Life,* "You have to credit Ben. He did what a champion does at such a crucial moment: play the shot he thinks will work best and the devil take the consequence." In other words, Hogan, who almost always played the percentages, ended up doing just the opposite: safety last.

As Nicklaus later described the shot, Hogan "laying the face of his wedge back almost flat with the ground, hit the ball with a very decisive action and cut up a low-flying shot that was obviously loaded with backspin." Nicklaus thought it was going to be perfect, and so did the gallery, who began a hum of awe. The shot was true and beautiful, and it came down on the bank in front of the green. But Hogan had put so much spin on it that it rolled back into the water.

Hogan did what he could. He took off one shoe and sock, waded into the water, somehow was able to slash the ball onto the green, and then missed his par putt. Risking everything to stay in the race with a birdie, he had ended up with a bogey. Long afterward, in a television interview with Ken Venturi, Hogan said, "It's been 23 years, and there isn't a month that goes by that the memory of it doesn't cut my guts out."

The adrenaline was no longer flowing. Hogan walked slowly

with Nicklaus towards the 18th tee, feeling that he had left a piece of his life behind. He hit his shot into the lake and ended with a 7. He finished with a 284, tied with two others for fourth place.

Hogan's plight also affected his young playing partner; Nicklaus was unable to maintain his intense concentration. On the 18th hole, his approach shot landed in the rough to the right of the green. He then stroked a marvelous 35-foot chip shot six feet from the hole. It would mean everything if he could make that birdie, but he just missed.

Now it was Palmer's turn alone. He had played steady, error-free golf down the stretch. After watching Hogan flame out and Nicklaus miss his birdie, there was only himself to beat. Palmer was thinking, *one more par.*

He drove with a 1-iron across the pond onto the fairway. He pulled his 4-iron approach shot 80 feet to the left of the pin. He took a couple of deep breaths, adjusted the visor on his head, hitched up his pants, squinted over the ball, and chipped to three feet from the hole. On his way to the ball, he did what Nicklaus failed to do back on the 12th green—a lifetime ago, it seemed: pause to repair a ball mark.

Palmer kept his head still, took the putter back slowly, and struck the ball into the center of the cup. Then, with Arnie's Army yelling in joy, Palmer, smiling like an angel, kicking a leg in the air like a drum major's strut, grabbed his visor and flung it towards the gallery. He had done what he dreamed of doing as a little boy. He had won the U.S. Open.

He walked on air into the tent of broken dreams. No broken dreams for Arnold Palmer. Not this time.

Today, on the first green at the Cherry Hills Country Club, there is a commemorative plaque that sits atop a fountain. It reads:

ARNOLD PALMER, 1960 U.S. OPEN CHAMPION
CHERRY HILLS COUNTRY CLUB

Palmer drove this green in the final round, scoring 65 for a 280 total and victory.

7

1964
CHOSEN BY
THE GODS
Billy Mills in the 10,000-Meter Olympic Finals

Now bid me run,
And I will strive with things impossible
                                                    —Julius Caesar

The first race for the gold would not begin until 4:30 in the afternoon, but early on the morning of October 14, 1964, the crowd began streaming into Tokyo's majestic National Stadium. A steady rain was falling and umbrellas were open everywhere. The red clay track was turning spongy. It was the opening day of track and field, the heart of the Olympic Games: world class runners and jumpers and throwers fighting for their country, fighting for themselves, fighting for the *gold*.

This was the first time since the rebirth of the modern Olympics in 1896 that an Asian country was host. Tokyo was supposed to have held the games in 1940, but a new world war raging in Europe had put an end to that, and the Olympic Games were not resumed until 1948. Now the Japanese were making up for lost time by offering what the columnist Arthur Daley in the *New York Times* called "a dream production of exquisite beauty." It was a pageant that perfectly reflected the Japanese sensibility—flowers everywhere, paper lanterns and soft lights glowing behind paper walls.

Although only preliminary heats for the sprints and hurdles were being held this morning, a gathering of 72,000, mostly Japanese, but spiced with spectators from many of the 94 competing nations, were sitting patiently through a two-hour lunch break. Four days earlier, at the opening ceremony of the 18th Olympiad, a 19-year-old Japanese runner, Yoshinori Sakai, streaked onto the track carrying the Olympic torch aloft. He ran around the track and then up 154 green-carpeted steps, flanked by flowers and giant artificial peacocks. At the summit he stood at attention, stretching the torch towards the black cauldron. Solemnly, he waited, as if to give the crowd—the spectators in their seats, the 5,500 athletes on the field, and Emperor Hirohito in his royal box—a pause for reflection. Then he dipped his torch into the saucer, and the combustion caused a great flame to shoot up into the sky. One wonders whether Sakai's pause was also for his own personal reflection; he was born in Hiroshima on August 6, 1945, the day the first atomic bomb was dropped and changed the world forever. Planes flew over the stadium trailing Olympic rings and doves soared into the sky.

The first rush for gold in track and field on this 14th day of October, 19 years after the signing of the peace on the battleship *Missouri,* would be the 10,000-meter event, a distance of 6.2 miles. It wasn't a race likely to touch the hearts of American spectators; throughout the history of the modern Olympics, American athletes had never shown proficiency at distance running. Only once had a runner from the United States taken a gold medal at a distance beyond 3,000 meters, and that was a fluke. It happened in 1908 when an Italian runner, Dorando Pietri, won the marathon but was so exhausted that he needed help to cross the tape. That was against the rules, and the medal was awarded to the second man home, Johnny Hayes of St. Louis, Missouri.

Thirty-eight qualifiers would be running 24 laps around the track, some of them versatile enough to have also qualified for the 5,000-meter race or the marathon, or both. *Track & Field News,* noting that 14 of the entrants had run the 10,000 in less than 29 minutes, called it "the greatest field in history."

There was, however, one clear favorite—the world record holder, Ron Clarke of Australia. Clarke had become a wonder boy in 1956, when at the age of 19 he set a world Junior (under 20) record for the mile: 4:06. For that feat he was given the honor of carrying the torch into the stadium to open the Olympic Games later that year in Melbourne, his home town. After that Clarke married, started a family, and put running aside, instead choosing to play Australian Rules football. (His younger brother, Jack, became a legend in that sport.) He returned to competition six years later and, in 1963, was entered in a 10,000-meter race at Okina Park in Melbourne. It was seven o'clock at night and there were, Clarke said, 23 people watching. He broke two world records held by the immortal Czech runner Emil Zapotek—the six miles in 27:17.8 and the 10,000 meters in 28:15.6. That was the start of an astonishing five-year string for Clarke in which he broke 18 world records in almost every category, from two miles to 20,000 meters.

At Australia's Olympic trials for the 1964 Games, Clarke had won both the 5,000 meter and the 10,000-meter race. He came to Tokyo primed in both events. The most popular runner in the race as far as the home crowd was concerned was 24-four-year-old Kokichi Tsuburaya, son of a samurai, seeking the highest honor for his country. But Clarke's most dangerous challengers would probably come from among Pyotr Bolotnikov of the Soviet Union, who had won the gold medal at Rome in 1960 and had held the 10,000 world record until Clarke broke it; Murray Halberg of New Zealand, the gold medalist in the 5,000-meter race in 1960; Bill Baillie, also from New Zealand, a veteran with a powerful finishing kick; Mamo Wolde of Ethiopia, a young runner but a comer; Bruce Kidd of Canada, a teenager, already recognized as one of the finest distance runners in the world; and Mohamed Gammoudi, a Tunisian army sergeant who had been winning races impressively in the past year. The only American considered to have a chance was 18-year-old Gerry Lindgren of Spokane, Washington, who had been winning a lot of races. The other two Americans entrants—ignored by everybody—were Ron Larrieu of UCLA, who held the U.S. record for six miles, at 27:54, and a complete unknown: U.S. Marine lieutenant Billy Mills. *Track & Field News'*, would later call the race "the greatest 10,000 meters of all time."

Billy Mills was nine years old when the idea entered his mind, he recalled for me in a long interview in November, 2000. His father, Sidney Mills, had shown him a book about the Olympics—not a real book, but clippings and photographs, stapled together, of Olympic champions in action. The thing about the book that Billy Mills remembered was the sentence that said,

"Olympians are chosen by the gods." After that, he wanted to be chosen by the gods.

The god of his childhood was the Sioux warrior, Crazy Horse. William Marion Mills was an Oglala Sioux and had grown up on the Pine Ridge Reservation in southwestern South Dakota, the land of Crazy Horse, where he was born, on June 30, 1938. Pine Ridge is one of the most careworn communities in America. The statistics scream out: the unemployment rate in the late 1990s was above 70 percent; the death rate from alcoholism was four times the national average, with no treatment center on the reservation; the rate of fetal-alcohol syndrome among children was 33 percent higher than for whites, and the suicide attempt rate among children was almost epidemic. Nevertheless, as Ian Frazier says in his book, *On the Rez*, "There is greatness here, too, and an ancient glory endures in the dust and the weeds."

Crazy Horse helped Billy Mills endure his own bleak childhood. The thing about him that struck Billy, aside from his fame as a martyred warrior who wouldn't sign a peace treaty with the United States, was that he looked like an *Eyska,* a mixed blood, with a lighter complexion, sandy hair, and green eyes that were the same as Billy's. Billy Mills still claims that, to an Indian, the only thing worse than a non-Indian is a mixed blood. His father was one-fourth English and three-fourth Sioux. His mother, Theresa Big Crow, was the opposite—one-quarter Sioux, three quarters English, French, and Spanish.

Billy was the 11th child in a family of 13, only eight of whom lived to adulthood. His mother died when Billy was seven. Sidney Mills became an inspiration to the boy, telling him Native American stories framed by the sounds of nature: wolves howling in the wind, leaves rustling in the distance, eagles flapping their wings. But he always emphasized to his son, "We don't tell stories just to tell stories; we tell stories to teach a lesson. Anything you can learn life values from is sacred."

The secret, Sidney told his son, was to find the passions within himself, the positive desires. Once he knew what those passions were he would become self-motivated and his dreams would have a chance to come true.

A year later, Billy Mills went off the reservation for his first track meet, a cross-country race. Before he left, he had told his sister Estelle, who was sick in bed. "I'll win a ribbon for you 'cause you can't come and watch me race." He returned from that county track meet with a third-place ribbon for running. A Catholic priest had taken him to the meet, and as they drove down the dirt road towards the Mills' house, Billy noticed billowing smoke and saw his dad out in the yard, burning a mattress and burning clothing. He learned that his sister had just died from tuberculosis and that his father was burning everything so his other children wouldn't get sick.

When he was 12, Billy's father died. About a week later he was sitting on the steps of his house with his best friend, Butch Eagle, a gifted young athlete. Thinking to comfort Billy, Butch said, "You'll probably go on to do something famous in sports." Billy thought Butch was making fun of him, but Butch Eagle went on: "I've read a lot about great athletes. They're either poor or orphaned and, Billy, you're both."

Billy was sent to the Haskell Institute in Lawrence, Kansas, a school for orphans and for children who were full-blooded or part Indian, and poor. He was small, 5-foot-2, 104 pounds, and couldn't make the track team. But over the summer he grew seven inches, and, as a sophomore, won his first cross-country race. Then he won another. After his third race, which he also won, he went over to the school library to read an article about himself that someone told him was in the local paper. The school's athletic director, Tony Cofa, found him there. "You had great time yesterday, Billy, 9:28. But, uh, how many times have you read this story about yourself?"

"Twelve," he said.

"Come on, Billy," Cofa said, "you should also read something that's happening locally, something that's happening nationally, so that you can relate *your* moment in time to other issues. That's how you learn things that will be important to you."

Billy was now 16, and for the first time he began to look at the paper seriously. He still remembers the first time he did that—May 3, 1954—and the story read: Brown vs. the Board of Education. In Topeka, Kansas, the Supreme Court had voted unanimously to eliminate segregation in schools. No more separate but equal, just *equal*. Later he would understand that those years represented the turmoil of America seeking "the betterment of America," as he put it. But he also realized that Native American issues had become insignificant. "We kind of slipped under the carpet," he told me, "and lay dormant in an America that was otherwise engaged in the issue of race and recognition." He kept wondering: How do I fit in this America? He grew to understand that his running, his attempt to excel on the track, to fulfill the dream his father had handed down to him, to be an *Olympic* champion, was also a running for identity, for an understanding of who he was.

Coming to that understanding wouldn't be easy, not at Haskell and definitely not at the University of Kansas. The university was in Lawrence, down the road from Haskell geographically, but in every other way a separate nation. Having starred in track at Haskell—he broke the school's two-mile record as a sophomore with a 9:08 and later ran a 4:19 mile, a notable time then for a high schooler—he received scholarship offers from 18 colleges. He chose Kansas because its track and field program was as good as that of any other university, if not better, and its coach, Bill Easton, was the Vince Lombardi of track. Billy became a member of a team that won the outdoor NCAA championships in 1959 and 1960. In 1960, he won the Big Eight conference's indoor and outdoor two-mile races. He also won the Big Eight cross-country championship, breaking Wes Santee's school cross-country record with a time of 9:28.1. And in the first 10,000-meter race of his life, he became the first Big Eight athlete to run it in 31 minutes or less.

But his college career was a disappointment to the school and to himself. He knew he should have done better, but he was held back by a feeling he could never shake—that society was rejecting him. He couldn't get into a fraternity because he was an Indian. In his junior year he asked if he could room with two other runners, one white and one black. He couldn't. "The town of Lawrence decided that three men of different colors shouldn't live together," he told a reporter. Billy also remembered that the Kansas basketball team traveled to New York to play LaSalle at Madison Square

Garden. A member of the team was Dee Ketchum, now a chief of the Delaware tribe in Oklahoma. His teammates were all black. One New York newspaper wrote that "four slaves and a savage started for the University of Kansas."

Bill Easton, a dogmatic coach, was a major source of Billy's discontent. Easton was the first white person he had worked closely with, and the experience was jolting. Before one race Billy asked Easton, please, could he use speed in a race, not just run to set the pace. "Billy, you don't need speed," Easton said. "You're an Indian. Indians run forever. Negroes are fast." Coach was applying the cliché that black athletes are great sprinters only; Indians are long-distance runners only. Billy would protest that he needed to develop speed as well as distance to become a world-class runner. Easton came to think of his argumentative Native American as a head case.

In his junior year, Billy participated in the Division I cross-country championships at Michigan State, finishing third. A photographer came to take a picture of the leaders. He asked Billy to step out of the way. "You, the guy with dark skin," he said. Right after that Billy went to Louisville to take part in the AAU cross-country championships. He was by himself, and he couldn't stand it any longer. He went up to his hotel room on the sixth floor, opened the window and stood on a chair, ready to jump. This powerful impulse for some Native American young people, feeling unempowered and helpless, to seek the way out through suicide, grasped Mills around the throat. But suddenly, underneath his skin, he began to feel his dead father's energy. He remembered a note his father had left with him when he was a little boy: "Mind your desires, know yourself and succeed." Shivering, he cried out to himself: Don't! Don't!

In the last race of his collegiate career, at the national championships on Randall's Island, in New York, Billy was entered in the three-mile run. He was rooming with Pat Clohessy, an Australian who was attending the University of Houston. They were friends, and the night before the race Clohessy suggested that they run together and slowly move up. Billy said, "I never can sleep the night before a race, and the coach gets everyone up to eat breakfast at 6 A.M."

"Jeez, Billy, this is your last race," Clohessy said. "Can't that bloke let up on you?" Billy decided that the Australian was right; he would sleep in and go down for breakfast at 9. When he came into the hotel restaurant Easton was there, waiting for him. Easton had always insisted that his athletes dress for public appearances, and Billy was wearing a sports shirt and no tie. The coach told Billy he looked like a tramp and said, "I'm kicking you off the team." Later, he came back to Billy, cooled off. "We wasted our money bringing you out here," he said, "but I feel sorry for you. I want you to run."

In the race Billy wanted to lay back, and his coach was hollering to him to get up to the front. Billy wouldn't; by now he wanted to do it his way, stalk the field, and then close with a rush. Easton, disgusted, yelled, "Get up front or get off the track!" Billy got off the track. Easton called him a quitter, gave him some money and his plane ticket, and sent him home.

So there he was, back in Lawrence, by himself. School had let out a month earlier, and the campus seemed haunted. He didn't want to run anymore; he felt that his dream was dead, and he went back to Pine Ridge to think it all through. He could go back to school; he still had requirements to fulfill before he could graduate. Maybe he could teach. Or he could join the Marines. In his funk he hung around the reservation too long. He was there to witness the death of two men he had known as a child; they died together after drinking anti-freeze. Jolted out of his stupor, he decided to go back to college.

One wonderful thing had happened to him at Kansas. In 1961, he met a young woman named Patricia Ann Harris on a blind date. She was an art student, a year behind Billy, blonde and blue- eyed, from Coffeyville, Kansas. They were instantly attracted to each other. Pat came from a middle-class white family; her father and mother had been divorced, but when they were told about Billy they were happy for her. It wasn't so easy on Billy's side: Nobody in the family had married a white person, and they felt that Billy was giving up his heritage. But Billy and Pat were in love, and that was all there was to it. They were married in January of 1962. In April, Billy enlisted in the Marine Corps Reserve. A month later he graduated from the University of Kansas. In October, with Vietnam heating up, he was called to active duty and sent to officers' candidate school at Quantico, Virginia. In December, he was commissioned a second lieutenant and transferred to Camp Pendleton, California, where promising Marine athletes were already training for a shot at the 1964 Olympics. The urge was on him again.

Pat Mills didn't know then about the origin of the urge. In the first months of their marriage, Billy, laced with insecurities, didn't know to what extent he could share his deepest feelings with a white woman. Gradually, he learned how to share everything with Pat, until finally he told her the secret of his childhood, the oath he had been keeping for many years—that he wanted to be chosen by the gods and become an Olympian. He showed her the workbook where he had written down his ambitions, among them a *gold medal*. She told him it wasn't too late to fulfill his dream.

At Camp Pendleton, the more he worked out, the stronger he felt. From 50-mile-a-week workouts, he raised it to a hundred miles or more. At Kansas he had only been able to do five to ten pushups and pull-ups. Now he was doing 40 or 50. He was at his full growth—an inch under six feet, 155 pounds, a compact body, with broad and bony shoulders, a large chest that allowed for expanded lung capacity, and thinner legs than you would see in most competitive runners. But the legs were strong. He wore his black hair in the short-cropped Marine style that made his brown, pockmarked face stand out more. He was as hollow-cheeked as Sinatra; his green eyes were fired with a hard glare, and his mouth was set in a firm, determined line. He looked like a Marine.

At that point he found another white person he could share his secret with, who would become his mentor. In 1920, Earl Thomson had won a gold medal for Canada at the Antwerp Olympics in the 110-meter hurdles. Then he came to the United States and coached track and field for 28 years at the Naval Academy. In 1962, he retired from the Academy and went to Camp Pendleton to help train the Marines' track and field team. "Tommy" Thomson was a man of firm bearing who understood modern athletes—that they had to be guided in a flexible way, that they were all different. When Billy met him he felt, here was a Bill Easton who would *listen,* who would offer encouragement. He told Thomson about the precious dream that had been handed down from his father, to become an *Olympian.*

"What do you want to do at the Games?" Thomson said.

"I want to run the 5,000," Billy said, "and the marathon, but especially the 10,000. And I want to win a medal."

"Lieutenant," Thomson said, "why don't you try for the *gold?* If you try to win the gold medal you may end up with your medal."

Billy said, "That's in my notebook—the gold medal, 10,000."

"Then I want to help you," Thomson said. "How fast do you think you can run the 10,000?"

"I know I can run 28:50."

"That's not fast enough. You'll have to do better to have a chance in Tokyo."

Mills spread his hands wide. "Maybe I can take 25 seconds off?"

"On a given day," Thomson said, "28:25 is fast enough to win. If you think you can do that, lieutenant, let's get to work on it." Billy wrote in his notebook: "28:25. Believe! Believe! Believe!"

They marked off part of a grass field at Pendleton where Billy would do his workouts. Thomson would help him, time him, but never let him know the time unless he fell way off pace. With the psychological lift he got from his new mentor it began to come together for Billy. His running week consisted of slow 15-mile runs, fast ten-mile runs, intermittent speed runs, drudgery and more drudgery, but he never let up. He became a slave to his own drive.

In June of 1963, at the Arizona Relays, he won the mile in 4:05 and the two-mile in 8:54. Next, in the Los Angeles Coliseum Relays, he finished second in the 5,000 meters. Then, in July of 1963, he traveled to Belgium for the CISM (Conseil Internationale du Sports Militaire) games, which featured runners from the NATO countries. There, he ran the second 10,000-meter race of his life. He took the lead with 500 yards to go, then found that he lacked a kick, the finishing burst that most of the great ones had. Mohamed Gammoudi did not lack a kick. He swept by Billy like a bullet train, then another runner passed by him, and then a third person. Billy finished fourth. Afterward, Gammoudi said to Billy through an interpreter, "All you need is more speed."

Speed. He had come out of high school doing 60 seconds for a quarter of a mile. He had come out of college with Easton pounding at him to run from the front, gaining only four seconds, doing 56 seconds. Easton's words haunted him: "You don't need speed. You're an Indian. Indians run forever." With Tommy Thomson he started developing speed.

Four months before the 1964 Tokyo Olympics, Billy began to concentrate diligently on the last 300 yards of the 10,000. He wanted to run those critical yards as efficiently as he could; that would allow him to run as fast as he could. By then he had constructed a seven-step training program. The seven steps consisted of sheer endurance work, speed endurance, sheer speed, rest, and recovery. The last two steps were mystical, a gift of his heritage, maybe a gift from the gods: visualization and spiritual empowerment.

Visualization was not in the athlete's lexicon back then; Billy learned about it as a child on the reservation from wise elders, who offered vivid dream pictures of the Indian past, mixed with visions of the future. So Billy was visualizing that he could run with the best in the world for six miles of a 6.2 mile race. With a lap to go, he visualized himself in position to spring past the leaders. Ron Clarke was always the leader ahead of him. Spiritual empowerment, the seventh way of running, meant that he wouldn't allow himself to do anything that would detract from his spiritual and psychological build-up. Tommy Thomson, who approved of Mills's approach, cautioned him: "Why are you only thinking about Ron Clarke?" Billy said, "Because he has the world record."

But before the visualization could be put to use, he still had to qualify for the Olympic 10,000-meter race, and he felt that he needed more help. He called upon an old friend, Cliff Cushman.

Cushman, who was from Grand Forks, North Dakota, knew about the Indian communities and reservations. In high school he had raced against Haskell runners, including Billy Mills, and they became friends. Cushman then enrolled at Kansas; he was a year ahead of Billy. In 1960 he was captain of the Kansas track team. He ran cross-country, ran the 440, the 800, and the mile, he triple-jumped, and he made the Rome Olympics in the 400 hurdles, winning a silver medal and coming back a hero. Cushman and Billy roomed together for a semester, and Billy would sneak into Cushman's closet and stroke his USA Olympic uniform, Wow, he would think, this is the greatest athlete I know.

After graduation, Cushman joined the Air Force and became a pilot. And, in the summer of 1964, he and Billy were reunited at Pomona College in California, where they were both training for the Olympic trials. But bad luck befell Cushman; he tripped in the qualifying race for the hurdles and didn't make the team. He was set to go home but Billy asked him to stay. "I need somebody to time me in the 10-K trials," he said. "It's my last shot to get in the race. I want to run somewhere between a 28:25 and 28:50."

Cliff looked at Billy strange. Billy caught the doubt in Cushman's eyes. He said, "I need to do a 28:25 in Tokyo."

"Okay, sure, Billy," he said.

"And Cliff," Billy said, "If I fall off the pace and it becomes tactical, quit giving me my time. Just encourage me." Cushman smiled. What if the leader slows things down, and the other contenders decide to stay with him? Billy thought. What do I do?

Turned out he wouldn't need to be timed. The race went off on a day when the Los Angeles Coliseum track was baking in the sun. Right away Billy saw that the race was going to be tactical. On the fourth lap Gerry Lindgren forced a 65-second lap, opening up a 50-yard lead over everyone but Billy, who stayed with him. At the three-mile mark, Peter McArdle, an accomplised American distance runner, dropped back with a stitch in his side. With two laps left, Billy looked back—there was no one with him. He and Lindgren had broken the field. When Lindgren kicked, Billy let him go. Lindgren broke the tape 45 yards ahead of him, in 29:02. Billy ran the race in 29:10—45 seconds off what he'd told Tommy Thomson and Cliff Cushman he hoped to do. It seemed like a poor effort to some, but it had been an unusually warm day. Billy's 29:10, someone said, would have been 28:40 in Tokyo's cool weather.

It didn't matter. Billy was excited. He was now the only American athlete to qualify in two distance events—the 10,000 and the marathon—and he had beaten Ron Larrieu for second place in the 10,000. That was particularly encouraging because, a few weeks earlier, Billy had run second to Larrieu in a six-mile race. So the three of them—Lindgren, Larrieu, and Mills—were on their way to Tokyo to represent the United States in the 10,000-meter challenge. It was a huge challenge for them, because no American had ever won a gold medal at this distance, and they were competing against a field of world-class international runners, runners who loved the distance and understood that it was suited for them.

Billy's wife Pat had been able to come to Tokyo with their 11-month-old daughter, Christy, but they couldn't see much of each other. Billy and Lindgren roomed together in the Yoyogi Olympic village. By now they were good friends. Billy was eight years older than Lindgren, but they had much in common, not the least being an overwhelming desire to run the race of their lives. Billy was awed by this manchild with an almost emaciated face, who was known to wake up in the middle of the night back in Spokane for a ten-mile workout, and who, once a month, would do an 88-mile mountain run. The two took strength from each other.

They also analyzed the competition, their talk always coming back to the greatness of Ron Clarke—how hard it would be to stop him. Clarke, according to Roberto L. Quercetani, author of *Athletics,* a history of modern track and field, was "the most efficient running machine ever seen until then. He was never frightened by the prospect of having to take upon himself the burden of setting a 'hot' pace. By his courage and his example he extended many of his rivals around the world to marks they had never dreamt of."

Rather than work on the Olympic track, Billy found a park at the rear of the Olympic Village where he could pretty much run by himself. It was called the Meiji Shrine, a beautiful area with dirt paths that ran through grass and verdant plants and trees and the music of birds. Billy measured out three laps for his sprints. He was now doing a quarter mile in 49.6, a lot better than his 56 seconds at Kansas. But now, to kick in, he wanted to make sure he had speed for the last 200 meters.

Four days before the race, Billy went over to the Olympic stadium and did a workout by himself—a warmup in the morning, six miles of easy, relaxed running, then four miles in the afternoon, plus a few wind sprints. Then he put on his spikes and decided to try to run 200 meters out of the blocks. The field was almost empty, but Billy spotted a German coach and asked if he would time him in the 200. The coach said sure. So Billy burst out of the blocks, pumping his arms, lifting his knees, running 200 meters on the curve. When he finished he asked the German, "What was my time?"

"Oh, not too fast," he said. "23:4."

Billy exclaimed, "Wow, wow, yeah, yeah!"

The coach, puzzled by his reaction, asked, "What event are you in?"

"The marathon and the 10,000," Billy said.

The coach said, "Whoa, very good." Billy figured that at least his speed was ready. Two days before the race, Billy and Lindgren went over to Meiji shrine to run together. In the press buildup, Lindgren had come to be considered a darkhorse possibility. Reporters remembered the earlier dual meet between the United States and the Soviet Union, in which Lindgren left the Russians in the dust in the 10,000 and also beat all the American challengers. For the first time, hopes were lifted that Lindgren might not only improve on the 1960 sixth-place finish of America's Max Truex, but might pull off a miracle.

Billy Mills received a quite different treatment from the press. Throughout his stay in Tokyo, not one writer covering the Games from *anywhere* had said anything to him. The United States leading wire service, the Associated Press, described Mills as a 1,000-1 shot.

As Billy began his jog with Lindgren, he felt at peace with himself, maybe for the first time since he had began to concentrate on his lifetime dream. Then, suddenly, Lindgren, running beside him, tripped on a tree trunk and twisted an ankle.

"Go back and ice it right now, Gerry," Billy said.

"No, I'll keep running, it'll be okay," Lindgren said. When the two came back to their room 45 minutes later, Lindgren's ankle was swollen. He iced it, but he still felt a little pain, and it never really left him.

So it came down to the day of the race, and Billy and his roomie began to dress for their great adventure which, for Billy, was not so much an adventure as a crusade. He looked outside. It was raining pretty hard, but he didn't care. The last time he had seen Pat he had told her about this strange feeling that had come over him— that everything was falling in place. "I'm going to surprise a few people tomorrow", he told Pat.

"Of course you are," she said.

On the bus taking the athletes to the stadium he sat beside a woman athlete from Poland. She told Billy she was a high jumper. "What event are you in?" she asked him. He told her it was the 10,000-meter run. That excited her. "And today is your final. Who do you think is going to win?" Billy didn't answer her. She repeated, "Who's going to win? Clarke of Australia or Bolotnikov of Russia?" Billy felt that he had to say, *me*. But he didn't know how it would sound to her. Finally, he said, "I think I can win—me, Billy Mills."

"Oh," she said. There was no more talk between them.

He was sitting quietly in his sweats when he heard the loudspeaker call the 38 contestants for the 10,000-meter run. He rose slowly, peeled down, and moved towards the starting line. He was wearing the number 722 on his blue-and-white USA jersey. He looked around. There was Lindgren, wearing 720; Mamo Wolde of Ethiopia, 616; Mohamed Gammoudi, 615; the handsome and dashing Ron Clarke, 12, with the gold-and-green sash under his number. Though it hadn't rained in the afternoon and the track was drying out, it still looked soft to Billy. He decided he would wear three-eighths-inch spikes instead of quarter-inch spikes to handle the surface better.

He had forged his strategy with Tommy Thomson's help and constant encouragement. He would run with the lead pack, try not to lag farther behind than fourth, always stay within contention of the leader. If a leader broke, Billy wouldn't necessarily respond with his own break; the leader might be going faster than he could run. He wanted to keep on the edge, but not go over the edge.

He was on the edge, all right. For some reason, as he moved into position among all his rivals, a disturbing vision came to him. He was back in Pine Ridge, contemplating the death of his mother from tuberculosis. He was seven years old and his older brother Sid told him about going to the bank to borrow $500 for the funeral expenses, and the banker saying he couldn't lend him the money because he had failed to make a previous loan payment. "All you have left to repossess," the banker told Sid, "is a dead body." Billy thought, well, that was why he was here, trying to play the warrior role for his family as well as for himself. Trying to obliterate the sorrows of the past. Trying also to overcome his low self-esteem. He felt he had come a long way—his strength now was not just the strength of the body, but the strength of the will. He remembered someone saying to him: "Look after your body. Temper it with pain. And your body will amaze you." Now the ultimate test had arrived.

The gun was raised. The crowd was expectant, so quiet that the starting shot was heard all over the stadium, and they saw the 38 runners stampeding like cattle, pushing, pulling, tugging for running room. The biggest roar came from the Japanese spectators rooting for their Tsuburaya, watching him run among the leaders. A Japanese sportswriter in the press box, Yoichi Furukawa, remembered, "We were thinking the winner would be Clarke, and I was just watching Clarke and Tsuburaya."

Immediately, Billy found himself back in ninth place, boxed in. The first lap—there would be 24 altogether—was run in a swift 64 seconds. But in the second lap, he struggled clear and joined the lead flight with Ron Clarke, Mohamad Gammoudi, Mamo Wolde, the Russian, Leonid Ivanov, Gerry Lindgren, Murray Halberg of New Zealand, Kokichi Tsubaraya, and another Russian, Nikolay

Dutov. Within 600 yards, Clarke took the lead, and Billy tucked himself as much as he could behind the pace-setting Australian. During the fourth lap, in second place behind Clarke, he felt a bolt of sunshine wash over him. He wondered if anyone else in the race had been touched by the healing light.

In the ninth lap Halberg, the 1960 5,000-meter champion, began to drop back. Nine runners were ahead of him, bunched together. Then a blazing 66.4 lap reduced the field. As they approached the halfway mark, five runners remained in the first flight: Clarke, Wolde, Gammoudi, Dutov, and Billy Mills. That's when Billy started worrying about the fast pace. He began a period of self-doubt, asking himself, can I stay with them? Then, inevitably, he thought about quitting.

What was it about Billy Mills and quitting? Had Bill Easton planted the word in his guts the day he taunted him off the track? Was he courting his inferiority complex, protesting too much that society was to blame for his failures? Why was the word "quitter" corrupting the passion that had inspired him since childhood: mind your dreams, know yourself, and succeed? Once again, he felt trapped between his work ethic and the shadow that was darkening his desire.

He looked into the infield. If he was going to quit, this would be the moment to do it. Nobody knew him; who would care? Then he remembered what an Oglala Sioux elder had impressed on him when he was young: "Bravery, Billy, is not being the toughest kid on the block. Bravery might be the tenacity to just hang in there." Billy temporized: I'll take the lead for one more lap, then I'll quit.

And at the 5,000-meter point, he did take the lead, for the first time. He had run half the race in 14:04, only seven seconds slower than his best for that distance. That scared him, too. Could he keep up the pace? He was passing the stands where he knew his wife was sitting. And he visualized her, and she was crying. Why was she crying? She was crying because he was quitting, forgetting what he had told her, that the competition wasn't with Ron Clarke or any of the other runners, but with himself. And suddenly he remembered why he was running; he was running for his identity.

After the 14th lap, Dutov was gone and Mamo Wolde was beginning to fade. But Billy ran on, taking the race one lap at a time, lap after lap after lap. At the 5,600-meter mark he was again running with complete confidence. Sometimes he would drop his hands down to his sides, flex them to release the tension, then raise them to the pumping position. He was running within himself, staying tight behind the Australian machine who was running so effortlessly. Not a hair on Clarke's head was out of place; he seemed to be controlling the race, either setting or forcing the pace, trying to burn out his competitors. Four times Billy faded back, as much as 15 yards. Each time he came on again, settling behind Clarke.

Entering the next-to-last lap it was Clarke, Gammoudi, and Billy, all alone. Clarke looked over his shoulder and let up briefly; later he said he did that because he thought the race was his. But to Billy it seemed that what Clarke really wanted was someone else to do the pace-setting so that Clarke could save himself for a strong finish. And it suddenly struck Billy, ooh, Clarke can be beaten. So Billy broke to the front, with Clarke behind him and Gammoudi just behind Clarke. And then it was just *one more lap, one more lap.*

Going into the final lap Billy was to Clarke's right, even with him, Gammoudi a few yards behind. But now they were running into traffic from runners who had been lapped and were all over the track. In fact, one straggler on the pole had Clarke boxed in. Billy thought, ah, an opportunity. He remembered watching Clarke on film in the 1963 British Empire's Commonwealth Games. Clarke had found himself boxed in by a fellow Australian, Tony Cook, and Cook ended up beating him. Billy thought he should try it. Clarke was boxed in and would have to slow down, and then Billy would start his own kick.

But with 300 yards to go, Clarke refused to slow. He nudged Billy, trying to get him to move out. Billy ignored the nudge. Clarke bumped him again with his right arm that was tucked tightly against his body. A third time he caught Billy hard, causing him to stumble out into the third lane. Billy thought he was going to fall because his legs were stiffening and his right knee was sore. But he didn't fall, and he continued his pursuit of Clarke.

And then, into the gap between Clarke, who was near the rail, and Billy, who was on the outside, swept the Tunisian in the red shirt, Gammoudi. But the gap wasn't wide enough, so Gammoudi raised his hands and shoved hard against Clarke's shoulder, slapping him with his left hand while simultaneously pushing his right elbow into Billy. The shoves knocked Clarke into the curve, and knocked Billy farther to the outside. And Gammoudi blazed into the lead.

Later, Billy felt that Gammoudi's moves had been a blessing. If Gammoudi hadn't shoved him and Clarke, Billy would have gone into his own kick and Gammoudi might have come from behind on him. Clarke, also, might have come from behind on him. Furthermore, Gammoudi had pushed Billy onto ground that was firmer than it was close to the rail.

But at that moment the shadow fell over Billy once more. Bumped and bruised, he felt that it might be too late to catch the runaways. For a stride or two, far on the outside, he seemed uncertain, seemed to be thinking about giving it up. But he quickly took hold of himself, crying out to himself—*one more try, one more try.* Then it was just a matter of *when* he should go. He made up his mind 150 yards out, even as both runners were pulling away from him, to wait, wait.

Gammoudi had a big lead now, but Clarke was moving fast and closing ground. Billy picked up the pace just a bit going into the final curve so that the two runners wouldn't open up too big a lead. Gammoudi and Clarke had 15 yards on him, but he made five back. With 105 yards to go, they had ten yards on him. Billy was thinking: I've got to go 110 yards in the time it takes them to go 105.

He came off the curve and knew now was the time. After two more strides he felt the divine thought: *I can win. I can win.* He started lengthening his stride and started to pump.

But again he found himself boxed in—right in front of him was a German straggler. The German looked back, saw Billy, and quickly moved into the fourth lane. Billy was free! And he was visited by an incredible rush of adrenaline. He felt fresh, renewed. It was the feeling that came over Roger Bannister in 1954 just before he kicked to break the 4-minute mile barrier—a feeling, Bannister said, that "the moment of a lifetime had come."

Now, in his moment of a lifetime, Billy could *see* the finish line. *I can win! I can win!* He moved out, arms pumping, legs pumping, knees lifting higher: Lift! Reach! and put down! He had practiced his kick hundreds of times in his mind—to run as efficiently as he could so as to run as fast as he could.

Going down the backstretch, he was closing on Clarke and Gammoudi. Fifty yards from the tape, still in third place, he was already exulting: *I won. I won.* He flew by Clarke, who, stony-faced, was looking straight ahead, running with everything he had left. Then Billy came abreast of Gammoudi.

When those final seconds were televised in the United States, the sports announcer Bud Palmer was calling, "Gammoudi's the leader, with Clarke just behind him!" There was no mention of a third man. Suddenly, someone else in the television booth started hollering hysterically: "LOOK AT THIS! LOOK AT BILLY! LOOK AT BILLY! ARRGHH!" Then Palmer regained control of the scene and in an excited voice, but with some decorum, said: "What a tremendous surprise here! Billy Mills of the United States wins the 10,000 meter!"

There is a soul-satisfying photo of Billy at that moment of surprise, when the tape snaps on his chest. His arms are outstretched, his mouth agape, his eyes closed, his head lifted towards the heavens. The look is one of supplication, mixed with ecstasy and relief, the halo of this runner whose central thought is, I am with the gods.

A puzzled Japanese official ran up to him, asking, in English, "Who are you? Who *are* you?"

It was a logical question, because almost nobody knew who this "722" was. "Billy Mills, I'm Billy Mills," he cried. Then, in a moment of fright, he asked the official, "Oh, my God, did I miscount the laps? Do I still have a lap to go?" And the official, speaking slowly so that Billy could understand him, pronounced the most beautiful words this self-doubter from the Pine Ridge reservation had ever heard: "Finished. Finished. You are the new Olympic champion!"

Billy sunk down on the grass to take off his shoes. Tony Cook, the Australian runner, who had just finished eighth, looked at Billy and thought, "Oh, poor Billy, got a blood blister or something and had to drop out of the race." Then Cook focused on the scoreboard, searching for his own name. What he saw was Billy Mills's name, *on top*—and with a record Olympic time of 28:24.4, almost exactly what he planned to run in this 10,000-meter race. Mohamed Gammoudi, three yards behind, finished in 28:24.8. Clarke was in third place at 28:25.8, and Mamo Wolde, the Ethiopian, was fourth, 28:31.8. All four had broken the Olympic record. But none had broken it better than Billy Mills.

The officials started to escort Billy towards a little corner off the track, where press conferences were held. But Billy didn't want to meet the press right away. Still feeling pumped, he wanted to run a victory lap with an American flag in one hand. He also yearned for an eagle feather from his nation, given to *warriors,* to carry in the other hand. He wanted to run around a track that he now envisioned as being "the great circle of being," what his tribe referred to as "the endless universe." Circling the endless universe at this time would also make him heal better in his head. But a Japanese official said, "Must wait, must wait."

"Why?" Billy asked. "Let me out! Let me go!"

The official said, "We must not detract from the dignity of the injured runner."

There was a runner down on the track, and it snapped Billy back to the main purpose of the Games—not the victory, but the pursuit. So they took him to the reporters, every one of them a stranger—hey, not even a hello from one of them while he was in Tokyo. But now they wanted to know everything. "What nationality are you?" one of them asked. "I'm 7/16ths Sioux Indian," Billy said. Then they started on him: "A Sioux warrior, wow!" one of them said. "A Sioux brave," hollered another. Someone sang out, "Custer's last stand!" And Billy began to hear the writers' mentality, the same old clichés white folks had laid on Native Americans without bothering to understand their history.

Fortunately, they had brought Pat down from the stands, and husband and wife hugged and cried together. Billy got through the press stuff and finally they led him towards the victory stand. Along the way he saw signs meant for him, but without his name—"Go, U.S. Marines." "USA. We're Proud of You"—because they didn't yet have a name for Billy Mills. But they did know he was a Marine, and he was an American, and now they were throwing him kisses. Billy felt so proud standing up there, with the silver and bronze winners, Gammoudi and Clarke.

Avery Brundage, president of the International Olympic Committee, with tears in his eyes, draped the gold medal around Billy's neck. Later Brundage would tell the press: "It was the greatest display of pressure running I have ever seen by an American." When they played the national anthem Billy Mills cried on the victory stand, a ceremony that for him was both beautiful and painful. He had achieved his dream of winning a gold medal. But he had won it for an America that he felt didn't understand him, and he still wondered, how do I fit into this world?

If he could have heard the reaction back home, he would have known. The *New York Times* splashed a streamer headline over its front sports page: MILLS OF U.S. SETS OLYMPIC MARK OF 28:24.4 IN WINNING 10,000 METER RUN. Underneath it was a large photo of Billy in his magnificent stretch run, pulling ahead of Gammoudi.

Red Smith's story in the *New York Herald Tribune* called the race "a shocker which makes everything that follows an anticlimax."

Billy Mills returned to the United States a hero and, in his own Native American community, a "warrior." In a ceremony on the Pine Ridge reservation the chiefs gave Billy a name—*Makcoe Theê'la,* which means "Respects the Earth." They also gave him his headdress of eagle feathers; he had become a chief because he had accomplished deeds. Three respected Pine Ridge Elders—Ethan Red Cloud, Ben Black Elk, and Fool's Crow—"sang my songs and danced my deeds," he told me.

In 1984, Billy fulfilled his lifelong dream of running his victory lap in Tokyo's National Stadium. Bud Greenspan, the longtime producer of splendid documentaries for the Olympic Games, was working on a special in which eight Americans would return to the scene of their Olympic triumphs. Billy was one of them, and he returned to Tokyo with his wife. While he was there, he prevailed on the film crew to go out with him to the Olympic stadium so that he could run his lap, 20 years later. It was raining and he'd recently had knee surgery, but that didn't bother him. He walked and jogged around the track. With 20 yards to go, he heard someone clapping. It was Pat.

In 1985, Hollywood made a movie about Billy, Running Brave, *starring Robby Benson, that further raised him in stature. But mostly he has done it himself by developing into an inspirational public speaker. Over the years he has raised millions of dollars for Native American charities and has become a mentor and role model to Indian children all over the country. In Pine Ridge, Billy Mills Hall was built not long after his Olympic triumph. In 1999, the organization he is spokesman for, "Running Strong For Native American Indian Youth," established the Billy Mills Youth Center on the Cheyenne River Sioux Indian reservation in South Dakota. Billy hopes it will help the children to gain self-sufficiency and self-esteem—attitudes, that as he knows, can take a long time to find.*

In the last summer of the twentieth century, I had a phone conversation with Ron Clarke. He had just opened a new super sports center in Queensland; he would also be a commentator for Australian television at the Sydney 2000 Olympic Games. We chatted about the past, about Tokyo, 1964, about that enduring contest of wills between him and Billy Mills. "In the end," Clarke said to me with typical Australian understatement, "I have to say his winning the gold medal made so much difference in his life. I think it was a good piece of fate that he won it."

A sporting goods company invited Billy to attend the Sidney Olympics. He was happy to go, and hoped to see Ron Clarke. They did meet at the Olympic Alumni Center, and had a good talk. Clarke, as he had said to me, mentioned the role fate had played in the race. Billy smiled. "Ron, that's not fate. You were up against insurmountable odds. My victory in Tokyo was God-given, you were up against a God-given gift. There was no way you could have won."

With a grin Clarke said, "If it was a God-given fate, why did God have me do all the work? You just sat on me."

Billy put his arms around the opponent of his life. Smiling, he said, "No, Ron, I was hanging *on you."*

The two left each other in good spirits, with a sense of completion between them.

8

1968
THE GAME
OF GAMES
Harvard–Yale

In 1923, the 11th commandment was delivered to the Yale football team by its coach, T. A. D. Jones. "Gentlemen," he said, "you are about to play football for Yale against Harvard. Never again in your lives will you do anything so important."

So deeply is the annual Harvard-Yale contest woven into the mythology of both institutions—it has been going on for 85 years—that it's known to their sons and daughters simply as "The Game." And on the chilly afternoon of November 23, 1968—five years to the day of the assassination of John F. Kennedy, five months from the assassination of Bobby Kennedy, who had played in The Games of 1946 and 1947—the two squads pretty much agreed with Jones's dictum. Neither team had lost a game—Harvard unbeaten for the first time since 1920—which meant that one would have to win and the other would have to lose.

It was one of the loudest crowds ever to attend The Game. The noise level was so fierce down at ground level of Harvard Stadium that the Yale coach, Carmen Cozza, would keep his headphones on most of the time "so that I could hear myself think." It was a capacity crowd, 40,280, and a 1968 crowd, matching in noise the clamor of a year that had been so loud, and so dispiriting. These spectators were filled with excitement because it was The Game and for two hours or more they could separate themselves from their wounded country. And, hey, this was a contest of importance. Why, a record 350 sportswriters, many of them the best in the country, had come to bear witness to—imagine—an Ivy League football game.

This was the game to be at, "the last great nineteenth century pageant," as a president of Yale, A. Bartlett Giamatti, referred to The Game.

For Tad Jones's Yale, a victory would be particularly sweet. It was riding college football's longest winning streak—16 straight victories over two seasons—and was rated 18th in the nation. Eight of its players had made the All-Ivy League team, two of them rising high above all the others: Brian Dowling, who would be immortalized as the quarterback "B. D." in a comic strip that Gary Trudeau, then a Yale undergraduate, would call "Doonesbury"; and Calvin Hill, who would go on to an illustrious professional football career as a running back with the Dallas Cowboys.

Harvard, a seven-point underdog, didn't have anyone to equal the magnitude of Dowling and Hill, but five of its players had made the All-Ivy team. It was a squad of driven seniors, led by—and inspired by—halfback and captain Vic Gatto, one of the greatest running backs in Harvard history. Gatto's seniors, he felt, were driven in part by the growing turmoil in the country. "We had seniors who were Vietnam vets," he told me. "We also had guys on the squad who belonged to SDS (Students for a Democratic Society). But all of them were extremely responsible." Harvard's Ivy League offensive guard was a fierce blocker named Tom Jones, "who was also a talented thespian," as the player guide described him, thus anticipating his later Hollywood success as Tommy Lee Jones. A Texan, Jones roomed with a Southerner from Tennessee, Al Gore. A friend of mine, who was at Harvard at the same time, remembered "Gore and Jones walking around the campus all the time wearing bib overalls, trying to look country."

During the week, emotions at both colleges had run high. In New Haven, Carmen Cozza watched his team's final practice and thought about his seniors. Never before had he had such a talented group, especially Hill and Dowling. About Hill, Cozza said, "He was the one player I had in 32 years who probably could have been a star at any position on the team." As for Dowling: "He had an aura about him. The students hung signs from their windows that said things like, 'God wears No. 10.' Well, you almost believed it." And the coach thought, "What am I going to do without them?"

In Cambridge that week, Vic Gatto remembered that "every practice had 300 alumni on the field, and reporters were everywhere." Gatto took it as his job to keep the players focused, urging them, among other things, not to attend a pep rally the day before the game. "It was kind of a family thing. We weren't going to play up to the fans, We were going to concentrate our energy on the playing of the game."

But almost before they knew it, Harvard found itself behind by three touchdowns.

The first quarter was an omen of the frustrations to come. Every time Harvard got their hands on the ball they couldn't seem to move it. The biggest surprise, Gatto told me, was "an impenetrable defense from Yale. We were stunned, because *we* were the team that had been so dominant on defense. It was heartbreaking the way we started." It was particularly heartbreaking for Gatto when a weak hamstring gave way and he limped off the field, thinking that his college career was over.

Meanwhile, Brian Dowling was as fluttery as a hummingbird. Late in the first quarter, the Yale quarterback moved his team 80 yards. The key play was Dowling's 32-yard reverse scamper run over the Harvard left tackle. With the ball on the Harvard two, Dowling sprinted out to his right as if to pass and, instead, skipped along the right sideline into the end zone, untouched. Skip Bayless kicked the extra point.

Early in the second quarter, it was fourth down for Yale on the Harvard four. Dowling went back to pass, scrambled hither and yon, somehow able to elude Harvard pursuers. Finally, trotting towards the right, he spotted the player he always looked for in such situations, and he lofted a patented Dowling floater to Calvin Hill, who was all by himself in the end zone, the ball coming out of the sky almost like a Frisbee and being cradled in Hill's hands for the touchdown.

The Yale strategy was plain. Because Harvard's secondary was so strong, Yale would run and throw off the "I" formation, run little plays off-tackle or outside, and work the pass option often. Mostly it was a Dowling-and-Hill thing.

That second touchdown was historic, giving the 6-foot-4, 225-pound Calvin Hill a career total of 142 points, breaking the Yale record set in 1931 by Albie Booth. Actually, Hill was not in top shape for the game. The previous week against Princeton, running as he always did, Michael Jordan–style with his tongue hanging out, he had bit his tongue when he was tackled. They had to close it with 15 stitches and then the tongue became infected. He spent Saturday and Sunday in the infirmary, though he did sneak out on Saturday night to a Jimi Hendrix concert. "Every time Jimi hit a high note it just killed me, that tongue was throbbing so," Hill told me. He didn't return to practice until the last one on Thursday. Now he was playing in silence, the eloquence coming from his moves as he put Yale into a 14-0 lead.

With eight minutes to go in the second quarter, Harvard found itself deep in its own territory, and forced to punt from its end zone. The punt was blocked by safety Ed Franklin, and Yale took over on the Harvard seven. And there was Dowling, once again, scrambling all the way back to the 30-yard line, eluding tacklers, looking for an open man, looking for Hill. Instead he spotted end Del Marting all by himself in the end zone and threw a 30-yard strike for the touchdown. Yale went for two points, when Dowling again found Marting. Now it was 22-0 and it looked like a rout.

"Dowling's control of the game seemed complete," Jerry Nason would write in the *Boston Globe* the next day. "The Johns were being psyched by his wild scrambling and off-balance throwing and his uncanny ability to brain-pick what every Ivy expert rates as the finest defensive unit in the league."

On the other side of the field, Harvard coach John Yovicsin, a green Tyrolean hat on his head, was steaming in frustration. Early in the game, he was heard to growl at his quarterback, George Lalich: "Three downs to go five yards and we didn't make it. Loosen up—let's go!"

But it was hard for Harvard to loosen up with a dismembered running attack. Gatto was in the dressing room, trying to get himself back in shape to play. The other breakaway back, Ray Hornblower, was hobbling on a bad ankle he had injured the week before. All year

Harvard had essentially been a running team. Now they had to pass, and Yale seemed to know all the tendencies of quarterback Lalich. As one Yale player put it, "We saw the runners limping and said, 'Let's focus on the quarterback and the game is ours.'" At that time Lalich had completed only two of six passes for 22 yards.

Coach Yovicsin walked over to where the second-string quarterback, Frank Champi, was manning a phone. "I want you in there," he said. It was a startling decision, one that would be long remembered. Yovicsin later explained in a television interview why he felt he had to pull George Lalich. "During the season George gave us a very fine and consistently solid performance," he said. "He handled our offense well and he kept us loose. He gave the team a feeling of general confidence that coaches sometimes can't give. It did bother me to have to take him out of the game; he deserved so much to climax his career in a real brilliant fashion, and I wanted it even more than he did. But Yale gave us some different things defensively, and we just couldn't engineer anything; with four minutes to go in the half we were 22 points down. I just felt we needed something to inspire our team, to convince everyone—including me—that we could get back in the game. And the best solution, I honestly felt, was to put Champi there."

The decision was made as Yale seemed to be driving towards still another first half touchdown. Calvin Hill took a pitchout from Dowling, broke loose around right end, running like a locomotive, running 10, 15, 20 yards downfield. Then the Harvard safety, Dan Conway, who was wounded in Vietnam ten months earlier in the surprise Tet offensive, hit Hill hard, and the ball flew out of his hands. Harvard recovered on its own 36. And the new quarterback went into action.

The late Harvard Sports Information Director, Baaron Pittinger, had once said of Frank Champi, "He wanted to be recognized as a person, not as someone playing a role. Frank is a very complex, introspective individual who is not, by any means, the typical football player."

Frank Champi's career up to that moment had not been what he or Harvard thought it would be. He came from a working-class

Italian background, and, from the age of three after his parents' divorce, was raised by his grandmother in the city of Everett, near Boston. At Everett High, Champi was an all-state quarterback for two years, passed for 23 touchdowns and 27 two-point conversions, and led Everett to 18 straight wins and 2 state championships. He seemed to be in Brian Dowling's league. He was also an outstanding javelin thrower and a fine basketball player. In his senior year he was president of his class and a straight-A student. He was intelligent, studious, and sensitive, and could throw a football on a line 90 yards.

When Champi first began to make a name for himself at Everett, he figured he would wind up at one of the big New England football colleges, Boston College or Holy Cross—his highest aspiration at the time. But in his senior year he began to hear from Ivy League schools. Princeton wanted him badly. Its backfield coach, Cosmo Iacavazzi, flew to Boston and spent a day with him. "He pretty much convinced me to go to Princeton and I sort of gave him a verbal O.K.," Champi said.

But then he met with the father of Bobby Leo. Leo had been three years ahead of Champi at Everett, an all-state running back who then lit up the sky at Harvard in sparking the Crimson to consecutive wins over Yale in 1964, 1965, and 1966. Leo's father and some other Harvard grads from Everett thought that Champi should go to Harvard, and got Yovicsin to talk to him. The Harvard coach told Frank how well he would fit in there. So Champi decided on Harvard rather than Princeton.

It turned into a nightmare.

"In my freshman year at Harvard," Champi told me 30 years later at his home in Newburyport, Massachussetts, "it was such a huge adjustment I just couldn't think straight. Whoo! That was brutal for me. I played so poorly because I couldn't focus in on football; I was trying to stay alive academically. I started the freshman year as first-string quarterback, highly touted, and by the end of the season I was like the last-string quarterback."

Frank looked in great shape then, at age 51, a little thick in the middle but not much beyond his playing weight in college of 195 pounds, compacted on a firm, 5-foot-10 frame. "I came from a public high school," he said, trying to explain his discomfort that first year. "Kids who came from the upper class had a decided advantage. So it was a struggle." Later, as we talked, he kept coming back to his ambivalence with Harvard, the course of his football career still flowing like an open wound.

From the beginning, his one inviolable asset at Harvard was his right arm. Coach Yovicsin once told a sportswriter that Champi had the strongest arm of any quarterback who had ever been at Harvard. Then he spoiled it for Frank by adding, "That's because he was a javelin thrower."

"That put me in a separate category," Champi told me, "like I wasn't really a quarterback. I was a javelin thrower." Football became less fun and more of an ordeal. "As a sophomore, I worked my way up to third-string quarterback." As a junior, he came to the team with a strong determination to succeed. "I was fourth-string at the beginning of that fall of 1968, but within a week I beat out the third-stringer." The next week, he beat out the second-string quarterback and felt that he had done well enough to be the first-string quarterback.

But the job went to the senior, George Lalich. Lalich was a sophisticated young man whose father had boxed professionally under the name of Danny O'Keefe. He didn't have the arm Champi had, but he was a leader who played with coolness, and he was very tight with a group of seniors who had developed an extraordinary bonding. "He had the respect of those seniors," Champi said. "I didn't know them very well. I was a loner. I tended to keep by myself."

So Champi waited through game after game during the 1968 season, "figuring that I'd get a chance if things didn't work out for the team." He played in Jayvee games to keep his arm in shape, and he snuck in here and there with the big team. But coming up to the Yale game, he had thrown exactly 12 passes all season long for the varsity.

Now he was being sent into The Game to try to salvage what was rapidly slipping away. "All I remember," Champi told me, reflecting on that long-ago moment, "is that I really got angry. When Coach put me in, he said he had confidence in me and all that, and that's fine and dandy. But the way I took it is, hell, I'll be damned if I'm going to be made a fool of here. He's sticking me in and I'm gonna be a scapegoat." His voice rose, the words tumbling out in disorder. "So my attitude was, I don't give a damn what happens. I knew the team expected this quiet, soft-spoken quarterback. Well, they're not going to get it. I said, I'll play my game. Actually, it worked in my favor to be angry at the beginning. I didn't go in there with nervous butterflies. Then, as I got focused, I wasn't angry any more. I just wanted us to win the game."

Over on the Yale side, Brian Dowling was puzzled. Yale had notes on every Harvard player, he thought, but not on Champi. His name had never come up.

From the Harvard 36, Champi drove his team downfield. With 42 seconds left in the half, the ball on the Yale 15, Champi faked a handoff to running back John Ballantyne, swung around, and threw a perfect spiral to sophomore end Bruce Freeman, the pass coming straight and true into Freeman's hands in the end zone.

Harvard was at least on the scoreboard. But the extra-point try missed and the Crimson went into the clubhouse trailing Yale by 16 points.

In the Yale dressing room, calmness prevailed. Well, why not, with Yale ahead 22-6. "It was a routine, relaxed halftime—maybe too much so," Dowling told me. Calvin Hill had a similar memory of the moment: "I wonder if we didn't relax a little bit too much. You know, if you blink, you empower the other team."

Cozza told his offense to run more sweeps and sweep passes. But he liked the way his team was performing, especially the quarterback. Every time Dowling touched the ball, it seemed, he was moving the Bulldogs into touchdown range. But the team had been hurt by fumbles. The way Dowling was playing, Yale might have made the score even more one-sided, but for the fumbles. Still, the defense was doing a super job. And with Gatto out and Hornblower limping, all Yale needed to do was to keep the quarterback in check as they had in the first half—until they put in that other guy.

In the Harvard dressing room, there was still some uncertainty about that quarterback situation. Champi had gotten Harvard on the scoreboard, but guard Tom Jones, for one, thought the new quarterback looked "scared to death." Other players were worried because the quarterback calls most of the plays, and Champi didn't know the playbook well. He had never even taken snaps in practice with the first team because Yovicsin didn't like to alternate Lalich with anyone; he wanted George to know he was number one. That left Champi a stranger to the first-stringers—not exactly an ideal situation for a reclusive personality. Several of the players used the same term to me when describing Champi: "He marched to a different drummer." But Vic Gatto said, "I liked Champi a lot. He wasn't a leader in the standard sense; physically he was. He was a very interesting guy."

The "interesting guy" was benched to start the second half. Lalich called three plays that didn't work, and Harvard punted. Mike Bouscaren fielded the ball on the Yale 16, was hit hard, and fumbled. Bruce Freeman recovered it on Yale's 25.

And there was Frank Champi, back in the game at quarterback.

His first call lost a yard. His second was a rope to sophomore tight end Pete Varney at the Yale one-yard line. His next call was to fullback Gus Crim, who steered through a big hole for the second Harvard touchdown. Harvard's offensive line was really blowing away the defense now. Rich Szaro kicked the extra point.

Yale 22, Harvard 13, two and a half minutes into the third period.

For the first time in 25 consecutive quarters, Yale would be unable to score a point in that third quarter. But they should have. Twice, Dowling had his team moving, and twice fumbles killed the drives. The first time, fullback Rich Levin fumbled on the Harvard 46. The next time, with the ball on the Harvard 35, Calvin Hill broke down the sidelines, heading for the end zone. But here came Pat Conway again, smashing Hill hard on the 10-yard line, the ball squirting out of the running back's grasp.

But Yale was holding Harvard, and early in the fourth quarter Harvard had to punt. At the Harvard 40, Dowling went to work again. A first-down rush gained five yards. On second down, in the pocket, Dowling fired a pass to tight end Bruce Weinstein to Harvard's 22-yard line. Two more runs, with a penalty sandwiched in between, brought the ball to the five, whereupon Dowling scampered in with another option-run touchdown. Yale 28, Harvard 13.

The Yale coaches debated going for two points instead of one, but Carmen Cozza felt that with ten minutes and 44 seconds left in the game, a one-point kick would be more prudent. That would give Yale back its 16-point lead, and Cozza thought that Harvard would never be able to overcome that margin— not against this Yale team, on this day. If anything, despite the fumbling, Cozza felt that there would be time for Yale to strike again.

And that's how the fourth quarter began to settle in. Yale held Harvard twice. First, with third and one on Harvard's 31, Champi tried to sneak in and was stopped at the line. He tried it again, now fourth and one, with the same result. Later, Ballantyne made a 15-yard run, but, on their own 45, two Champi passes failed and Harvard kicked again. Now Yale had the ball on its own 45. The clock, showed 6:10 to go, and Yale began, rat-a-tat, to move the ball. Dowling completed a pass to Weinstein. Levin ran for the first down. Dowling completed another pass to Weinstein on the right sideline; first down on the Harvard 32. It was getting a little cold in the late afternoon sun, and the wind was up. Some people on the Harvard side began to rise and leave the stadium. A Harvard member of the class of 1969, Robert Edgar figured the game had been lost. Edgar said to his roommate, "Let's go back to the club. We need a drink." They headed out of the stadium towards Mount Vernon Street and their private club, pleased that they had beaten the post-game crush.

On the Yale side, nobody was leaving. Everyone seemed to be on their feet, waving a white handkerchief. The stands seemed bedecked, a botanical garden, white flowers fluttering in the wind. That ritual had its origin somewhere in the bowels of Ivy League lore, the white hankies to be waved when the smell of victory pervaded the air—a precursor of the white towels to come in all sports, used less for celebratory purposes than as weapons. Along with the hankies came a thunderous chorus from the Yale crowd: "We're number one!" In retrospect Calvin Hill wasn't sure it was such a good idea. "Those white handkerchiefs might have infuriated them," he said.

One of the infuriated was Bob Dowd, an offensive tackle for

Harvard. "We could see hundreds and hundreds of white handker-chiefs waving on the Yale side," he told John Powers of the *Boston Globe*, "and every time we came up to the line we were taking it pretty good from the Yale players—a lot of crap about how big a game it was and how badly we were losing. So we decided we were going to stick it to 'em."

Yale was only 32 yards away from still another touchdown. Dowling dumped a screen pass to Bob Levin, who found a clear path down the sidelines, streaking almost 20 yards until he was hit, and, still on his feet, tried to lateral to Hill. The loose ball was pounced upon by Harvard defensive end Steve Ranere at the Crimson 14-yard line.

Today, Ranere practices internal medicine in Boston. He reminisced with fervor about that moment. "My roommate, Michael Georges, made the hit on the fullback," he told me, "and I picked it up on our 14-yard line. Suddenly I got this incredible feeling that we were going to do it. I can't underrate the electricity of that moment. It was incredible to be in the game in the fourth quarter with Champi. I still quiver when I think about that game."

Frank Champi went back onto the field with three and a half minutes left to play, knowing he would have to take the team 86 yards to score. But now, the anger having seeped out of his body, he was fully focused, feeling better about himself. "The whole team was working as one team," he told me. "There was a sense that we were doing well, that we might get in close."

The first offensive play for Harvard lost two yards. Then John Ballantyne, gimpy leg and all, took a handoff in the backfield, a dou-ble reverse, and ran 17 yards. Scrambling out of the pocket, Champi looked for a receiver but was sacked by Yale tackle Jim Gallagher. A disastrous 12-yard loss. Hold it—a flag had been thrown at midfield, and defensive holding was called on Yale. So instead of third and 22 on the Harvard 17, it was first and 10 on the Yale 47.

On first down Champi found Bruce Freeman, who took the pass and ran it to the Yale 30. First down again. A Champi flat pass to fullback Crim went incomplete. Then, the quarterback was tack-led eight yards back. It was third and 18, and a crucial call was com-ing up. Little more than a minute was left in the game.

Champi took the ball and scrambled to his left, three Yale players converging on him. "The way I remember it," he told me, "is that I was hit, and as I was going down I thought I saw Crim out of the corner of my eye and I tried to lateral the ball to him. Just as I tossed the ball, this tall lineman hit my elbow. The ball rolled around on the ground as I was going down. I did see a man and I wanted to get it to him. I just did what was instinctive."

It was not Crim who was out there, but a 220-pound offensive tackle, Fritz Reed, and he scooped up the loose ball and, clutching it tightly to his chest, churned 23 yards to the Yale 15. Had God switched sides?

On the next play, Champi stepped back, rolled right, out of the pocket, dodged some white jerseys, saw Bruce Freeman in a crowd, and went for him with a pass. "It was a flood pattern," Freeman said. "Three of our men were out there and only two Yale guys to cover. We were all on the right hash mark. I raced down the right sidelines. Frank hadn't been able to pass yet; he was scrambling. So I turned back and just tried to find a soft spot, and I saw the pass coming, a beautiful pass— he throws a very level ball—and all of a sudden it was there. Crim took a man out, and I just put my head down and coasted in." 29-19.

Someone had thrown out the kicking tee. John Ballantyne picked it up and disdainfully threw it back towards the bench. There would be no try for one point at this time.

Pete Varney, the 6-foot-3, 230-pound sophomore tight end, was the receiver Champi wanted to find for the two-point conversion. And there he was, hooking into the end zone and Champi fired. Defensive back John Waldman came up behind Varney and batted the ball away. But down flew a flag; Waldman had grabbed Varney about the waist. "He was trying to pull my arms down," Varney said. Another two-point try coming up.

Champi was thinking of maybe a quarterback sneak now that the ball was nestled only a yard and a half from the goal line. But Fritz Reed remembered it had failed twice before. He asked Champi to give it to the fullback. "I wanted me to be blocking for Crim," Reed said. Frank growled, "Okay, but it better go." And he had one more word to his teammates: "We've come this far, it would be a shame not to get this."

Everyone thrust off the line as Champi slipped the ball to Crim. The fullback drove left, over Reed, whose man lay smothered in the ground under him. Yale 29, Harvard 21.

The only thing Harvard could do now, with 42 seconds left, was to go for the onside kick. It was a play, Yovicsin told a reporter later, that Harvard had practiced every day but had never needed until this point in the season. Up in the stands, on the Yale side, the white handkerchiefs had been put away, and everyone was standing, imploring their team to hold on. The crowd rocked back and forth tensely, almost with a sense of foreboding. The Harvard fans, on the other hand, were crazed, up on their feet, screaming hoarsely. "The crowd noise was so overwhelming," remembered Yale's Ed Franklin. "Nothing has ever compared to that game."

Harvard's kicker, Tommy Wynne, was standing directly behind the tee, but as he approached the ball he veered away, and it was Ken Thomas, a defensive back, who squibbed the ball towards the right. Thomas had been chosen because in practice he had shown a knack for kicking the ball in a way that made it roll and maybe take a big bounce.

"The kickoff came to my side," said Bill Kelly, a Harvard sophomore who was standing on the line because he had good hands, "but it didn't bounce right, and I thought, uh-oh, this isn't what we practiced." The ball seemed to roll right into the chest of Yale's Brad Lee, who, for a second, seemed to have it. But, no, the miracle ball was loose, bouncing on the grass. Kelly saw the ball lying there, with nobody around it, and thought, "This is amazing—all I have to do is fall on it." And he did, cradling it in a fetal position.

At this point Brian Dowling came up to Coach Cozza with Calvin Hill, and begged him to put the two of them into the game. "My impulse was to get involved and not be a passive observer," Dowling told me. "I had played safety in high school and Calvin had played linebacker."

In his memoir, *True Blue,* published in 1999, Cozza disclosed that he was tempted—he really wanted to do it. "We were in a three-deep mode, and I would have put one of them in at safety and the other at defensive halfback. But then I told them I wouldn't do it because it would have meant taking two players out of the game. I said, 'We would destroy two young men if we took them out now.' Looking back 30 years, I don't regret that decision. I would have let down a wonderful team by sending in Brian and Calvin. We had gotten that far because of the talents of all the players, their dedication, their commitment. You don't win 16 in a row with one individual or even two individuals, or even two superstars."

Harvard's ball on its own 49, and Champi back to pass. The Yale line charged in on him, one of the Bulldogs almost grasping him in an embrace. Somehow, Champi shook him off, turning left. A big Yale lineman was just behind him but couldn't grab him and Champi found himself clear, running hard (he had "quick feet," Cozza would remark later), running 14 yards before a Yale lineman flung his hand into Champi's face. "I felt my head turn around," Champi recalled. The official called it a 15-yard penalty for the facemask violation, bringing the ball down to the Yale 15.

Thirty-two seconds left.

The crowd was howling—the Yale side of the stadium in dismay, the Harvard side in hysteria. Champi raised both arms, calling for quiet. Quiet never came. He took the snap, looking for Freeman in the end zone, but the pass was batted down.

Twenty-six seconds.

Again, Champi raised his arms, begging for quiet. Again the noise remained deafening. Again, the pass was broken up.

Twenty seconds. And here came Vic Gatto, hobbling in. Trainer Jack Fadden had strapped up the Harvard captain as best he could. "I couldn't walk," Gatto told me, "but somehow I could run." He was bringing in a play from offensive coach Pat Stark—a draw play to Crim.

Bill Narduzzi, Yale's assistant coach, immediately knew what the play was. "Draw!" he hollered. "Draw!" The players on the sidelines picked it up. "Draw play! Watch the draw!" they yelled in unison. It didn't matter that Yale knew. Champi executed perfectly, slipping the ball to Crim, who broke clear to the left of the center and, for a moment, thought he could go all the way. But the secondary ganged up on him inside the ten-yard line, finally taking him down at the six. "I just wanted that first down," Crim said.

"I just wanted to make the game more respectable. I never thought about the possibility of a tie until I got to the sidelines."

Fourteen seconds.

Champi took the ball, scrambled right, then left, was closed in, tried to burst through, but fell. He was downed at the eight, a loss of two yards. Someone called time out.

Three seconds.

Champi trotted to the sideline, and listened to Coach Yovicsin. Yovicsin called a pass to Varney, with Gatto the secondary receiver.

"I'm out there on the wing on that play," Gatto told me. "The idea was for me to try to run out and do a hook pattern. I did. I saw Frank scrambling. I had to find an opening. I had to hook all the way back."

Champi called it "my best scramble of the day, because I remember I scrambled and scrambled back there, and found myself in the middle of the field And at that point I actually stopped for a second. Because I expected to get hit, I really did. I stopped, waiting to get hit; I had gone this way and that way and didn't know where else to go. Then all of a sudden I didn't see anybody, and nobody hit me. *It was like I was being shielded by something.* It was almost metaphysical. So I said, 'O.K.,' and I moved out again, and that's when I spotted Vic Gatto. It was amazing, given our small size, that we saw each other at all."

Champi unloaded the ball just as he was being hit by a Yale player, and Gatto caught it in the gut, standing in the end zone with four white jerseys around him, toppling over in the grasp of one of them. The clock on the scoreboard said 0:00.

Hundreds of Harvard fans had been standing ten deep beyond the end zone, and when Gatto fell into payland they broke loose and rushed onto the gridiron. "People are all over the field!" shouted Ken Coleman, who was calling the game on the radio. "There is no time left, but they have the right to go for the extra points. They must go for two points! If they get two this will be *two* undefeated football teams!"

It took 15 minutes to clear the field. "Everyone was jumping on me," Vic Gatto said, calling the experience "very profound."

The play the Harvard coaches called for Frank Champi was "the roll right, turn in" to Pete Varney. It would be executed this way: balanced line, Varney six yards out to the left; Bruce Freeman, tucked on the line at the right, to head downfield at the snap; Gatto, flanked to the right, to go straight downfield; Ballantyne back and to the left of Champi, to flare out to his left to draw off a defensive back; Gus Crim, behind Champi, to block to his right.

Champi took the snap, made a half roll to his right, then quickly turned as Yale linemen attacked. Varney raced downfield six yards, then hooked back inside for the pass. As he was turning, Champi let the ball go, aiming high for the sure-handed ball hawk. He knew that when the ball arrived Varney would be there.

The most memorable moment in the entire game was this last one. On the film, Varney's back is to us. All we can see is his big number 80, his feet off the ground, a half-yard inside the end zone, his arms high in the air, holding the ball. Yale defensive back, No. 15, Ed Franklin, who earlier blocked a punt that led to a Yale touchdown, has his arms hooked around Varney, but he knows it's too late. The referee, facing the camera, is waving his arms overhead, a flash of white handkerchiefs waving from behind him, Harvard handkerchiefs. "It's TIED! TIED! TIED!" Ken Coleman screams. "It's bedlam at Harvard Stadium! The crowd pours out on the field. The Yale team is stunned. Harvard team is being mobbed by its fans." Once more, Coleman cries out: "HE FIRES IT TO VARNEY! IT IS TIED! THE GAME IS TIED!"

Bob Edgar, Harvard '69, and his roommate, were turning on Mount Auburn Street, about to enter their club for the redemptive drink they felt they so desperately needed. "We heard this roar, this deafening roar," Edgar said. "It was an outer-worldly roar, and we said to each other, 'Oh shit, we should have been there.'"

The Harvard crowd had now turned into a mob, were down on the field, grabbing any Crimson jersey they could, carrying Champi on their shoulders, carrying Gatto on their shoulders.

A Yale alumnus from New York City, who, shamed by his everlasting sorrow over the outcome, asked anonymity, confessed: "I walked across the field thinking 'This is the end. There is no God, no God!' It was the worst thing that ever happened to me. It took me months to get over it. By the time I came to the open end of the stadium they were giving out this goddamned newspaper."

It was a *Harvard Crimson* "Extra" with a conventional front page headline that said Harvard had "drawn" with Yale. But on Monday, the *Crimson* captured the headline of a lifetime: HARVARD BEATS YALE, 29-29.

Vic Gatto was in the locker room, dressing, when Calvin Hill came through the door and walked over to him. The two embraced. "Congratulations, you deserved it," Hill said. Then Gatto and Hill, together, went over to Yale's locker room. Brian Dowling was in the shower, but he came out and shook hands with Gatto.

Dowling, who had had a tremendous afternoon—scored two touchdowns rushing, threw for two touchdowns—was tactful when talking with the press, speaking graciously about Harvard's comeback, masking as best he could his disappointment. One of the writers asked him, "How's it feel finally to lose a game?"

"Gee," Dowling said, "I thought it was a tie." Later he told me that the one consolation on the sidelines during all that late momentum shift, when he couldn't get back on the field, "was that the worst thing that can happen is a tie. We can't lose."

Calvin Hill, his mouth still sore, was about to board the bus to return to New Haven. But he just couldn't do it. Besides, he'd heard about a party at Radcliffe, and that's where he went. When he got there he noticed an attractive young woman in the distance. Earlier in the evening Janet McDonald had been heard to say, after meeting a football player, "I hope I don't meet another one, they don't even know how to talk."

Calvin came over to her, held out his hand, "Hi, myth'name I'th uh—Cal Calhinhill." Janet threw up her hands. "Oh, no," she said, "not another one." Janet, who was then attending Wellesley, was a suite-mate of Hillary Rodham's; she married Calvin Hill three years later.

That fall day of 1998 in Newburyport, Frank Champi talked to me about his life after Harvard—"an odd biography," as he put it—how he, an eccentric, fit in there. It reminded me of what a Harvard official once said about the kind of student the school was looking for: "What we're after is not the well-rounded person, but the lopsided person who will make up a well-rounded class."

Champi, lopsided or not, majored in English (he also earned a Master's degree at Harvard in education). I asked him what he had written his undergraduate thesis on.

"Hamlet," *he said.*

"How did you come to pick 'Hamlet' to write about?" *I asked.*

"I think it has to do with being a son in contest with his father. I'm not a typical Harvard graduate. My father felt it was a stigma when, in 1969, I was the first-string quarterback and quit the team." *Harvard lost its first game against Holy Cross. Its second game was against Boston University.* "The captain of the BU team," *Champi said,* "was Pat Hughes. He was a teammate of mine at Everett and later had a good pro career, mostly with the New York Giants. Early in the game, Hughes sacked me. I'm lying on the ground, Hughes is on top of me—he's doing what is called trash talk now—'you can do better than that, Frank.' And I'm on the ground thinking, this is ridiculous. That's when I decided to don't want this anymore. I quit football.*

"In those days, people were questioning a lot of things. And one of the things that was on my mind was the fact that here are these men, my age, dying over there in Vietnam, getting shot and maimed. And I was playing what to me was a child's game in comparison. And I've never really been a good schmoozer. Much to my father's disappointment I never joined the Harvard Club and rubbed elbows with rich and powerful people. Anyway, I originally thought of the idea of identity when I was in a psychology course; and I did my thesis on* Hamlet.*"

I had been talking with him a long time and Champi wanted to get out in the fresh fall air, go down to the field and throw the football. He does that a lot. He says he can still throw a spiral close to 90 yards. "Sometimes, when I throw a football," *he said, his voice dreamy,* "it's the same as when I was throwing a javelin. I loved doing that. I always think of throwing the javelin as a form of meditation. And sometimes when I throw the football, it's the same as when I threw the javelin. I'm there by myself. And I throw the thing, and for a few moments I can focus on what I'm doing and it drives out the rest of the world."

9

1971
THEY LEFT IT
ON THE TABLE
Frazier–Ali, I

The only event described in this book that I actually attended was the first of the three epic fights Joe Frazier and Muhammad Ali waged for glory and redemption in the 1970s. Held at Madison Square Garden on the cold night of March 8, 1971, with snow flurries in the air, it was billed in advance by Ali, the poet laureate of the age, as "the biggest sporting event in the history of the whole planet earth." For me, the fight did live up to Ali's pronouncement, and I've got plenty of company; one newpaper carried this screeching headline: "After the Fight the Century Ended."

The Garden was packed to capacity that night with a crowd so ebullient that it looked as if it was maybe heading for the Savoy Ballroom to hear Count Basie play and Billie Holiday sing and to dance the night away. Except that Basie was unavailable; he was at the fight. As was Miles Davis. As was Elvis. As were the Beatles, some of the astronauts, some senators, and a galaxy of stars of stage, screen, and television. Coretta Scott King, was there, too, along with many civil rights figures of the time: Jesse Jackson, Andrew Young, Ralph Abernathy, Julian Bond, all bonded to the fighter who wouldn't commit to the agenda of the establishment world. It was a night when all the people, emerging from taxis and limousines, were beautiful. The guys were wearing long coats of leather or ermine or mink and sequined capes and tangerine jump suits. The dolls were in décolletage, in tight yellow maxis, white mini-suits, velvet hot pants, and knee-length jackets of leopard and wolf—and diamonds were their best friends. All of them seemed to know they had bought a ticket to a cause, not just a fight.

The cause for Muhammad Ali's crowd was rooted in what he'd had to live with the last 43 months away from the ring, after he said, "Cassius is not my name any more, it's Muhammad Ali;" after he aligned himself with the Nation of Islam, resisted the draft, and told everyone that he had no troubles with them Viet Cong. The government wanted to send him to prison and throw away the key, and only the judicial system saved him. Meanwhile, the fight authorities, "in the best interest of boxing," stripped him of his heavyweight title and sent him into purgatory. Now he was back, more strident than ever, and the Ali crowd was there to see whether he was truly back.

For the Joe Frazier crowd, the cause was more complex. He was the blue-collar worker excelling at his trade. Nothing had come easy for him. He was a fighter who never took a lazy breath in the ring, nor a step back; he swarmed after his opponent, ignoring the pain it took to get in there. Nor was he a braggart; like Joe Louis, he was the obedient American Negro. So the Joe Frazier crowd was a contaminated mix, some genuinely wanting him to win because of his honest professional standards, others not caring one way or another, just wanting him to destroy his opponent because they hated Clay/Ali. Joe Frazier was their white hope.

Yet even if he did win, as his corner-man, Eddie Futch, said before the fight, Frazier's popularity "would sink to zero." Futch remembered what happened to Ezzard Charles after he took the heavyweight championship away from the beloved Joe Louis—he was ostracized by the boxing public. "Louis was a symbol of the black man's struggle to achieve equality and the better life," Futch said. "Ali represents a new hope—a pride, a dignity, plus an articulation that the black man has never been able to achieve in the white community, the quality of speaking and being heard."

Ali was certainly being heard by Frazier, who was sickened by the words. Over and over, Ali was calling Frazier a tramp, a bum, a gorilla, and the worst thing of all, a *Tom*. Yet in his innocence Frazier felt that he would overcome. All he ever wanted was respect, especially from his fellow African-Americans. But he didn't *crave* respect. Fighting was his profession, not his life. One of the detectives who was guarding him that night because he had received several death threats said, "I like Frazier. I hope he shuts up that draft dodger. This is more than a fight—it's the politics of the country."

So it would all be settled in the ring, since it was the best fighting the best. For the first time in the history of the heavyweight division two undefeated heavyweight champions would be fighting each other. Muhammad Ali was unbeaten in 31 fights, 25 of them knockouts. Joe Frazier was unbeaten in 26 fights, 23 of them knockouts. It would be a test of oddly juxtaposed skills—speed vs. strength; cunning vs. aggression; trash talk vs. fist talk; feline ferocity vs. dogged ferocity. A test of wills, too. "Frazier and Ali," someone said, "were fighting for the championship of each other."

It was 10:45 in the evening, fight time, and Muhammad Ali was coming into the ring first. He was wearing a scarlet robe trimmed in white satin—a Santa Claus dancing and prancing down the aisle, cutting and stabbing the air with his jabs. With him were his supplicants, each one bent over like a monk, holding onto the one ahead of him by the shoulders, a conga line swaying toward the altar: his putative manager Herbert Muhammad, the son of Elijah Mohammad; his trainer Angelo Dundee, his corner-men and cut-men and various tight-mouthed bodyguards from the Nation of Islam.

Then Joe Frazier strode out of the catacombs from the opposite side of the Garden, garbed in a green mini-robe, his face a mask of unconcern. He swung along briskly, his retinue half the size of Ali's: his manager, Yank Durham; the corner-man Eddie Futch, the cut-men and several New York City detectives. Proceeding to the ring, the two fighters sat on their stools. Alistair Cooke, writing for a British newspaper, would note that Ali "assumed his stool as the heir apparent must await the depositing of the crown by the Archbishop of Canterbury."

Then the principals were on their feet, naked to the waist—Ali in red velvet trunks, red tassels flopping on his white boxing shoes; Frazier, sporting green satin brocade trunks decorated with gold flowers. I was startled to see the contrast between the two men: Ali, 6-foot-3, 214 pounds, with an 80-inch reach; Frazier, 5-foot-11, 207 pounds, with a 73-$\frac{1}{2}$ inch reach. The announcer, Johnny Addie, pulled down on the microphone and introduced the fighters in a strangely subdued voice:

"Ladies and Gentlemen: From Louisville, Kentucky, here is Muhammad Ali. His opponent, from Philadelphia, Pennsylvania, the heavyweight champion of the world, Joe Frazier."

The third man in the ring was Arthur Mercante, Jr., a seasoned referee, who, at two o'clock that afternoon, was told he had the job; Yank Durham had insisted on an experienced referee who would keep the bout under firm control. He was satisfied with Mercante, who would be paid $750. (Later, the ref told people he would have worked this fight for nothing.) The fighters would be earning somewhat more; each man was guaranteed two and a half million dollars.

Mercante summoned his fighters to the center of the ring and gave them his final instructions. Ali was staring defiantly at Frazier, shaking his head back and forth, words frothing from his mouth: "Look out nigguh, I'm gonna kill ya." Frazier fixed his antagonist with the stare of a man who has been buffeted too long by the taunts of his opponent. Back in his corner Frazier remembered that he had hoped to go into the ring with a clear mind, a peaceful mind. But then he heard the bell ringing and thought, it's ringing for me, and, snarling, this fearsome body puncher was on Ali at once, claiming the first swing. It was a right meant for the head, not the body, and it just missed. Ali, now all grim business, retaliated with three crisp jabs—a long left and a right to the head, and a left to the body. The crowd roared. But Frazier, bobbing and weaving, kept sneaking in, taking a shot to the head and a shot to the body before breaking a solid left into Ali's midsection.

Ali gripped Frazier around the head, tying him up. Arthur Mercante moved in and told Ali, "Stop holding!" Freed, Frazier stalked Ali once more, popping him with a left and a right to the head. Ali backpedaled to the ropes; all his career he had been a backward "leaper." As he once explained, "If a man finds himself in a tough spot, he can help himself by stepping back lightly until the danger is over." But Frazier found him there and landed a hard left hook to the jaw. Ali, however, shook his head as if he was dismissing a servant. Frazier responded by sticking out his chin, inviting his antagonist to a free shot. Later, he said he had done it "to let him know he couldn't hurt me."

Still, Ali was scoring. Angelo Dundee commented after it was over that his fighter "had Frazier completely frustrated and came close to knocking him out in that first round." Indeed, that round Ali seemed like his old self, a dancer *en pointe,* floating like a butterfly and stinging like a bee. But starting in the second round, he danced mostly flatfooted. It soon became obvious that during his years in exile, although he had become bigger and stronger, he had lost foot speed.

Still, there was nothing wrong with his arm speed, and round 2 went even better for him. Throughout the three minutes, Frazier was taking three hits to one, sometimes four to one, five to one. But just as the Ali crowd began smooching for Ali, out of nowhere Frazier struck with a stunning right to the jaw. Now the Frazier crowd was up and roaring. The rest of the round, however, was all Ali—12 solid hits to maybe three for Frazier. Mercante and the two judges, Artie Aidala and Bill Recht, awarded the round to Ali. Returning to his corner, scornful as ever, Ali waved Frazier away as if he was a speck of dust on his scarlet trunks. Between rounds he stayed on his feet to show the crowd he was breezing.

But Frazier wasn't paying attention. He was sitting in his stool, listening to Eddie Futch recap what he had told him in training camp, that "Clay has only one type of jab—long and straight—and he needs time to throw it. If he misses his first jab, he can't bring his fist back to throw another one without you getting inside."

Frazier knew he would have to absorb more punishment. So what, he thought, Ali might hit me a few times, but not enough. I'll reach him.

He'd once said of himself, "Joe Frazier is a natural person, like other people, a human being. Not a loudmouth. Not a machine you wind up to beat up. Not a animal." He despised Ali for making him seem like an animal, always rapping that he was going to give Frazier a ghetto whipping. Frazier rasped back, "What he know about the ghetto?"

Growing up black and dirt-poor in Beaufort, South Carolina,

Joe Frazier knew all there was to know about ghetto life. He was born on January 12, 1944, the youngest of seven brothers in a family of 13 children, the son of a sharecropper who lost his left arm in a shooting over a woman. "When my mother was in labor with me," Frazier said, "people hung around the house to see if I'd come out borned with one arm, like my daddy."

The family lived in a six-room shack with an outhouse down the road. The land was owned by a white man and needed constant tilling. Frazier's mother was a churchgoing Baptist who taught him about the serenities of the Bible and the certitude of religion. The boy was proud of his father. "With one arm he tied his own shoes," Frazier recalled. "When he died, there wasn't room for all the cars in his funeral procession."

At the age of six, he was working beside his father, tending to the hogs and listening to his father describe Joe Louis's last fights. Inspired by the Brown Bomber, the boy stuffed grass and hay and bricks into a large bag, hung it on a tree and banged away at it, concentrating on hitting it with his left hand. Freudians might say he was compensating for his father's lack of a left arm. Credit Freud with giving Frazier his awesome left hook.

At age 13, he learned first hand about the miseries of being the wrong color. He was walking on the road when a white man jumped out of his car and hollered, "Hey, nigger, whatcha doing?" It was the first time he'd heard the "N" word spoken quite that way. "He grabs me and hits me," Frazier said, "but I start hittin' him back, and every time I hit him I draw blood. I have him down in the dirt now, and blood's all over the place, and the cracker is saying, 'Hey, man, we can talk this over, can't we?'"

Soon afterward he fell in love with a 15-year-old girl named Florence Smith. He used to steal gasoline from school buses and put it in his father's car so he could visit Florence. They had a boy they named Marvis, and Frazier quit school and went north to Philadelphia to earn a living for the family. When he got a job, he had Florence and the child come north. His first job was toting slabs of meat in a slaughterhouse. It built his muscles, but he was eating a lot of that meat and he ballooned to 230 pounds, "My legs were so fat I couldn't get my pants on," he recalled. It was at that point that he found the Police Athletic League gym and Yank Durham found him.

Durham, a tall, stoop-shouldered man, fooled around with fighters at the gym, dreaming, like so many small-time fight managers of the day, that he would find one he could groom for greatness. Durham saw that the fat kid didn't know how to box, but he liked his work ethic. Frazier got up every morning at 5 to run, in every kind of weather, then went to work, and then went to the gym and spent his late afternoons sparring, skipping rope and punching the bag. He also began to learn things from Durham.

They called Frazier "the slaughterhouse kid" because of his occupation, but also because of what he began doing to his opponents. He won the Golden Gloves heavyweight crown in 1962, 1963, and 1964, and won a place on the Olympic team. At the Olympic semifinals in Tokyo, his left hook demolished the Russian heavyweight in the second round, and he came back home with a gold medal.

But he didn't have any money. Yank Durham, noting that a syndicate of white businessmen in Louisville had financed Cassius Clay when he came back from the 1960 Rome Olympics with a gold medal, got 270 white and black citizens from the Philadelphia area to put up $250 to make Frazier a corporation. With the security of a weekly paycheck, Frazier turned pro, and his career took off. In the next three years he won all of his 19 fights, except for a split decision with Oscar Bonavena. Soon he would establish his right to challenge for Ali's crown.

Before the bell rang for round 3, Ali waved at Frazier and spat an obscenity at him. Frazier spat back. The referee hollered at both men to stop the damn talking. Frazier wasn't talking now; he was attacking. Ali scored first with a left hook to the head, but Frazier drove him back to the ropes, pounding Ali in the body. Ali tied him up, but Frazier broke loose, bobbed in again, jabbing lefts and rights to Ali's head. Ali fought back with two lefts and two rights to Frazier's head. Frazier took the punishment, then blasted Ali with a hard right hook to the head and a left hook to the ribs.

It was a round of nonstop action, punctuated at the bell by a barrage from Frazier of lefts and rights to Ali's face. When it was over

Mercante warned both fighters—Ali for holding and Frazier for having too much Vaseline on his face. But it wasn't Vaseline that gave Frazier his first round from the three officials; it was his recklessness. Going back to his corner, Ali gave the press a genial wink. But it was beginning to occur to some that Ali's ceaseless belittlement of Frazier, from the time of his exile until this very moment, might have been a smokescreen to disguise his own misgivings, even fear, about this opponent he never understood. But once again he refused to rest on his stool.

In round 4, Ali began peppering Frazier with jabs and hooks and then moving out of range. He seemed to be fighting in flurries now, sticking his opponent, then falling back to the ropes to save strength. Falling back, not darting back—that was the difference so far between this Ali and the earlier Ali; he was moving flatfooted. Was he a bit tired already? When Ali did come back to the center of the ring, where he had easier maneuverability, Frazier would try to push him back to the ropes. He would have liked to have done what Firpo did to Dempsey—hit him a hook on the head and tumble him out of the ring; let him land on some of his press buddies down there. Near the end of the round, a Frazier left hook sent a trickle of blood out of Ali's nose and opened his eyes wide. All three officials gave the round to Frazier. This time Ali took to his stool.

As Frazier stalked out to start the fifth round, Ali caught him with a hard hook to the face. Angelo Dundee's eyes lit up; he thought Frazier was hurt. But Frazier did an Ali, flapping his arms and dropping them to his sides, inviting Ali to pop him. And when Ali did send two jabs to his opponent's face, Frazier just laughed at him. "He's conning you. Go after him!" Dundee hollered at his man. Yank Durham also wasn't happy about his own fighter playing Ali's game. "Don't go jivin' him!" he shouted "He gets a rest when you do that. Keep the pressure on him." The round went to Ali.

Before the fight, Ali had predicted that Frazier would fall in the sixth round, and then he did nothing to make it happen. When Frazier bulled him onto the ropes Ali hung limply, allowing himself to be hit. And he *was* hit—a smashing left to the head from Frazier and a left hook to the jaw. Ali stayed on the ropes, snapped two jabs to Frazier's face, and Frazier laughed. Ali was attacking in flurries, then pulling back. Frazier was growling at him, as if to say, C'mon, I'm ready for you. The round went to Frazier.

Between rounds, Dundee screamed at Ali: "Get your butt off them damn ropes and quit playing. You got to score." Yank Durham was in a better mood; he liked what was happening. "Stay down," he said to Frazier. "Stay low and you keep him off stride. Make him breathe on your back and go right for the belly. You're doin' beautiful."

Frazier felt O.K. but he didn't look O.K. His mouth was bloody, and welts were growing around his eyes. "He looked like a man who has pushed his face into a beehive," someone said. But he rushed out to meet Ali for round 7. Ali held out his left hand like a lance, one more gesture of contempt for Frazier, and then seemed to settle down. It was a tough, no-nonsense, blue-collar round. Frazier was scoring with booming left hooks to the body, remembering the golden rule: "Kill the body and the head will die." But late in the round, Ali caught him with a hook of his own and followed with a right-left combination that seemed to jerk Frazier's eyes up to the sky.

"That shook him," Durham muttered to Eddie Futch, "but he's all right—not hurt." Dundee also felt a lot better. "Now you're doing your thing," he told Ali. "Dance and those tassels will start swirling really pretty." Although two of the three officials gave the round to Frazier, the Ali crowd had obviously seen it otherwise. When their man came out for the eighth they were on their feet, and the roar of "Ali! Ali! Ali!" thundered through the Garden.

Then, inexplicably, Ali reverted, plopping back on the ropes, taunting Frazier with gestures. And, for the first time, the Ali crowd started to boo their man. At one point, a disgusted Frazier pulled his opponent off the ropes, deposited him in mid-ring, and pounded away at him. Everyone gave the round to Frazier.

At the end of eight rounds, the fight stood this way on the officials' cards: Mercante had it 4-4; both Arthur Aidala and Bill Recht, 6-2, Frazier. I was sitting in the middle of the press section and, around me, there was disagreement as to who was ahead. The writers who tended towards Ali, partly because of the symbol he had become in a sullen America, put him slightly ahead; he had, after all, landed most of the punches. The writers who leaned towards Frazier because of their distaste for the "slacker," or who were simply neutral, thought Frazier was in front by a hair, that he had landed the more punishing hits. I felt it was dead-even. I had come into the Garden hoping for Ali to pull off the sports comeback of the century. But now I wasn't sure who I wanted, for I was feeling admiration for the dead-game Frazier.

Whoa. *Dead?* Why that word, used twice? It was because at ringside, the word "dead" seemed to hang in the air. Roger Kahn, author of *The Boys of Summer*, once told me, "Whenever I go to a heavyweight fight with two really strong fighters, just when it starts I get this little pit of fear in my gut. Nothing else in watching sports has ever created that same sensation. Did you ever feel that?" I told Roger that I never had; such a fight always gave me a jolt of excitement, one that I never felt in any other sport. But now, at the end of that eighth round, what I was thinking of, subconsciously, was death—death in the ring.

In the top of the ninth round, the Frazier crowd sent him out with cheers. But Ali, shammin' no more, greeted the express train with a left and a right and two more lefts and rights to the head, without a return from Frazier. Ernie Terrell, a heavyweight of the era, who was once stung by Ali, told me that "Ali invented a new way, like Charlie Parker did with bebop: stick, stick, move, move, move, bang, and grab." Ali was doing just that, and blood was trickling from Frazier's nose. In a flash, everyone in the Garden was up.

But Frazier remained resolute. As Ali was maneuvering towards the ropes, the champ caught him with a hard left hook to the jaw, then another hook to the jaw and a left and a right to the body. There was a minute and a half to go in the round and it was all fury. And then Ali turned it around. Once more he became a backward leaper, at the same time returning Frazier's fire with four hooks in a row that not only blunted the attack but, for the first time, left a stunned concern on Frazier's face.

The crowd was on its feet, stunned, too, wondering how Frazier had been able to survive this blitzkrieg, wondering, too, whether he would be able to come out for round 10.

Cassius Clay was born in Louisville, Kentucky, on January 7, 1942. "I was marked from birth," he said, "because I had a big head.

They said I looked like Joe Louis in my crib." One day, Cassius Clay, Sr., walked his little boy down the road to a particular telephone pole. "Put your hand on that," his Daddy said. The boy wanted to know why. "Joe Louis was here once and he leaned against that pole for five minutes while he was talking to people." Cassius, Jr., put his hands on the pole and never wanted to let go.

The Clays were said to have been descended on the white side of the family from Henry Clay; perhaps that's where Cassius inherited his gift of oratory. His mother, Odessa, and his father, who was called "Cash," were light-skinned, middle-class Negroes. Odessa cleaned houses in white neighborhoods. Cash was a sign painter with a bad temper. When Cassius was 12, someone stole his bicycle and he ran to a policeman to complain. He picked the right cop, a white man named Joe Martin, who ran the Louisville Recreation Center. Cassius swore that he would lick the kid who had his bike. Martin said he would help him get revenge; he took the 89-pound boy to the gym to teach him how to box. Right away, Martin understood that he was seeing a prodigy—and not only in the ring, where he would win 108 of 116 bouts, taking the American Athletic Union's and Golden Gloves championships in 1959 and 1960. He also had a prodigal imagination. "His mind," Martin told *Sports Illustrated*'s Mark Kram, "was a jumble of fears—ghosts, violence, blood, emotionally wild before a fight." The only skill he seemed to lack, finishing high school 376th in a class of 390, was that he couldn't read.

Never mind. Ali came to the Rome Olympics in 1960, a tightly muscled 178 pounds, and won the light heavyweight championship. He wore his gold medal back to Louisville, where he was feted with a downtown parade. That reception persuaded a group of white Louisville businessmen, most of them distillers, to form a corporation to underwrite his professional career. This was a kid with speedy fists and dancing feet and *charisma*—and smarts. When he was 15, still fighting under Joe Martin's supervision, he went to a Louisville hotel where he knew Angelo Dundee was staying with his outstanding light heavyweight, Willie Pastrano. He told Dundee that he expected to become heavyweight champion of the world. The conversation was one-sided, Clay lollygagging about how he was a student of boxing. As Dundee later remembered the young fighter,

"He understood the scenery of it, and he knew the psychology of it. He was a born psychologist. That's why you couldn't bullshit him." Cassius Clay made it clear to the trainer that if they could get together, he, the 15-year-old, would be CEO and Dundee would be his chief operating officer.

But first the distillers decided to send Clay to San Diego, in 1960, to learn about life at Archie Moore's Academy of Boxing. Moore had been in the boxing game since 1936, had won the light heavyweight championship in 1952, had come close in a heavyweight title fight against Rocky Marciano. From Moore, Ali learned not just how to perform in the ring, but what food to eat, what diets to observe, what roots and herbs to try, and how to dress; Archie himself once walked around London the day before a fight wearing morning clothes and a bowler, stroking a malacca cane. Clay loved being there with the coolest of all guys, except for one thing. Moore's students had housekeeping chores to do when they were off duty, and when they asked Clay to pitch in he threw a fit. One thing Archie Moore couldn't teach him was humility. In Mark Kram's 2001 history of Frazier–Ali, *Ghosts of Manila*, Kram reported Moore's reaction to Clay's petulance: "His egos and fears are always in battle and sometimes it leaves him empty inside. He's always going to be a lonely and hollow man."

Working out of Dundee's Fifth Street gym in Miami Beach, after the trainer agreed to take him on, Clay fought his first six fights in Miami and Louisville and won them all. Next, in Las Vegas, he met a heavily coiffed wrestler named Gorgeous George. "He was always saying how pretty he was," Clay remembered, "and he had the crowd crazy." After seeing Gorgeous George perform Cassius Clay went from extrovert to narcissist.

In 1962, also beginning to get mean, Clay was booked for a fight with his old teacher, Archie Moore, now 49. Clay announced that Moore would fall in four rounds and saw to it that he did. The crowd booed as he humiliated the old champ, banging him around at will, shouting, "Where's the dishes? Where's the laundry?" After the fourth-round knockout, Moore paid his respects to Clay: "Never show up other fighters, son. You may be coming down yourself one day."

When he turned into Muhammad Ali that fiftful streak of cruelty became part of his character. He turned defiance into defilement, most memorably in a 1965 fight with Floyd Patterson, who was then only a ghost of his heavyweight championship past. Ali never liked Patterson, for, among other reasons, always referring to him as Cassius Clay, and now he sought revenge. Before the fight Ali poured out insults, calling the decent Patterson "a white man's rabbit." In the fight he made the rabbit endure 11 rounds of taunts and snarls while proceeding to cut him to pieces. From there, Ali went on to mash everyone else in his way, sometimes tempering his attack with mercy, sometimes, if offended by the opponent, showing no mercy at all.

Ali could hardly believe Frazier was up and ready to go, after what he had done to him in round 9. Looking at his opponent between rounds, Ali shouted, "He's out!" Angelo Dundee was elated, too. "We're home free," he thought. Yet here was Joe Frazier, rising from the dead with a big lump over his left eye, his features resembling pitted mashed potatos. Ali looked at that face once and decided to go head-hunting.

But it was Frazier who got in the first licks of the tenth round—a left hook to Ali's jaw and a right to the ribs. And Ali, tired from his assaults in the previous round, moved in and started grabbing. The problem for Frazier was that as soon as Arthur Mercante pulled him off, Ali would grab again. Once, in close, Ali rasped, "Don't you know you're in here with God tonight?" "Well, God's gonna get his ass whipped," Frazier said. Crouching as he advanced, throwing a succession of hooks aimed at Ali's head and body, Frazier thought, something's got to get through soon. But the officials gave the round to Ali.

As round 11 began, the cry: "Ah-lee! Ah-lee! Ah-lee!" boomed through the Garden. Inspired by his fans, Ali rushed out and began sprinkling jabs at Frazier. But then he started grabbing again, and Frazier was yelling, "Let go of me!" He maneuvered Ali into a corner and tried to get to his head with a series of lefts and rights, but Ali had his face covered with his gloves. They continued to trade punches in a neutral corner, and then Frazier caught him—a searing left hook to the jaw, followed by a bomb to the heart. The light went out of Ali's eyes and his legs began to buckle.

Years later, in *Playboy*, Muhammad Ali explained what a blow like that does to someone: "Your mind controls your body and you don't know where you're at. There's no *pain*, just that jarring feeling. But I automatically knew what to do when that happened to me—sort of a sprinkler system going off when a fire starts up."

What he did now was to stagger away from Frazier, hoping to hang on until the round ended. He could feel his jaw swelling as he stumbled around, backpedaling, with eyes and mouth agape. Was he playing possum again? Frazier wasn't sure, so he moved carefully; he had always been taught that an opponent is most dangerous when hurt.

Ali *was* hurt, and as soon as the bell rang Dundee and his cut-man, Chickie Ferrara, were in the ring, directing their fighter to his stool. They worked furiously to revive him, splashing him with water, holding ice to his jaw, kneading his tired legs. Sportswriters at ringside began to sense an imminent end to the fight. Alistair Cooke later wrote that the round was "a nightmare that no one who saw it will ever forget."

Before they let Ali out for the 12th round, Dr. A. Harry Kleinman examined Ali. It was Dr. Kleinman who had given the fighters their pre-fight physical and proclaimed that both of them were in the best condition of their lives. "We should see an awful lot of fistic dynamite," he said. Doctor Kleinman didn't like the fistic dynamite that had puffed Ali's jaw, but otherwise he seemed all right, and the doctor sent him on his way.

Frazier went out wanting to finish it, muttering to himself, What's holding this guy up? He immediately penetrated with two commanding hooks to the jaw, causing Ali to roll like a landlubber swaying on a ship's deck. But Frazier was weary, too, and his punches weren't stinging the way they had. The one thing he knew now was that he couldn't be hurt by his enemy. Late in the round Ali threw a left-right-left to the head, and Frazier laughed in his face.

Yank Durham didn't think it was so funny. He kept hollering at Frazier to be alert: "Down, Joe, down! For the body! Bring the right over! Don't wrestle him, Joe—let the referee do the work."

When the bell rang for the 13th round, 20,000 people were on their feet. The Frazier crowd felt this was it; all that remained was to watch the execution. The Ali crowd was beginning to understand that their saint would have to perform a miracle. But he had done it before, and he had three rounds to do it again. No miracle came in the 13th. Ali's punches had lost their steam.

Before round 14, Joe Frazier asked Yank Durham what round it was. The manager lied. "Three to go," he said. He didn't want his exhausted fighter to let up. In Ali's corner, Angelo Dundee was imploring his guy to make one last noble stand. "Get you butt off the ropes!" he screamed. "Goddammit, dance! You're blowing the fight. You're giving the guy your title."

Ali responded. He came out stinging Frazier with jabs and a series of lefts and rights to the head. There were moments when he was back up on his toes, dancing as Dundee had asked. As the round was coming to an end, he ripped Frazier with a volley of punches to the head, tying the champ up. The Ali crowd was joyous, screaming out their fighter's name, sensing that the fight was now too close to call, that the last round might become the miracle of miracles.

Between rounds, Angelo Dundee looked at both fighters as they clung to their stools. My God, he thought, two guys with busted jaws. Again, Dundee screamed at Ali: "He's dead—take him out! You gotta do your thing. You don't know what them judges are thinking. Don't let them take away your title."

Now at last it was round 15. The two fighters met in center ring, and Arthur Mercante had to take each one's hand and force them to touch gloves, one of the rituals of the sport. Ali knew that to bring off his miracle he had to go for a knockout. But he forgot one of the golden rules of boxing: you never hook with a hooker. Twenty seconds in, Ali threw a hook at Frazier that landed. So what did the champ do? Frazier reached back with a left hook that "went all the way to home," as he said afterwards. It crashed into Ali's swollen right jaw. "Bam, then boom—got him short and hard, and *accurate*," Eddie Futch said. All of us near ringside could see the jaw blowing up like a balloon. And for the third time in his career, Ali hit the floor.

There are two photographs that show it all. In the first, Ali is on the left, his right arm out straight from the hook he'd just thrown, his left arm above his navel. Frazier's missile has just hit its target; his arm still ripples with muscle—you can almost feel the blow yourself. Ali is still upright, but his right leg is off the canvas. In the second picture you see Muhammad Ali sliding back, vacant eyed, his mouthpiece showing, both knees buckling, Joe Frazier hovering over him, his left hand cocked again.

Ali once said, "I may get knocked down a thousand times but my heart never goes down." Now he managed to jump right up at the count of 2. He took the mandatory 8 count and the fight continued. Frazier, was all over him, sending slashing blows, lefts and rights to Ali's head, to the midsection, to the hips, wherever he could find bone and sinew. In Ali's corner, Dundee was as pale as death. One of the cornermen was crying out, "Oh, God, oh God!" Ali, his eyes glazed, closed with Frazier, hanging on. The crowd was hysterical as Frazier worked to put his man down for good. Nobody heard the bell toll except the referee, who threw his body between the gladiators to end what has been called "the most dramatically fought fight in history."

Ali staggered over and patted Frazier on his shoulder. Frazier patted Ali back. Neither man spoke. A hush had fallen over the crowd as Johnny Addie prepared to announce the tally. Some fans started the chant, "Draw! Draw! Draw!" The Ali crowd would settle for that. Then Johnny Addie called out the results: The referee, Arthur Mercante, 8-6-1 for Frazier; judge Artie Aidala, 9-6 for Frazier. That's when bedlam gripped the Garden; judge Bill Recht's 11-4 for Frazier was irrelevant. People rushed towards ringside, but the police had blocked it off. Ali was already moving towards his dressing room, with a cordon of cops around him. When Joe Frazier realized that he had won he leaped into Yank Durham's arms, "You done it, Joe, you done it," Durham said.

Backstage, Frazier was there for the press, but Ali had disappeared.

Two sports reporters from *Newsweek,* Sandy Padwe and Peter Bonaventre, pursuing a tip, had rushed over to Flower Fifth Avenue hospital, where they saw Ali being helped out of a black limousine by Dundee and his corner man, Drew Bundini-Brown. Frazier hung out in his dressing room for an hour. His left cheek was swollen and discolored, his face lumped with knots, blood still seeping out of wounds. He was a mess, but there were truths he wanted to get off his mind. "Clay underestimated me," he told the reporters crowded around him: "Thought I was flat-footed. Kept talking to me, telling me he'd kill me. That's ghetto talk, but I gave it right back to him, and that inspired me. I knew early that I could take anything he could give me. He could cut me, but he couldn't hurt me."

One writer asked Frazier, "Is there anything you want right now?" Frazier said, "Yes, I want Clay to come to me and apologize for all the rotten things he said about me. I should have made him crawl on his hands and knees the way he said he was going to make me crawl." It was a litany that Frazier would repeat for the rest of his life.

Then Frazier dismissed the press to tend to his pain. "Someone put some ice in the sink and I'll soak my whole head in it," he said. And he did.

Muhammad Ali had spent the night in the hospital, tending to his jaw and his immense fatigue. A week later Joe Frazier went into a Philadelphia hospital. At first, no one knew what was wrong. It was serious, some doctors thought life-threatening. Frazier had high blood pressure, a kidney infection, and exhaustion. Doctors worried about a possible stroke. But two weeks later, when the *New York Times'* Dave Anderson and the sports publicist, Joe Goldstein, visited Frazier in the hospital, they were relieved to find the champ sitting up in bed with a smile on his face.

The inevitable rematch with Ali took place on January 28, 1974, before an inevitable sellout crowd at Madison Square Garden. Yank Durham had died the previous year and Eddie Futch was now Frazier's manager. Frazier respected Futch, but he missed the guy he had grown up with. Frazier lost a unanimous decision.

Thus, there had to be a rubber match with Ali, who was now the heavyweight champion of the world, having upset George Foreman in Zaire in 1974. Frazier-Ali III was held in Manila on October l, 1975. At ten in the morning, under the burning Manila sun.

In the first five rounds, Ali was the batterer, raining back-to-back lead right hands all over Frazier. In the sixth round, Frazier blasted away at Ali's innards, then caught Ali once again with two profound left hooks to the head, the hardest shots, Angelo Dundee said afterwards, he had ever seen thrown. The Frazier barrage continued against Ali into the sixth, seventh, eighth, ninth, tenth. The champion of the world was thinking that what he was going through had to be the closest thing to death he would ever know.

But he was still alive, and in the 12th round there *was* a miracle: Ali regained control of the fight. He found Frazier's face, particularly his left eye, and pecked away at it. When the round ended, Frazier told his handlers, "I can't pick up his right." That was because his left eye was shut tight. In the 13th, in the savage Manila heat, he could barely hold on, and round 14 was a massacre—Ali smashing Frazier's left eye with nine straight right hands. At the bell the referee had to guide the half-blind Frazier back to his corner.

Eddie Futch had been in it three different times when fighters died in the ring. He would not allow a fourth man to die here. He signaled to the referee that the fight was over.

"No! No! No!" Frazier cried, "you can't do that to me!"

"Sit down, son," Futch said. "It's over. No one will forget what you did today."

Not long ago, at the Boxing Hall of Fame in Canastota, New York, I sat around a breakfast table drinking coffee and talking about the past with the old heavyweights—Ken Norton, Jimmy Ellis, George Chuvalo, Bob Foster, Ernie Shavers, Ernie Terrell—all of whom had fought losing bouts either with Frazier or Ali, or both. The conversation was about the the punishment each had dealt out, and the punishment each had absorbed, especially in their fights with Frazier and Ali, who had created what someone at the table called "the greatest sports rivalry of the century." Ernie Terrell, a large and dignified middle-aged man from Chicago, perhaps said it best about the Frazier-Ali heritage: "In the end, what they did was that they both left it on the table. That's the greatest thing you can say about a fight and fighters who fight."

10

1975
BODY ENGLISH
Cincinnati Reds
vs. Boston Red Sox

On a warm and humid afternoon in July of 2000, I drove into Cooperstown, New York, for the annual induction ceremonies at the Baseball Hall of Fame. The chosen ones were to be Sparky Anderson, manager of the Cincinnati Reds during their terrorizing reign as "the big Red machine"; Tony Perez, the Reds' first baseman during those years; and Carlton Fisk, the stellar Boston Red Sox catcher during the 1970s. This induction was of special interest to me because all three had been involved in the sixth game of the 1975 World Series at Fenway Park—a game that would be remembered, as the writer Roger Angell noted, "as long as we have any baseball memory—and here they were, by some sort of heavenly dispensation, walking hand-to-hand into the Hall of Fame."

That sixth game was the diamond embedded in an equally memorable World Series—"a set of games that almost transcended winning and losing," as *Boston Globe* columnist Ray Fitzgerald wrote, "a string of pearls to be tucked away in the drawer and brought out from time to time." Every fan who was there, or who saw the game on television or listened to it on radio, knew it was something special.

Now at Cooperstown, 25 years later, that game dominated the conversation once again, though there was plenty of competition from players who had preceded Anderson and Perez and Fisk into the Hall of Fame. Up and down the historic town's elm-shaded Main Street, sitting like Santa Clauses behind tables, were such icons as Johnny Bench, Yogi Berra, Whitey Ford, Bob Gibson, Juan Marichal, Willie Mays, Joe Morgan, Brooks Robinson, Frank Robinson, Mike

Schmidt, Warren Spahn, and Carl Yastrzemski. Fans waited in long lines for an autograph from those giants. For them it was a street of dreams, the shrine where their heroes would live on forever.

The day before the induction ceremonies, Anderson, Perez, and Fisk sat together up on the stage of the local high school, taking questions from reporters who wanted to know what it was they were feeling at this defining moment of their lives. The three of them, having just come off the golf course, seemed more inclined to talk about their golf game. But when a sportswriter asked them to look back a ways, to that World Series of 1975—what they had felt through the seven games, especially that sixth game—he immediately got their attention. It was Carlton Fisk who seemed to understand better than anyone else about the impact of the past on the present, when, thinking of 1975, he said, "It's come full circle here."

The sky was hazy, the temperature a balmy 64 on that Tuesday night of October 21, 1975, and the grass was a deep velvet green. Fenway Park had never looked better. Look up into the sky— a hunter's moon gleaming down on everybody. After three days of rain, the sixth game of the World Series would finally be played.

The pregame ceremonies had just concluded. Duffy Lewis, 87 years old, the last survivor of the most acclaimed defensive outfield in Red Sox history—Lewis, Harry Hooper, and the immortal "Gray Eagle," Tris Speaker—had just thrown out the first ball to his New Hampshire neighbor, Carlton Fisk. Fisk brought the ball back to Lewis and hugged the old man, who had played in the glory years, the Red Sox winning world chanpionships in 1912, 1915, 1916. In 1918, when the Red Sox became world champions again, Hooper wasn't there; he had been sent to the Yankees. Babe Ruth was there, and he pitched two victories. Two years later, the Red Sox committed what *Boston Globe* columnist Dan Shaughnessy called "baseball's original sin"—three pennants in 83 years, but not a world championship after the Babe left Boston—by sending Ruth to the Yankees. Shaughnessy further refined his biblical observation with the title he put on his book documenting the Red Sox wilderness years: *The Curse of the Bambino.* But now, even though the Red Sox trailed the Reds by three games to two, there was hope. After three games in Cincinnati, they were *home,* and Luis Tiant was their pitcher. Win this one and they would stay alive for a seventh-game clincher.

Sparky Anderson, surveying Fenway Park, was tickled by its dimensions. "It's not a ballpark, it's a shooting gallery," he said, referring to the leftfield wall, known in New England folklore as "the green monster" because it has devoured so many pitchers. For a right-handed batter it was an easy shot to the wall—310 feet from home plate to the leftfield foul pole. The wall was 37 feet high, with a 25-foot-high screen on top whose only purpose was to keep windows from being broken on Landsdowne Street; a batted ball that hit the screen was a home run.

As Luis Tiant began to warm up, the cry *Loo-eee! Loo-eee!* echoed through the capacity crowd of 32,500 fans who had come to love this pitcher. And why not? Back in 1970, Tiant had been thrown on the garbage heap by the Cleveland Indians, who thought an arm injury had finished his career. They sent him to Minnesota, who sent him to Atlanta, and he ended up at Louisville, a Red Sox farm team. He told the people in Louisville that his arm was still good, and the Red Sox gave him a chance, for which they were bountifully rewarded. Tiant became a 15-game winner in 1972; won 20 games in 1973, and 22 in 1974; was 18-14 in the current season of delights, and was now starting his third game of the World Series. Almost single-handed he had kept the Red Sox afloat, winning the first and fourth games, that one, according to Roy Blount, Jr. of *Sports Illustrated,* by "delivering 163 pitches in 100 ways." He was the "pride of Cuba," age 34, maybe a little older, with a daunting face, puffed cheeks, long sideburns, a Fu Manchu beard, and a gentle disposition.

Preparing for the Red Sox, Sparky Anderson focused on the Tiant dilemma. It wasn't the pitcher's extensive repertoire that perturbed the manager—a lively fastball, a slider, a knuckleball, a change-of-pace floater, a "hesitation" pitch, and a variety of curves, thrown every which way. It was El Tiante's delivery that had him worried—a relic, seemingly, of some ancient tribal rite. Tiant started with the ball and glove above his head. From there he would flash a respectful look at the heavens, then wheel around so that the batter often saw the blur of number 23 on his back before he saw the blur of the ball being delivered. Adding to the effect was the leg kicking in the air at the last moment. When a runner was on first base the delivery rose to witchcraft. Tiant would bring his arm and glove down to the belt line in a series of stutter steps—a delivery that inspired caution in baserunners and attention from umpires looking for a balk. As for the eventual pitch, Pete Rose said, "In the National League we don't have anybody who throws a snapping curve that takes two minutes to reach the plate."

Now Rose, the Reds' leadoff man, picked off a Tiant curve that reached him in somewhat less than two minutes and slashed a line drive into leftfield. Carl Yastrzemski, 36 years old, with aching shoulders and knees, but still the clutch guy in his 15th year with the Red Sox, raced to his left and dove for the ball, sliding and slipping on the damp grass, and made the catch on his back, his legs in the air.

Tiant walked the number two batter, rightfielder Ken Griffey, but got second baseman Joe Morgan, who would be named the National League's most valuable player in 1975, to foul out. Next up was Johnny Bench, the most dangerous Red in this danger-loaded lineup—Johnny Bench, who won his first MVP at age 22, in 1970, and won his second two years later. El Tiante poured in two quick strikes to Bench and then caught him off stride with a low outside slider. Bench waved at it.

In the bottom of the first, Gary Nolan, Cincinnati's starting pitcher, easily dispatched first baseman Cecil Cooper and second baseman Denny Doyle. But Yastrzemski came through again, driving a 3-and-1 pitch on a string into leftfield, which brought up Carlton ("Pudge") Fisk. The Reds knew Fisk as a dead pull hitter and gave him the right side of the infield. But Fisk found room between shortstop and third and slapped a hot groundball into leftfield. With two men aboard and Fred Lynn on deck, Sparky Anderson had two pitchers warming up already; he didn't want this game to get away from him.

Lynn, who had come up to the Red Sox late in 1974, at the age of 22, had compiled a brilliant record in the current year, his rookie season. Not only was he a beautiful centerfielder to watch, reminding oldtimers of a young Dom DiMaggio, he batted .331, led the league in doubles with 47 and in runs scored with 103, hit 21 home runs, and drove in 105 runs. He would become the first player ever to win the league's Rookie of the Year award and the Most Valuable Player award. His only competition for the rookie prize was his teammate, Jim Rice, who batted .309, hit 22 home runs, and drove in 102. Rice was lost to the club in September when he was hit by a pitch that broke his wrist. When I spoke with Lynn many years later I asked him if Rice was missed. "It would have been absolutely different if he'd played," Lynn said. "It was like the Reds not having Johnny Bench."

Nolan's first pitch to Lynn was up above the shoulder. His second pitch was a fat hanging slider, and Lynn hammered it into the centerfield seats, the first World Series home run by a rookie since 1967, when another Red Sox rookie, Reggie Smith, did it. Lynn was pummeled by his teammates when he crossed home plate, and the Sox had a quick 3-0 lead.

The Boston crowd breathed a little easier, even though they understood that a three-run lead in Fenway Park meant nothing, especially with the wind blowing out to leftfield. But the fans sat back, feeling comfortable as they watched Tiant at work, keeping up the cry—*Loo-eee! Loo-eee!* Hearing that chant, Tiant felt secure. He struck out Tony Perez and retired George Foster and Dave Concepcion. When Tiant himself came up to bat in the Red Sox second, the chant of *"Loo-ee!"* serenaded him even when he struck out, prompting Joe Garagiola in the television booth to say, "Tiant's got a chance to lead the Series in standing ovations." He hadn't lost a game since September 7, and now he hadn't allowed an earned run at Fenway Park in 38 straight innings. Tiant's streak continued in the third inning, and also in the fourth, but the Reds' reliever Fred Norman matched him, keeping the Sox from scoring despite several threats.

The Red Sox rightfielder, Dwight Evans, 25 years old, in his third season with the Sox, opened the bottom of the fourth with a screaming double down the right field line. Shortstop Rick Burleson (they called him "Rooster") walked to put men on first and second, and that brought up Tiant again. This time he popped a bunt into the sky that dropped between the pitcher and first baseman, and the sacrifice moved Evans to third and Burleson to second, with one out. The budding rally fizzled out, however, when Jack Billingham, the Reds' third relief pitcher, easily erased Cooper and Doyle.

In the top of the fifth, Cesar Geronimo hit a half-liner to Dwight Evans, and a pinch-hitter, Ed Armbrister, walked. Pete Rose, up for the third time, fouled off a bunt attempt, worked the count to 3-and-2, and then fought off seven Tiant pitches. The eighth pitch came down low but in the strike zone and Rose lined it into left-field, Armbrister hustling all the way to third. Ken Griffey, then 25, was in his second full season with the Reds and could run faster than anyone on the team; he had batted .305, and 38 of his 141 hits were infield hits. In this World Series, he had already legged out three doubles. Tiant got ahead of him with two fastballs. After the second one, a called strike, Tony Kubek in the NBC booth said, "He needs another like that."

But Tiant's 2-and-2 pitch was a slow overhand curve, coming in chest high and over the plate, the same kind of pitch that Rose had struck for the first hit off Tiant, and Griffey clubbed it. It was flying deep, deep, to centerfield, and Fred Lynn was giving chase, his back to the plate. On the warning track, Lynn took one quick look at where he was, leaped for the ball, and ran out of room. His back crashed into the concrete wall under the 379-foot marker, and he half-slid to the ground and lay there, motionless. Dwight Evans ran over for the ball, firing it back to the infield, "holding" Griffey to a triple. Then he bent over his teammate.

Lynn was lying on his back, his cap off, both knees bent awkwardly, his arms behind his back, still not moving. The Fenway Park crowd stood silent, fearing the worst. Lynn later remembered that he wasn't unconscious; he understood that he had just run out of space. What made him apprehensive was that he'd lost all feeling in his lower body. But soon he began to feel a tingly sensation down his spine. And he was helped, slowly, to his feet. The pain was there, at his tail-bone, but at least he could move around. They gave him his cap and left him alone in centerfield. The crowd reacted with nervous applause. It was true, as Roger Angell once observed, that Sox fans have an "oppressive, Calvinist cloud of self-doubt." They seemed at this point to find it hard to believe that they had been robbed of calamity.

Griffey's two-run triple cut the Red Sox lead to 3-2. Joe Morgan popped up for the second out, but Johnny Bench atoned for his two strikeouts by golfing Tiant's low pitch off the "green monster." Yaz played the carom perfectly, holding Bench to a single, but Griffey was in with the tying run. Tony Perez struck out to end the inning, but it was a new ballgame—3-3—and for Red Sox fans some of the joy had been sucked out of the game.

It was in 1970, Sparky Anderson's rookie year as manager, that Cincinnati began to be called "the Big Red Machine." Johnny Bench and Tony Perez were the first elements to fit in the machine. Then came Pete Rose, Ken Griffey, George Foster, Joe Morgan, Dave Concepcion, Cesar Geronimo. But, if anything, Sparky loved his defense most. He had moved Rose from the outfield to third base, Perez from third base to first base, where he was much happier. "With Bench catching, Morgan at second base, Concepcion at shortstop and Geronimo in centerfield," the manager said, "up the middle you couldn't drop a bowling ball from ten feet in between these guys." In 1975, the Reds led the major league in the field, but also in runs scored and stolen bases. They won 108 games and clinched the pennant on September 7, the earliest ever for a National League team. But the big Red Machine was still looking for its first world championship.

The tie held up through the sixth inning, but Griffey led off the top of the seventh by smashing "a 19-hopper," as Joe Garagiola described it, past first base. Joe Morgan followed with a line-drive base hit. The Red Sox manager, Darrell Johnson, walked slowly out to the mound. "How do you feel?" he asked Tiant.

"I get him. I get him," Tiant said. Johnson left him in. Tiant did get Bench, on a flyball to Yastrzemski, and Perez on a fly to Evans, with Griffey moving to third after the catch. Now all he had to do was take care of George Foster and he would be out of it.

He got one strike, but on the next pitch Foster connected— a line drive that seemed to carry and carry, banking high off the centerfield wall 400 feet from home plate, scoring Griffey and Morgan. Concepcion made the final out, but the Reds now led, 5-3. When the Sox went out 1-2-3 in the bottom of the seventh, the silence deepened.

Cesar Geronimo, the first batter in the Reds' eighth, sang the executioner's song on Tiant, hitting his first pitch long and high, the ball streaking down the rightfield line and finally landing on the fair side of the foul pole. That made the score 6-3, and Tiant received his last standing ovation of the World Series—a heartfelt but muted *Loo-eee,* without the exclamation mark; the fans were down. Roger Moret came in and mopped up the Reds.

In Boston's bottom of the eighth, Fred Lynn stepped in to face Pedro Borbon, the Reds' fourth pitcher, who had shut down the Sox in the previous two innings. Lynn hit a shot towards the mound that caught Borbon on his right leg. He started after the ball, but Johnny Bench, out of his duck blind, hollered for the pitcher not to throw the ball; Lynn had it beat. The veteran third baseman Rico Petrocelli battled Borbon all the way, hitting foul balls, taking pitches, staying alive at 3-and-2, and finally getting the walk. Sparky Anderson walked slowly towards the mound and then motioned to the bullpen for Rawley Eastwick. Eastwick, who had shut down the Red Sox in four of the first five games of the Series, came in to face Dwight Evans. The last time he had faced Evans, he had allowed the home run. This time, he struck him out. The number eight batter, Rick Burleson, came to the plate and a pinch-hitter, Bernie Carbo, moved into the on-deck circle. When Burleson popped up for the second out, Carbo waited, thinking that Sparky Anderson would change pitchers.

The Reds' manager felt that he knew everything there was to know about Bernie Carbo. He had managed him back in 1970, a kid everyone thought had infinite possibilities from the time he was the first draft pick of Reds in 1965, drafted ahead of Johnny Bench. The first thing Anderson did with Carbo was switch him from third base to the outfield, and the kid who writer Pat Jordan said, "could easily pass for a flamenco dancer," hit a home run in his first time up. He went on to bat .310, with 21 home runs, and was National League rookie of the year. The next year Carbo slipped almost a hundred points, ending with a .219 average. In 1972, he was traded to St. Louis, and two years later found himself in Boston as a part-timer. In the 1975 season, he hit 15 home runs and drove in 50.

Another thing Anderson knew about Carbo, a lefthanded batter, was that lefthanded pitchers got him out a lot easier than righthanders did, and Eastwick was a righthander. But because Eastwick had been working with such brilliance, Anderson decided to defy the percentages. When Carbo heard plate umpire Satch Davidson holler, "Batter up!" he said to himself in surprise, *he's going to let me hit?*

Carbo took Eastwick's first pitch for a strike. All he wanted to do was not strike out—to try to put the ball in play some place. Before the next pitch, Joe Morgan gestured for the outfielders to move back. Eastwick was trying to keep the ball inside on Carbo. Two of his pitches came too far inside, and the count went to 2-and-1. On the next pitch Carbo took a home run cut and missed.

With the count 2-2, Sparky Anderson suddenly had an epiphany. "I knew McEnaney could strike him out," Sparky would write in his autobiography, *They Call Me Sparky*, referring to his left-handed relief pitcher, Will McEnaney. "I took one step up the dugout steps, then spun around and went back down. I have no idea why I did that. I had never done it before and never did it again." The next pitch headed in high, and then Carbo saw it dipping into the strike zone. Frantically, he "chopped at it like a man cutting sugar cane," Ray Fitzgerald wrote in the *Boston Globe*. Pete Rose called it "one of the most pathetic swings I've ever seen." It was a swing of desperation, but Carbo was still alive. Eastwick felt that he had Carbo set up and would now throw the best fastball he could—in and low.

But something went wrong; the ball traveled up and out, and Carbo jumped on it. He knew he had put the ball in play, but he wasn't sure where it was going. Joe Garagiola, calling the game on television, watched the ball flying on a line to deep centerfield, "going way back, way back." There was a pause from Garagiola, and then he bit off two words: "We're tied!"

Carbo, ringlets sticking out from his cap, watched the ball sail out and, after rounding the bases, fell into the arms of his teammates. "When I came home dancing all the way," he said later, "it was the happiest moment of my life." Dwight Evans remembered that joy. "We all had to hug him—it's funny how we all become kids." That was a refrain I would hear from almost everyone I interviewed about the game (as well as other games in this book). As Roy Campanella once said, "You gotta be a man to play baseball, but you gotta have a little boy in you." Listen to Pete Rose, the biggest kid of all, chattering at the Sox third base coach Don Zimmer after Carbo's home run that tied the score. "Win or lose, Popeye," he said, "we're in the greatest game ever played."

It took only that swing of Carbo's to transform the Red Sox fans. They were standing and cheering and dancing in the aisles, pounding their neighbors and screaming in ecstasy; for the game was still theirs to win. They watched with equanimity as Eastwick retired Cecil Cooper to end the redemptive inning.

Carbo's majestic home run provoked Sparky Anderson more than anything else in this thriller of a contest, with all its Tiantesque twists and turns. Why hadn't he put in the lefthander to start with, or at least followed his gut instinct and pulled Eastwick for McEnaney? "After what happened in the eighth inning," he subsequently said, full of self-recrimination, "I could feel the devil getting ready to poke his pitchfork." But in the last half of the ninth inning the devil, nonpartisan as always, would poke his pitchfork at the Red Sox.

Dick Drago had come in to pitch the top of the ninth for the Red Sox, and the fastballing reliever wasted no time—he got Morgan, Bench, and Perez to ground out to the infield. In the bottom of the ninth, Denny Doyle was the first Red Sox batter. The crowd was full of élan now, ringing bells and clapping every time Eastwick threw a ball to Doyle; the noise was so loud that Doyle didn't even hear the umpire call ball four. The next batter, Yastrzemski, who was 7 for 22 in the Series, hadn't been asked to sacrifice all season long. But, trying to move Doyle along, he bunted and fouled it off. Then he tried to chop a ball past Pete Rose at third, but that also went foul. Finally, on the two-strike count, Yaz, ever the clutch guy when the pressure was at its highest, punched a single into leftfield, his third hit of the night, and Doyle made it to third.

With Carlton Fisk up and nobody out, Anderson came to

the mound and excused Eastwick for the evening. Better late than never, he called on McEnaney. On the Red Sox, everyone went into a huddle. Coach Don Zimmer ran over from third base to talk with Johnny Pesky, the coach at first, and then went into the dugout to see what Darrell Johnson was proposing. They all knew what the scenario would be: Anderson would walk Fisk to load the bases and try to work out of it from there; he had his infield playing in and his outfield was shallow. Johnson hoped that his next batter, Fred Lynn, would wrap it up for the Red Sox. A long flyball would do it.

Lynn did hit a high fly down the leftfield line. As Don Zimmer would later recall in his autobiography, *Zim,* these were the instructions he gave to Doyle, who was waiting on third base: "Bases loaded, nobody out. Anything that looks like a line drive, you can't go nowhere. We can't have you doubled up here. Anything in the air, I'll watch while you just tag up." Zimmer watched where Lynn's drive was going. It was shallow and veering towards foul territory. Foster came running in and chased it towards the stands. As he did, the coach started down the line and yelled to Doyle to tag up.

"But as soon as I realized it was too shallow to score him," Zimmer wrote, "I knew he was going to have to hold. I was stunned when I saw Doyle breaking for home. 'No!' I screamed, 'no, no, no!' Doyle thought I was yelling 'go, go, go!'"

At first, Zimmer thought Doyle was faking a break for the plate, but he just kept running. "I liked to die," Zimmer told a reporter after the game. The same thing had happened to Dwight Evans in the first game of the Series when he was on third. He heard what he thought was "go-go," took off for home, and was an easy out. He blamed himself for not hearing Zimmer correctly. Evans also wanted me to know that "Zimmer was the best third base coach, the best baseball man I ever played for."

Foster caught the ball at the foul line and fired home. It came in on one bounce, slightly wide of the plate. Bench took it with his gloved hand and swiped at Doyle, who slid in, a hapless feet-first slide on his back, and Bench had him. Double play. Petrocelli grounded out to end the inning. The game would go on.

In the top of the tenth, with one out, Dave Concepcion

singled and stole second. But Drago struck out Geronimo and got another pinch-hitter, Dan Driessen, on a fly to Carbo in leftfield; Carbo had stayed in the game after his home run, and Yaz had moved to first. In the bottom of the 10th, Sparky Anderson called on his eighth pitcher, Pat Darcy, a rookie righthander. Darcy had appeared in 27 games as a starter and a reliever, ending with an 11-5 record and a 3.58 ERA. He had a major league fastball, but lately his arm had been feeling tired; he wasn't sure why. It was lively enough in this inning, however, as he quickly sent Evans, Burleson, and Carbo packing. Still 6-6.

Pete Rose, coming up to start the 11th inning, said something to Carlton Fisk behind the plate. What he said was, "This is some kind of a game, isn't it?" Drago's first pitch brushed the back of his uniform, and Rose was sent to first. Ken Griffey, playing for the one run that would win the game, dropped a bunt in front of the plate. Fisk, quick as a cat, pounced on the ball and drilled a strike to second base that got Rose.

With Griffey on first—a speedster who would look for the chance to run—Drago peered down at the next batter, Joe Morgan, who was always a threat to a pitcher's serenity. The scouting report said you had to play deep for this lefthanded hitter and look out for low line drives that took off. Drago's first pitch was outside; his next one was a strike on the outside corner. In between, he was throwing to first to keep Griffey from taking off. Morgan stepped away, in need of his own serenity. He looked at his third base coach, Alex Grammas, wanting to see the sign. Would they send Griffey on this pitch? Would they call for a hit-and-run? In that case, Morgan would have to swing, no matter what. Or could he call his own shot? Morgan liked what Grammas's sign told him. He stepped back into the box and relaxed, looking for a pitch he could drive. And he found one, a fastball that he sent on a low screaming line towards the rightfield stands—just what the scouting reports had said.

Even before Morgan had settled in at the plate, Dwight Evans, the rightfielder, as he always did, was anticipating his role in this situation. If Morgan hits a drive between first and second, I've got to keep Griffey from making third base. If Morgan hits a gapper to right center, I've got to keep Griffey from scoring. If it's over my head, I've got to go in the stands. He knew that Morgan, for a little guy, had tremendous power. He also knew that most lefthanders, when hitting the ball down the line, tend to swing down on the ball, thus making it curve towards the line.

Evans started running almost at the crack of the bat, running with his back to the plate, but slightly to the right, anticipating that the ball would hook. He was thinking he didn't have a chance, but he was going to give it his best shot—had to. He was near the three-foot-high wall by the visitors' bullpen when he kicked high off the ground. The ball was behind his head when he flung his left gloved arm into the stands. And pulled out a plum! Bouncing back on the field, he whirled around and gunned the ball towards first base. But his throw sailed towards the grandstand and Yastrzemski had to go over to retrieve it. Nobody would be covering first, he thought, but the Rooster, Burleson, saw what was happening and had hustled over from shortstop. Ken Griffey, almost all the way to third base, could never get back in time. Double play. Bill Plummer, the Reds' bullpen catcher, who saw Evans' catch from up close, said that Morgan's ball would have landed two or three rows back in the seats. Sparky Anderson called it the greatest catch he had ever seen. But by then, in *this* game, Sparky had lost all perspective. So had everyone else.

In the bottom of the 11th, Darcy still showed no sign of arm weariness, easily retiring pinch-hitter Rick Miller, then Doyle and Yastrzemski. As the 12th inning was about to begin, Joe Garagiola looked at his scorecard and rattled off the names of the potential heroes of a World Series game that he felt was like no other: Lynn, Griffey, Bench, Foster, Carbo, Eastwick, Morgan, Rose, Evans, Yastrzemski, Geronimo, Tiant, Fisk. And now here was Fisk, chasing a foul ball behind the plate by Johnny Bench, taking it and falling back on his rear.

Rick Wise had come in for the Red Sox, the 12th pitcher of the night, a World Series record. Wise was the ace of the staff, with 19 wins. But after Fisk's catch, Wise allowed back-to-back singles to Foster and Perez. Then he reared back and got Concepcion on a fly to left and caught Geronimo looking at a third strike.

It was almost a half hour past midnight when Johnny Bench began to warm up Darcy for the bottom of the 12th. Bench was worried; his pitcher wasn't getting the ball over the plate. Would he have enough left to stay out of trouble? Bench looked over at Sparky Anderson, but what could the manager do? He had only two pitchers left: Don Gullett, who would start tomorrow, if there was a tomorrow, and Clay Kirby, who wasn't currently an Anderson favorite.

In the Sox dugout, Carlton Fisk, who would lead off, was removing his catching gear. Fred Lynn, who would bat second, was near by, picking out his bat. Lynn remembered Fisk telling him, "I'm going to get on. You knock me in." Fisk, feeling a little tired, wanted a lighter bat, and he asked Burleson if he could use his "pea shooter." As he strode towards the plate, holding Burleson's bat, Fisk liked the feel of it. Odd, he also felt his fatigue leaving him.

Pat Darcy's first pitch was ball one, high and outside. Darcy was a down-and-in kind of pitcher with his sinker, but he couldn't pitch down-and-in to Fisk, who ate up such pitches. But he also didn't want to walk the leadoff man. Bench signaled for a fastball, down but away.

There is a striking photograph of what happened next. Darcy is in his follow-through, the ball a whisper away from Bench's glove; you can see Bench, behind his mask, gazing down at the ball. Satch Davidson, the umpire, is crouched behind Bench, one knee on the ground, also looking at the ball. Fisk, his mouth open, has the fat of the bat down around his thigh, in line to meet the ball. In the first four rows, none of the spectators are smiling. One woman holds her face in her hand; nobody seems to be expecting anything special.

Fisk knew he'd gotten good wood on the ball; it was soaring high and deep, toward that green monster in leftfield. The only question was, would it end up fair? Watching it rise in a long arc, Fisk jumped, raising his arms to the heavens, and yelled at the ball: "Stay fair! Stay fair!" Darcy's body slumped and his face went blank as he looked up into the dark October sky. He knew that the wind was blowing from left to right, and that wouldn't be a help. He prayed that it would land foul.

Fisk, skipping sideways towards first base, began waving his arms frantically from left to right, begging the ball to stay fair and find the screen. Don Zimmer ran into the infield and, with *his* arms, tried to push the ball into fair territory. That moment still lights up his dreams. In the television booth, crying out to 60 million viewers, Dick Stockton was hedging his bet: "There it goes...A long drive...If it stays fair..." In leftfield, George Foster ran towards the corner and looked up, ready to catch the ball if he could, or pick it up if it hit the wall and throw the thing into second base. An instant later he knew it was over.

The ball hooked high in the sky, hooked to the left just enough to hit the foul pole and drop down, down, down, into George Foster's glove.

And Dick Stockton finished his sentence: *"Home run!"*

It was 12:34 A.M. when the ball struck that foul pole—an event, Red Smith said in the *New York Times,* "that was no more than punctuation, a period marking the conclusion of an utterly implausible tale." The Fenway crowd erupted in cheers and yells and hand-clapping, accompanied by Red Sox organist John Kiley playing Handel's "Hallelujah Chorus." Carlton Fisk, the joy on his face immense, took his turn around third and fought his way home through an unruly mob of young ruffians that had burst onto the field.

What insured the immortality of the home run was an act of God that only got revealed 25 years later in a *New York Times* article by Alan Schwarz. An NBC camera was inside the scoreboard behind the leftfield wall. According to Schwarz, the cameraman, Lou Gerard, had been told by the producer Harry Coyle to follow the *ball,* wherever Fisk might hit it. But Gerard was frightened. "Harry," he said, "there's a rat right here next to me the size of a cat, and it's moving closer."

"What are you gonna do?" Coyle asked.

"Maybe I ought to just stay with Fisk and see what happens." If he had gone with the ball, he would have had to move within sight of the rat.

So every movement of the midnight ride of Carlton Fisk was captured by a TV camera while its cameraman stayed clear of a rat. It was the first time, Schwarz wrote, that "a camera captured an athlete's emotions so immediately," as every baseball fan will attest. That brief segment of film has been shown repeatedly ever since—perhaps the best known sequence in the annals of a sport that has been extensively photographed.

When Sparky Anderson slowly walked out of Fenway Park to

the team bus, at one o'clock in the morning, Pete Rose tried to cheer him up. "Wasn't that some kind of game?" he said. "Are you nuts?" Anderson replied, "I just lost us the World Series and you're telling me it's the best game you ever played in?"

Rose looked Sparky in the eye. "This will always be remembered as one of the greatest games in history," he said, "and we were part of it." Then Rose added, "We're gonna win this thing tomorrow."

And so another capacity crowd came to Fenway Park for the seventh game, buoyed by the miracle of the night before, but unable to shake the self-doubt that had built in the mind of Red Sox fans through 60 years of failure. A banner was paraded through the ballpark, intending to mask fears, *We're Sending the Big Red Machine Home in a Little Red Wagon*, but it did nothing to ease the disquiet of the Red Sox fans. For a while, though, hopes rose.

It started out as a battle of southpaws—Don Gullett for the Reds, "Spaceman" Bill Lee for the Red Sox—two southpaws who hated pitching in Fenway Park. Lee always called the green monster "an automatic reason for massive depression," and he suffered accordingly. He had won 17 games for the Sox in 1975, but fell down during the stretch and was bypassed in the playoffs. When told he would be the starting pitcher for game two of the World Series, Lee said, "I don't know if I'll be ready. I've only had ten days rest." He was ready, pitching without fear in Fenway Park, allowing only one run on seven hits into the ninth inning. The Red Sox were leading, 2-1, when Johnny Bench opened the ninth with a double. Lee was relieved by Dick Drago, who gave up the two runs that lost it for the Sox. And here was the Spaceman, back again in the grand finale, pitching a surgical five innings against the Reds, scattering five hits and not allowing a run. The Red Sox took a 3-0 lead into the top of the sixth.

George Sullivan, a sportswriter for years in Boston, had also been a bat boy at Fenway Park and did a stint as public relations director of the team. The Red Sox were his team. In this final game of 1975, there came a moment in his life that he would never forget.

"It's the top of the sixth and the Red Sox are winning 3-0. I'm in the press box up on the roof, getting nervous, so I go out and walk along the roof down the leftfield line. I just had to walk. This might be the *world championship* tonight. *Finally.* As I start to walk down the roof, all of a sudden, behind me, Tom Yawkey's box flies open. And out comes the Red Sox owner, running to go to the men's room. He sees me. 'Hey, Sully!' this man who has suffered years and years of frustration hollers, 'This looks like it might be it!' And he flings his right arm to the sky, fist clenched, a beatific smile on his face.

"I say, 'Yeah, Mr. Yawkey! yeah, Mr. Yawkey!'

"I'm still up there, walking along the roof almost to the foul line, when Lee throws his 'moon ball' to Tony Perez, a slow, arching curveball. And Perez hits it and here comes the ball *right at me.* I can still see the white ball coming at me, it seemed, at eye level. It flew right over my head—in my mind it's still going." The Reds got two more runs in the late innings, and the Red Sox were shut down, and Cincinnati, at least, had driven off its own curse, winning its first World Series title in 38 years.

One more gala was held for Carlton Fisk in his Hall of Fame year of splendor, on the afternoon of September 4, 2000, at Fenway Park: the retirement of his number, 27.

Throughout its history the Red Sox organization has been frugal about whose number gets retired; only four numbers were up there on the facing of the rightfield roof—Bobby Doerr, their great second baseman of the 1940s and '50s, who wore No. 1; Joe Cronin, a shortstop, manager, general manager, and American League president, No. 4; Ted Williams, No. 9; and Carl Yastrzemski, No. 8. And now Carlton Fisk, who played in the majors for 24 brilliant years, best remembered for one at-bat.

Fisk walked along the railing in rightfield, slapping hands with his fans until he reached the pitcher's mound. The Sox would be playing the Seattle Mariners, and the players from both teams were crammed on the dugout steps to watch Fisk throw out the first ball. Fisk's catcher for the occasion, a chest protector over his more than ample stomach, was Luis Tiant, and his surprise presence wowed the crowd. Tiant caught Fisk's easy pitch and, with Tina Turner belting out "Simply The Best" in the background, the two old teammates warmly embraced and exchanged compliments. "He was the best catcher I ever had catch for me," Tiant said. Fisk said his relationship with Tiant "was the most special I ever had with a pitcher." For both of them, all the good memories were flooding in. Of the sixth game especially—the brave performance of Luis Tiant: the Fred Lynn home run and the Fred Lynn crash; the Bernie Carbo home run; the Dwight Evans catch; the Fisk body English knockout punch—"that one moment in the universe," Fisk said, "that was truly mine."

11

1980
DO YOU BELIEVE
IN MIRACLES?
U.S. vs. USSR

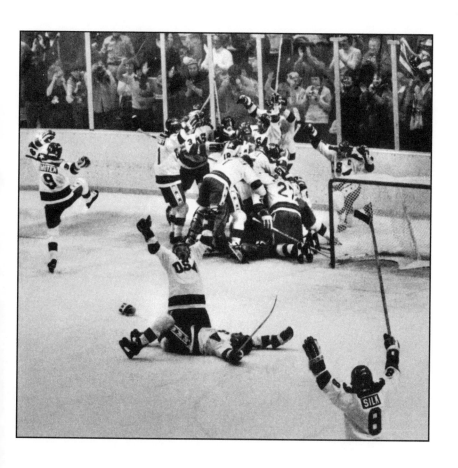

At FIVE IN THE afternoon of February 22, 1980, at Lake Placid, New York, Vladimir Petrov of the Soviet Union and Mark Johnson of the United States peered at each other, their lances at the ready, waiting for the referee to drop the puck to begin a hockey game whose dimensions would extend in time for years to come. "Now the dove and the leopard wrestle/at five in the afternoon," wrote Federico García Lorca in his poem eulogizing a young matador killed in the bullring at five in the afternoon. But who here was the dove, and who the leopard?

Petrov—at center—was the anchor of what aficionados regarded as the most productive hockey line in the world, including the professional players of the National Hockey League. It was a veteran trio, but still potent. At left wing was Valeri Kharlamov, the leading scorer in the 1972 Olympics, with nine goals and six assists, and at right wing was the 35-year-old team captain, Boris Mikhailov, intelligent, steady, intuitive, perhaps the all-around best of the Soviet offensive players. The United States coach, Herb Brooks, thought so, and tried to defuse Mikhailov by pointing out to his players that he looked like the sad-faced film comedian, Stan Laurel.

Opposite Petrov was a 5-foot-9, 160-pound, 22-year-old. Mark Johnson, son of the University of Wisconsin hockey coach, was a three-time All-American, college Player of the Year as a junior at Wisconsin. Johnson was wiry and sinuous, with a leopard-like sixth sense that told him where the puck was without seeing it. Johnson's left wing was Rob McClanahan, from the University of Minnesota, a speedy, tough workhorse who helped kill penalties when his team was shorthanded, and piled in on power plays when the other team was down a man. The right wing, Dave Silk, was out of Boston University. He had fought his way up from the fourth line by working his butt off, digging pucks out of the zone and passing off with deadly accuracy. If he wasn't one of the fastest guys on the team, he was one of the most motivated. Mark Johnson, Rob McClanahan, Dave Silk: this was the coach's first line, out there for the whistle and the face-off.

As the action began, the 42-year-old Herb Brooks was standing in back of the United States box behind his players, his piercing eyes nailed to the rink. With his camel's-hair sports jacket and flamboyant plaid pants, he looked like the "gentleman caller" coming to court Blanche Dubois in *A Streetcar Named Desire*. But he was no country bumpkin to his players, who had had to live with him for six months. Under his menacing stare they had played 61 pre-Olympic games, won 42 of them, lost 16, and tied 3, with hardly a word of approval from their coach. Brooks had come to be detested by his players. "Herbie was very confrontational," said McClanahan, who had played under Brooks at the University of Minnesota when the team brought two NCAA titles to the school. "He was in your face and hounded you all the time." That kind of talk never bothered Brooks. Actually it was what he wanted—anything to distance himself from the team. "I'll be your coach," he had said back in the beginning, "but I won't be your friend."

But by five o'clock on this afternoon, at the climactic point in their young lives, the players understood that except for Brooks's maniacal efforts they probably wouldn't be where they were— playing the best hockey team in the world, a team that had won 43 out of 44 Olympic contests and was going for a fifth straight gold medal. Under Brooks, the United States had a chance, at least, to take that medal away from the USSR. So, an hour before the game, Brooks had stood before them in the locker room. This zealot, who had been likened to a combination of Vince Lombardi and Bobby Knight, was about to transform himself into Knute Rockne, the legendary Notre Dame football coach known for his inspirational locker-room sermons. This

one would be a bit different. Brooks wouldn't make a speech senti-
mentalizing what had become a wary relationship between himself
and his players. But now that everything was on the line, it was time
to convey his respect to these guys by offering a positive slant. He had
never had trouble improvising when he gave them hell. But this was
new to him, so he pulled a piece of paper out of his pocket and read
from it: "You were born to be a player. You were meant to be here at
this time. This is your moment."

His players were stunned. This was the man who would say,
"I'm gonna work you till you die," who had an array of "Brooksisms,"
most of them loaded with bile, most of them also derivative. But not
today. Jack O'Callahan, a tough, unsentimental defenseman out of
Boston University, who ordinarily was one of Brooks's whipping
boys, thought it was kind of a nice thing the coach had done, because
it was the only time he had let his heart out a little bit. "He basically
came in the locker room," O'Callahan said, "to tell us, 'You guys are
American hockey players, and you earned this, and don't let anybody
tell you this is a fluke. It's not.' He made us feel that that we were right
at the edge of where we wanted to be—where we needed to be if
we were going to have a chance to win a gold medal."

Now it was game time and every one of the 8,500 red plas-
tic seats at the new Olympic Field House was occupied. Another
thousand spectators were standing wherever they could around the
rink. Ten days earlier, when the Winter Olympics began, it was ludi-
crous to even dream about the possibility of a Cold War match-up
between a USSR team—composed of Russians, Ukrainians, Latvians,
Lithuanians, and Byelorussians of the highest caliber—and a United
States team that was seeded seventh in the 12-team tournament, a
team filled with 21-year-old college kids. Most experts thought the
Americans probably wouldn't even qualify for the medal round.
When they did, spectators who had passed up the opportunity to
buy tickets for the medal-round games found themselves paying
scalpers up to $200 for a seat.

But the families of the 20 American players, who lived
together in a large house that offered them a communal setting,
never had to pay a scalper; they were believers from the beginning.

These fathers and mothers and grandfathers and grandmothers and sisters and brothers had been out there for every game, waving their American flags, yelling "USA! USA!" Now they were unfurling banners that said, "BRING ON THE RUSSIANS!" and "GO FOR GOLD!"

The puck dropped and the game was on. The Russians, wearing all red, were trying to take command, but so far the American kids, wearing blue helmets, white jerseys, and red pants, alive with speed and confidence, were beating them back. And their goaltender, Jim Craig, was holding fast. Craig had approached the game with one ambition. He wanted to have a good opening five minutes so as to send a message to his team: Be cool, everything's under control. That's also what the coach wanted. "Don't let the other team score on you in the first or the last five minutes of a period," Brooks said, "and play them all-out in the middle ten." The trouble was that in the first five tournament games, the United States had never enjoyed a settled first period; in all but one of those games the other side scored first. Now playing the Russians, it was crucial not to let them get ahead, certainly not by more than one goal, because once the Russians had a lead of two goals or more, they would blitz the other team. In their first three tournament games they routed Japan by 16-0; Holland, by 17-4; and Poland, by 8-1.

Back in the summer of 1979, when 80 potential Olympians gathered together to try out for the American team at Colorado Springs, Craig was a sure bet to be the United States goaltender. He had had an outstanding career at Boston University, where, in two seasons, his teams won 29 games, and lost only four. In 1978, he led BU to the NCAA championship. "He doesn't have the great foot speed, and his gloved hand is only so-so," Brooks told Gregg Wong of the *St. Paul Pioneer Press*, "but his greatest qualities are poise and tenaciousness. He'll give up a goal in the first period, then shut a team down the rest of the way."

Now, in the first minute of the game, Craig made his first save, kicking out the shot attempt, then moving fast and cutting his angle to cover the rebound. In the first five minutes the Soviet Union did not score. But the U.S. team was finding it difficult to mount an offense of its own. Just then, however, a cheer went up when defenseman Bill Baker, who had been the captain of Brooks's 1979 championship University of Minnesota team, spun a long pass to fourth-line wing Phil Verchota. Vladislav Tretiak, one of the best goaltenders in the history of the sport, pounced on the puck, but at least the U.S. had its first shot on goal. And so far the American defensemen—particularly Ken Morrow and Mike Ramsey—were keeping the Russians away from Craig. Suddenly the hard-riding veteran, Valeri Kharlamov, was racing down ice with the puck, alone. Seeing the two defensemen practically side by side, he would split them. As he blew in, Morrow and Ramsey, holding their ground, applied mustard to the bread and made a sandwich of Kharlamov. The Russian wing hit the ice, and the puck was gone.

But at 9:12 of the first period, the Russians broke through. Defenseman Aleksei Kasatonov, from the right point, rifled a shot that skimmed down toward the right of the goal with no screen. Jim Craig was up and ready. But the 19-year-old sensation, Vladimir Krutov, was there, barely able to get an edge of his stick on the puck, just enough to deflect it into the net. Craig never saw it. Damn, he thought, if we're going to lose, let it at least be a *good* goal!

The Soviet Union led, 1-0, and the nervous home crowd, whose cheers had rung out from the beginning, perhaps to cover up their muted hopes, started to boo. They weren't booing Craig. Fed by the reality of the situation and by their own insecurities, they were booing the Soviet Union.

Insecurities were running high in the United States at that time. President Jimmy Carter, up for reelection, had told the American people, perhaps imprudently, that there was a malaise in the country. The malaise, in truth, had started back in the 1970s. The Vietnam War had ended in 1975, but Americans weren't yet ready to deal with the 55,000 men who had died for their country, or to recognize the sacrifices that had been made by the returning veterans. It was a war that seemed forever painful to talk about. At home, the economy had gone sour, unemployment was high, and, on November 4, 1979, 52 Americans were taken hostage in their own embassy in Iran and would remain hostages for 444 days. As a symbol of the country's sorrow about the hostages' plight, President Carter canceled the annual Christmas tree lighting on the south lawn of the White House. Two days after Christmas, the Soviet Union invaded Afghanistan.

With the enemy ahead by 1-0, and Craig beginning to get roughed up, Herb Brooks was concerned. He didn't like the way the Russians were containing his team, pinching in hard and forechecking aggressively. Brooks decided to apply a new tactic—something that had worked for him in college at Minnesota, and that his Olympic team had practiced. He would have the strong-side winger (the player with the puck) make his break up the side boards so that the Soviet defenseman couldn't risk rushing in to confront him. Meanwhile, the weak-side winger would race all the way to the Soviet goal line to take a possible pass. The Russians were jolted by the change. Their defensemen couldn't pinch in and forecheck as easily; they had to fall back where the wings had penetrated, which allowed the U.S. offense to come out quicker.

At the 14-minute mark, the third American line hit the ice. They were called "the Iron Range line" because all three had grown up by Minnesota's Mesabi Range, where rich iron-ore deposits had been mined for more than a century. Buzz Schneider, the left wing, the only player to have participated in the 1976 Olympics, was from Babbitt; John Harrington, the right wing, was from Vienna; Mark Pavelich, the center, from Eveleth. Babbitt, Vienna, Eveleth—can't you hear the music? These Mesabi Rangers learned hockey by playing outdoors all winter in temperatures that were often 15 below zero.

Pavelich started the music back at the U.S. blue line by stealing the puck from Vladimir Golikov, center on the Russian's third line. He broke across center ice with Schneider, a two-on-one opportunity. He faked right, and when the defenseman rushed over to challenge him, he passed to Schneider, who was streaking down the ice. From the top of the left face-off circle, Buzzy pulled his stick back as far as he could, and with an extended follow-through blistered the puck towards the goal. The slapshot blasted into the top of the right corner of the net, over Tetriak's shoulder. The Soviet goalie seldom gave up such shots, but this one came in at a severe angle that fooled him just enough. Tie game: 1-1. Suddenly, a home crowd that had been sitting on their hands were up on their feet, cheering and waving all those star-spangled flags.

But the Russians were applying pressure. The other Golikov brother, Alexander, along with a sure-shot scorer, Sergei Makarov, came in on a two-on-one breakaway. Makarov took the pass from Golikov and screamed a 40-foot wrist shot towards Craig. The U.S. goaltender speared it with his left glove. But 30 seconds later, at 17:34, the two Russians were back, Golikov near the goal, dropping it again to Makarov. Craig made the save, but the rebound broke free; it was deflected off Ken Morrow's skate, and Makarov slipped it into the left corner. Once more, the USSR held the lead, 2-1.

What could one do against this veteran team that took advantage of every opportunity given them, and otherwise created its own opportunities? The Soviet coach, Viktor Tikhonov, had finally figured out how to counter Brooks's surprise of breaking his wings free. When the U.S. had the puck, Tikhonov had one of his burly defensemen, Vasili Pervukhin or Zinetula Bilyaletdinov, stay back ten feet in front of his own goal, while one of his forwards circled around the USSR blue line. Above all, the coach didn't want to see Mark Johnson break free on Tetriak. He regarded Johnson as, by far, the most gifted scorer on the U.S. team. In any case, a score by the U.S. seemed unlikely now, because with two minutes to go, the Russians were still attacking. One Soviet forward got the puck in close and Craig made the save. Then Mikhailov was in on the goaltender, squeezing off a shot from the slot. But Craig buried it. Altogether, in the first period, the Soviets fired 18 shots on Craig, and the U.S. had had only six. But there were still ten seconds left.

The one weakness that hockey experts had noticed about the USSR team in their recent games was a subtle slump in intensity. It may have been because of the easy time they had with their early opponents. But in the medal-round games, against Finland and Canada, the Russians had to come from behind both times to win. And now, meeting a superbly conditioned American team, who were also young—22 years old on average, against 28 years for the USSR—the Russians seemed to be playing more deliberately, husbanding their strength. Brooks had noticed the same tendency while watching films of the Finland and Canada games. He told his players to look for the chance to exploit Soviet tentativeness, and to never pass up any opportunity.

Right now the puck was in the United States' hands, with hardly any time to exploit anything. Ken Morrow had it, and dropped it to Dave Christian at the U.S. blue line. Christian, who came from Warroad, Minnesota, and played for two seasons for the University of North Dakota, had been a forward all his hockey life. But during the team tryouts, in 1979, Brooks had asked him to switch to defense. Well, if that was the only way he could play in the Olympics, what could he do? The Olympics were in his blood. His father, Bill Christian, had played on the United States' 1960 Cinderella team at Squaw Valley, California. So had an uncle. It was Bill Christian's goal that beat the Russians and enabled the U.S. to go on and beat Czechoslovakia for the gold medal. "I got a different perspective as a defenseman," Christian told me. "I'd always felt comfortable with the puck, not so much without it." Christian was with the puck now, but he had to hurry. There was no thought of scoring—just get it down the ice before the period ended. So he broke to center ice and cut loose with a 90-foot slapshot. But Tetriak was on it easily, and kicked it back out, it seemed, with careless disdain.

Was this the kind of tentativeness that Brooks had talked about, the tentativeness that created opportunity? Christian, weaving in the neutral zone 100 feet back, looked down and beheld an apparition: Mark Johnson, like an avenging angel, appearing out of nowhere. Johnson had been playing with a right shoulder that was tightly harnessed. In an earlier game with Czechoslovakia, in which the U.S. led by 7-3 deep in the third period, he had taken a cheap shot from a Czech defenseman, who crumpled him with a forearm, dislocating his shoulder. Brooks was so enraged that he screamed, "We'll bury the goddamn stick right in your throat. You're gonna eat it." His remarks were heard all over the world on ABC television. Brooks had no regrets except that his 72-year-old mother, watching the game, was one of the listeners.

Now Johnson had to get by two big Soviet defensemen who,

however, were slouching, expecting the buzzer to go off instantly. Another opportunity? The buzzer hadn't gone off yet. Johnson's linemate, Dave Silk, was also there, at the sideboards, thinking that the puck coming down the ice was just a shot in the dark. "Johnson was the only guy with the presence of mind to follow up," Silk told me. "Great athletes make great plays at opportune times." Johnson swirled between the two defensemen and feinted a move on Tetriak. As the goaltender fell to his knees, Johnson cut left, tucked behind the goaltender, and flipped it behind him. The puck slid into the net. But no light flashed. And then the buzzer sounded.

The Russians, thinking that the goal hadn't counted, started off to their locker room. But the goal did count. It had landed in the net with one second left; it was just that the period-ending buzzer had sounded at the same time that the goal judge, a beat late, hit his switch. Officials rushed back to the locker room to bring the Soviet team onto the ice for the ceremonial last-second face-off. Only four of them returned. One was the goaltender, who was not Vlatisav Tetriak, but was Vladimir Myshkin. Everyone thought Myshkin had been sent out so that Tetriak could sip his between-period tea. But Tikhonov, who later complained that his goaltender was "playing poorly," had benched him for the rest of the game.

The score was tied at 2-2 and the cry of "USA! USA!" swept through the arena. The home crowd was ecstatic. Parents of the players were hugging each other. Mark Johnson's father, Bob, the U.S. Olympic coach in 1976, had come all the way from Colorado Springs, where his Wisconsin team was playing a game, to see his son, who had been nicknamed "Magic," not just for the basketball-playing Johnson but for sprinkling his own magic over the ice. The father knew all about this Soviet squad—still the best in the world, it looked to him, and a team to be feared, especially when they were wounded.

Before Herb Brooks became a coach, he worked as a life insurance salesman in his hometown of St. Paul, Minnesota. One day, as Don Riley told it in the *St. Paul Pioneer Press*, Brooks stopped at the Stage Door Café to have chili for lunch and talk hockey with the guys. "If you're such a great hockey brain," one of them asked him, "why don't you become a coach?" Brooks replied as if he had been reflecting on the question for years. "I'd be a winner because I'm tough," he said. "Too many weak-kneed pussyfooters coaching today. The kids are crying for discipline. I'd sure as hell give it to them."

Sure as hell. In the late 1950s, when he was a star player for the University of Minnesota, Brooks hoped to make the 1960 Olympic team. He was the last person to be cut by coach Jack Riley. Afterwards, still bitter, he told Riley, "Well, you must have made the right decision—you won." Brooks did make the Olympics teams of 1964 and 1968, and then, in 1972, he became head coach at the university.

When, in 1979, he was hired to coach the United States hockey team for 1980 Olympics, he brought a dozen of his own college players to the Colorado Springs tryouts. He chose eight of them. The competition for the team's 20 spots was something of a sham; Brooks already knew the dozen kids he needed to give his team a chance against the Russians—if the team got that far. The problem was that all of the good ones had been drafted by a National Hockey League team. They were accomplished hockey players, all from working-class families. If they agreed to remain amateurs in order to qualify for the Olympics—to play six months for $7,500— they would deprive their families of income they needed badly. Things were tough in the country: inflation was high, jobs had been lost, and money was getting scarce.

An apt example was Jim Craig. In a profile of Craig that was televised during the Olympics, the host, Jim McKay, told the story of the goalie's dilemma. His mother had died of cancer, his father had lost his job running the food concession at a local school, and here was the son telling his father that the Boston Bruins had offered him a contract. He wanted to accept the offer to help the financial situation at home. "Jim," his dad said, "you're not fooling me. Pro hockey can come later. Right now you're going to fulfill your ambition to your mother— you're going to play in the Olympics for your country." Craig told McKay: "I model my life after my father. He's the greatest man I know."

Most of the other hopefuls felt the same way: they wanted to play for their country. With the help of Arthur Kaminsky, a lawyer and agent for most of the players, Brooks was able to persuade them not to sign professional contracts until the Olympics were over.

On the first day of practice, Brooks told his team, "I expect every man to give his maximum. Your team is your family, and you will give 100 percent." Rob McClanahan remembers one other thing that Herbie said: "You guys are going to learn more in the next six months than you learned in all the years you've been playing." He told them about the style of play they would learn—the international game rather than the North American game that the writer E. M. Swift in *Sports Illustrated* called "ugh, me fight, me chop, me muck."

What McClanahan and the other players enjoyed the most in those months were the practices, which were always different. They didn't have to do a lot of starts and stops; everything was circles, constant circles. If a player had the puck and didn't see another offensive player, he would not be allowed to dump the puck in; he would have to reverse, bring the puck back, and regroup. "That's what Herbie had us work on a lot," McClanahan said: "Come back, get to the blue line, regroup. Throw the puck back to the defenseman. And weave." Instead of standing—ordinarily the wings stand next to the boards, the center stands in the middle—each player had an option. He could go wherever he chose to go at the time, as long as he wasn't standing still. You must not stand still, you always had to be moving.

Early in their odyssey, the United States, on tour in Europe, played two exhibition games in Oslo against Norway's national team. In the first game Norway held the United States to a tie. A tie? Brooks was livid. As the players started off the ice he said, "No you don't. You didn't play to your limits." For the next 45 minutes, even when the lights had been turned off in the arena, he had them doing "Herbies"—skating back and forth, back and forth, at varying distances, relentlessly. It was a humiliating experience, so much so that the mild-mannered Mark Johnson battered his stick into the boards until it broke. Brooks couldn't see who did it, but he hollered out, "If anybody breaks a stick on the boards again, I'll skate you till you die." The next night they played Norway again. This time they won, 9-0.

Brooks struck once more in Lake Placid, when the U.S. played its Olympic opening game against Sweden. In the first period, taking his first shift with the No. 1 line, Rob McClanahan was slammed off the boards and felt a harsh pain in his right thigh. He limped into the locker room; the trainer found him swollen from his knee to his waist—a deep charley horse with contusions. All McClanahan could think of as he looked at that leg packed in ice was that it was the first game he was playing in the Olympics—a dream he had had since childhood—"and now I'm out."

When the first period ended, with Sweden ahead by 1-0, Brooks stormed into the locker room and saw McClanahan, out of uniform, his leg covered by ice packs. "You gutless sonofabitch," he said. "we've come too far for you to go belly-up on us now. You're going to play hurt. There's no tomorrow." McClanahan started screaming at the coach. Jack O'Callahan, the only player who hadn't dressed because of a knee injury, grabbed Rob to keep him from leaping on Brooks. When Brooks went out the door, McClanahan hobbled after him, still spittin' for a fight. Finally captain Mike Eruzione came over and told Rob to suit up. "We'll make it work, Rob," he said, "even if you can only give us a 20-second burst."

McClanahan did get back, standing on the bench to keep his leg from stiffening up, and taking short shifts, hoping he wouldn't cause his team trouble. After the game, which ended in a 2-2 tie, he left the arena on crutches. But he played in the next game against Czechoslovakia and scored the last goal of the team's 7-3 victory. As the tournament progressed, his injury eased off. In the game against West Germany, with the team behind, he scored the first U.S. goal on a breakaway, and later scored the goal that won it.

"It was a way to get our attention," Mike Eruzione said years later about Brooks's behavior. It also helped bring the kids together as a team. For a long while the Eastern players who came from Eastern colleges felt that Brooks was a creep. When they found out that the Midwestern players felt the same way it almost erased the regional tensions between the two groups. They became not a Boston team, or a Minneapolis team, but "Team USA."

When the second period began, the Americans couldn't believe that the second-string goaltender, 23-year-old Vladimir

Myshkin, was in the goal for the USSR. Myshkin, short and stumpy, was an able goalie—a year earlier, he had been the goaltender against the NHL All-Stars and shut them out, 6-0. But this year he hadn't been as sharp against NHL teams. And he was no Tetriak.

As it turned out, Myshkin didn't have much to do in the second period because the United States was only able to attempt two shots on goal. Fifty-eight seconds into the period, John Harrington went off on a penalty for holding. The Russians had been having trouble with their power play—the patterns had become too predictable. But they went out there, with Yuri Lebedev, Alexander Maltsev, and Vladimir Krutov together up front. Krutov took the puck on the right side and burned it to Maltsev, who broke away at center ice and flashed towards the U.S. goal. Coming in on Craig, he faked a shot that the goaltender moved on, then streaked left and slapped the puck into the back of the cage. The time was 2:15 and the Soviet Union led 3-2. The crowd turned to stone.

Actually, the score should have been much higher during the second period because the Russians challenged Craig mercilessly, taking 12 shots at him while Myshkin dozed in the other cage. At one point Craig was so bedeviled that he drew a penalty for delay of game after falling on the puck behind the goal line. The U.S., however, thwarted the power play. At another heart-stopping moment Craig made a brilliant save while being piled on by three Russians. In the last six minutes, Craig was challenged by Mikhailov, Petrov, Krutov, and Helmut Balderiis, the Latvian "Electric Train," but he held them all off. When the period ended, the crowd rose and applauded him. Largely because of Craig ,the United States was down by only that one goal, with 20 minutes to go.

Over the months they had played together, Mark Johnson and Jack O'Callahan had become good friends, and they would talk about how they were going to play against the Russians. "We've got to keep it close," Johnson said. "We can't let them get two or three ahead of us. If we can come in at the end of the second period either down one or tied, we'll have a shot at it." When the team did come into the locker room O'Callahan said, "I looked at Mark, and he looked at me, and we kind of smiled."

A week before the Olympics opened, the U.S. had played the Russians in an exhibition match at Madison Square Garden. Only 11,000 spectators showed up, partly because of the Soviet Union's invasion of Afghanistan. The fans booed each Soviet player as he was announced, except the goaltender, Tetriak; they knew about his prowess. They also figured it would be a blowout, and it was, the Russians winning, 10-3. "After the first period we're losing 7-1," Eruzione recalled. "The next two periods we stayed pretty equal. I think we kind of worked away, thinking—you know what?—if we ever get another chance we might be better prepared and ready to play at the beginning."

Now, in the locker room before the third period, Brooks told his players: "Stay with the system, no matter what." That was his mantra. His heart was in his throat when he said it, but he knew that they had to stay with it. Through practice after practice, game after game, the Americans had perfected that system: puck control as opposed to dump-and-chase, stick-handling to keep possession, speed, and the criss-cross weaving game with the puck instead of standing around waiting for it to come to you. Brooks also stressed the team's distinctive American qualities. "He recognized that we had to do things differently," Jack O'Callahan said, "but he maintained our North American grit—the feistiness and competitiveness that a lot of the Europeans didn't have in those days. That added another whole dimension to our game."

Above all, Brooks wanted his team to be superbly conditioned. For almost 20 years, the Soviet Union had been the fastest, best conditioned team of them all, able to rally when behind late in the game, as they had in their previous two crucial matches against Finland and Canada, their energy and resolve increasing rather than flagging. So far in this one they had played the two periods at full speed, but so had the Americans, and the Russians hadn't been able to pull ahead significantly. As the teams came on ice for the last 20 minutes, the big question was whether the age factor would work for the U.S. The other question on Brooks's mind—one that he shared with his team—was whether, after winning four straight gold medals, the Russians' desire was as urgent as it had been.

As the third period unfolded, the teams exchanged bursts of speed, racing down to their opponents' goal but unable to finish the charge. Sergei Makarov staged a breakaway and flew in on Craig, but couldn't get the shot away. Then it was the United States' turn, Mike Ramsey coming in on Myshkin. But the puck slipped off Ramsey's stick and he couldn't fire it.

At the eighth minute, Vladimir Krutov was sent off for "elbowing," a penalty Ken Dryden, the Hall of Fame goaltender for the Montreal Canadiens, who was doing the analysis for ABC television, called "rather questionable." So the U.S. had its second power play of the game. If the Americans had shown any one weakness throughout the tournament it was in exploiting power plays. This time the U.S. put heavy pressure on the Russians, speeding into Soviet territory but not quite able to pull the string on Myshkin. Mike Eruzione flashed in on a breakaway, but his shot went wide. Then, with 30 seconds left in the two-minute penalty, the Johnson line—Rob McClanahan and Dave Silk on the wings—raced onto the ice. Silk took the puck from the Soviets' defenseman Valeri Vasilev and immediately looked for Mark Johnson. And immediately saw him. And immediately slithered a pass from his left side to the slot, where Johnson was loitering. Two Soviet defensemen were down there to Johnson's left, and one of them, Sergei Starikov, found the puck on his stick. But, just as quickly, it slipped off Starikov's skate and trickled onto Johnson's stick. The man named "Magic" provided just that, speeding to his left, past Vasilev and Starikov, and slapped the puck into the empty area to the left of the fallen goaltender. Starikov, in frustration, pounded his stick into the ice.

The goal was scored at 8:39 and the game was *tied*, 3-3. Everyone went crazy. All the U.S. players stormed the ice, as they always did when they scored a goal—a contrast to Russian behavior; when one of their players scored, a teammate or two would maybe pat the goal-scorer on his helmet, and then just position themselves for the face-off. But these Americans were the young and the untamed, beginning to feel that maybe destiny was on their side. The crowd felt that way, too; they were up on their feet, exhaling in delight.

But a tie was not a victory. The Russian bear had been

aroused, and nobody knew what might come next. So joy was tempered by anxiety.

That clamor of the crowd felt so strange to Mike Eruzione as he gathered himself together in front of the bench, awaiting the call to action. On the bench, all you could hear was that steady roar; it sounded like the cascading noise of the Niagara Falls at which he had once wondered at as a child. Once you jumped off the boards and hit the ice, there was no crowd noise; you couldn't hear anything but your teammates. It was like being in a vacuum.

A vacuum. He still remembered the vacuum that had settled in his heart four weeks before Lake Placid, when Brooks bluntly told him he wasn't playing well, that he was thinking of replacing him, even though he was captain, unless he showed rapid improvement. The coach had called in a couple of players who had been borderline when he was picking the team; he was thinking about maybe moving one or two of them onto the squad: fresh bodies. Brooks threatened to make Eruzione assistant coach and sit him on the bench next to him. That was all Eruzione needed—to sit next to the guy who had destroyed his dream.

Brooks's threat scared the hell out of Eruzione, not so much for himself, although that was bad enough, but for how it would disrupt a team that was now a family. That's what he told his willful coach. Oddly enough, Brooks liked what he heard. It was what he had always wanted—a team bound to each other. It was why he had treated them the way he had, from the beginning, goading them without mercy, day and night, never laying on a priestly hand; the players had to become a family by themselves. Eruzione made it easy for his coach. In the next three exhibition games he scored five goals. He would not be banished. He became part of the second line, with Neal Broten, a center who they say could go 105 miles an hour on ice, and Steve Christoff.

Eruzione had never asked to be captain. Brooks was the one who wanted it. The team voted for him, with no little help from the lobbying of the coach. Eruzione never asked for anything in his life. He grew up poor in Winthrop, Massachusetts, a working-class town on the Atlantic Ocean a blue-line away from Boston. What he did have was strong family ties. He was one of six kids with tough but caring parents; in the Eruzione home, where three families lived, it was always *alla famiglia*. As a kid he was a talented athlete, played baseball and football, and learned how to play hockey in the sand traps of the local golf course. Not one Division 1 college offered him a hockey scholarship; he was 5-foot-9 and weighed maybe 150 pounds. At the last minute, he did get a hockey scholarship at Boston University when a student who had signed up with BU chose another school. In four years there, his last one as captain, his teams won four straight Eastern championships, but always lost in the NCAA finals to Midwestern powerhouses: Brooks's University of Minnesota, Mark Johnson's father's Wisconsin and Michigan Tech.

After graduation, Eruzione spent two years playing semipro hockey; no NHL team was interested in him. He was one of the guys who went to Colorado for the Olympic tryouts with only a 50-50 chance. He was a good skater, but not particularly fast, too small to hit hard, though his bashed-in nose would indicate otherwise. But he did have a knack for putting the puck into the net, often off the wrong foot. But so what? Things happened when he was on the ice.

Now, against Russia, with roughly ten minutes left, "the conehead line" was out there—Mark Pavelich, John Harrington, and Buzzie Schneider—named after school kids who once had to wear dunce hats, but appropriated from *Saturday Night Live*, and its "extra-terrestrials." Dave Christian and Bill Baker were on defense. Suddenly, Schneider waved to the box that he wanted a blow, and he skated off. That's when Eruzione jumped out on the ice, without his regular linemates, Broton and Christoff. The puck had gone behind the Soviet cage, where Harrington was fighting for it with defenseman Vasili Pervukhin. It stayed loose, but Pervukhin took it and tried to pass it off the boards to Sergei Makarov, who was skating hard to reach it. Pavelich got there at the same time as Makarov. He took the puck away and sent it down towards the slot just as he was being knocked over by Makarov.

Eruzione was inside the Soviet blue line when he saw the puck squirting towards him. He also saw the Soviet defenseman,

Pervukhin, in front of him. In a split second he reasoned: "If the Russian is going to stay, I'll use him as a screen and shoot. If he comes to me, I'll pass it by him." Eruzione saw Harrington and Bill Baker breaking to the net. Pervukhin stayed to cover them and Eruzione let it fly. It was a wrist shot, fired from 25 feet out, and he thought he had gotten a lot of it. The puck sped down ice, entering the net under Myshkin's arms. The goaltender went to his knees, both arms upraised as if he were surrendering to an armed intruder. Which he was. The puck could be seen hopping like a tadpole behind his feet into the ne.: 4–3, United States.

In the seats behind the net, the Americans' mothers and fathers and sisters and brothers were standing, their arms raised in exaltation. On the ice, Mike Eruzione, suddenly the American darling of the games, was prancing high like a show horse, clopping up and down on his skates along the left boards, a wide, self-satisfied smile on his face. A moment later he was buried by his teammates.

Would this be the goal that would mark the rest of Mike Eruzione's life? He had put the United States ahead, but there was still ten minutes to go, and ten minutes was a lifetime when you were facing the Soviet Union. When the Russians were about to be mugged by Finland with five minutes left, Krutov, Maltsev, and Mikhailov crashed through with three goals to put the Finns away. When they were down against Canada by 3-1, they rallied to win, 6-4. This would be the longest ten minutes of the American kids' lives.

Enter Mark Wells, who was Herb Brooks's last survivor. Wells had played college hockey alongside Ken Morrow at Bowling Green University; in his four years at center he scored 77 goals, with 155 assists. While Morrow was bearded, Wells was baby-faced; while Morrow was tall and strong, Wells was 5-foot-8 and a little lumpy. Still, Brooks always saw something in Wells, and he became one of the original 26 players picked for the team. One day in Norway with the team, when he went for a run, he hit a hole in the ground and snapped his ankle. "We don't think you'll be able to withstand the intense training to be an Olympian," Brooks told him, dismissing him from the team. That made Wells "angry, mad, sad, hit my heart." What he said to the coach was, "I'll be back."

A week before Lake Placid, he *was* back. No way could he match up with centers like Johnson, Broten, and Pavelich, but Brooks had a special mission for him, especially if the United States wound up playing the Soviet Union. He wanted Wells to be a defensive center and help shut down the big line: Mikhailov, Petrov, Kharlamov. Wells didn't have the speed to stay with Kharlamov, but he could get in his way, cross-check him, keep him in the neutral zone, shadow him, shut the main holes, and hit the holes where Kharlamov was circling back. Now was the time, with ten minutes left, and Wells took the ice with wings Phil Verchota and Eric Strobel—the "shut-down line," as it came to be called.

After Eruzione's goal there was a Soviet flurry—Krutov heading into Craig, only to have his shot bang off the top of the post; Maltsev loose, shooting and missing the rebound; Alexander Golikov firing one right into Craig's pads. And then, as the minutes ticked off—it seemed like a week, Eruzione said—it was the Russians who became frustrated. How well these American kids, with speed and youth, were playing the Soviet game: forechecking, skating the puck out, or passing it. The Russians began to play the NHL game, dumping the puck into the corners and chasing after it.

Many of the U.S. players felt that the Russians were growing tired. "I think they were coming off two tough games," Bill Baker said later, "and didn't have as much as we did at the end." Others wondered how much they were feeling the absence of Tretiak, the goaltender among all goaltenders.

In any case, the pressure eased off Craig, except the pressure deep within him to keep the Russians from scoring. Coach Brooks was also feeling the pressure, looking up at the clock every other second, it seemed, pacing back and forth, hollering "Play Your Game! Play Your Game!" What did he mean? "It was all about maintaining speed and skills and puck movement," Eruzione said, "and using the freedom he'd given us to be creative." So here was a Soviet defenseman loose, Slava Fetisov, 22 years old, streaking in and shooting, and Ken Morrow diving into the shot and smothering it. Here was Morrow's partner, Mike Ramsey, grabbing off a shot aimed at Craig.

It was 1:59 to go now and a face-off in the U.S. zone, the

puck taken by the U.S. The crowd was on its feet, as they had been since Eruzione's go-ahead goal, chanting in unison "USA! USA!"

1:12. Boris Mikhailov, the Soviet first-line wing, broke in on Craig, but shot too quickly, the puck flying wide of the net. Tikhonov, the Soviet coach, desperate now, was keeping the first line in as long as he could. "Our line was more than a hundred years old," said one Soviet citizen with Russian fatalism while watching the game in Moscow, "so what can we expect?"

45 seconds. Why hadn't the Russians pulled their goalie? Everybody was asking that, but the coach seemed paralyzed.

25 seconds. The puck was in the United States' zone, kicking around the boards behind the goal. Dangerous territory. Morrow and Ramsey were down there, trying to dig the puck out of the zone. It scooted into a corner and Dave Silk had it, but was having trouble clearing it. Battling for possession, Ramsey took a check from Zinetula Bilyaletdinov in the corner but held onto the puck. Mark Johnson was there, as always, and took the puck and flipped it around behind the net the other way. Then it was Morrow feeding Silk. Silk had it solid now, was skimming from the left corner all the way out to center ice, with Rob McClanahan providing police escort.

5 seconds. In the TV broadcast booth, play-by-play announcer Al Michaels shouted: "DO YOU BELIEVE IN MIRACLES?" Then, hearing the buzzer go off, he answered his question: "YESSS!"

Herb Brooks, a human factor at last, flung his arms up to the heaven, tears in his eyes, crying out one word: "WOW!" Then he stalked out, hiding himself in the men's room. Let the players have the glory; they deserve it. Throughout the games, Brooks hadn't let any of his players talk to the press, or be interviewed on television. It was like solitary confinement. "We knew that people in Lake Placid were happy, we knew people in Lake Placid were excited," Eruzione said, "but we didn't know the whole country was watching. We didn't know nothing. So we just played."

And now they just celebrated. One four-color photograph in *Sports Illustrated* says it all. The United States players, in their red, white, and blue uniforms, are sprawled in every direction. An American flag has been given to Mark Johnson; he is waving it, a look of astonishment on his face, while being hugged by Eric Strobel. Marty Pavelich, Mark Wells, and Neal Broten are among those sighted in the scrum, all piling over goaltender Jim Craig. Off to the side is Jack O'Callahan on his knees, his hands aloft, grinning, proud to display his badge of hockey honor: missing teeth. Under him on the ice is Mike Ramsey, laughing, his arms also flying high. Behind the frenzied players a calmer scene: the families of these players, now beginning to compose themselves, some taking pictures, all standing in pride with smiles on their faces.

The last players to leave the ice were the four musketeers from Boston: O'Callahan, Silk, Craig, and Eruzione. One for all and all for one. Eruzione, as usual, had the telling comment when, finally dressed, he stepped into the mob outside the Olympic Field House and told a reporter: "Everything we had to do to win, we did. They're the best team in the world, you know." Then he paused. "Wait a minute. No they're not. Maybe we are."

They would still have to beat Finland to prove it. The worst scenario for the United States was that if they lost to Finland by at least two goals while, in the other playoff game, the Soviet Union and Sweden tied, the Soviet Union would win the gold medal, and the U.S. would win nothing. If the U.S. tied Finland, they would win the bronze. If they beat Finland, the gold was theirs.

They came to work the next day fatigued from all the hullabaloo, but the adrenaline still flowing. It was a classic two-hour Herb Brooks session, full of Herbies—go this way and that way, up and down the ice—and of Brooksisms, some of them actually original. "You were lucky," he bawled at them. "You're too young. You can't pull it off." When practice was over he sputtered one last Brooksism: "If you lose this game, you'll take it to your fucking grave."

Well, they knew that. They had been talking among themselves about Finland. The Finns were a tough bunch, with a rock-hard work ethic. But they were almost as old as the Russians and lacked their stamina. The kids vowed to play their game.

And they did. After the first period Finland led, 1-0. The U.S. had peppered goaltender Jorma Valtonen with 14 shots, but none slid into the net. The Finns scored on a 50-foot slapshot that slid past Jim

Craig. Early in the second period Steve Christoff took a pass from Neal Broten and backhanded the puck through the goaltender. The game was tied. But four minutes later, with Buzzie Schneider in the penalty box, the Finns scored on the power play. When the period ended, it was still Finland out in front, 2-1.

In the dressing room, awaiting the last 20 minutes, Brooks, calm, seemingly unconcerned, spoke gently. "We've been a third period team all year," he said. "Just suck it up and do what you've done all year."

Dave Christian was one who sucked it up. At 2:25, he saw Verchota breaking in down the left side and fed him a perfect crossing pass. Verchota drilled the shot low from ten feet and it went through the goalie's pads. Tie game.

Four minutes later, Christian moved with the puck towards center ice and whistled a stinger towards Valtonen, who deflected it behind the net. Mark Johnson had it, heard McClanahan, out front, screaming for it, and he obliged his wing. McClanahan rifled the puck between the goaltender's legs. Then he looked at Johnson and Johnson looked at him. "All of a sudden," McClanahan told me, "we knew right there—*right* there—there was no way we were going to lose to the Finns. No way." The superfluous fourth goal came with 4:15 remaining, a Mark Johnson goal, scored deservedly by Johnson. That gave him 11 points in the tournament, five goals and six assists. The best of anybody.

When the game ended it was not quite a repeat of the orgy that followed the death of the Russian bear. But it was more meaningful—this was the game that won the *gold medal* for the USA. American flags were unfurled throughout the arena. One spectator said she hadn't seen so many flags since the 1960's, "when we were burning them." After the medal ceremony—Russia had beaten Sweden, 9-3, for the silver medal, Sweden took the bronze—the three team captains were called up to the platform for the playing of the anthems. When it came to "The Star-Spangled Banner," Eruzione sang his heart out. Then, up there all by himself, feeling lonely, he began waving to his teammates: "C'mere! Come on, get up on the stage! Come on!" And they all did.

Twenty-two years later, on the most public of stages, Eruzione did it again. This was the opening ceremony of the 2002 Winter Olympics in Salt Lake City. Officials had kept secret the identity of the person who would have the highest honor—putting the torch to "the flame of human aspiration," the flame that would light up the sky throughout the Games.

Who else could it be up there but Mike Eruzione? Again he was all alone, dressed in black, a happy smile on his still youthful face. Again he was waving to his 19 miracle-on-ice accomplices, imploring them to join him. "C'mon. C'mon!" And they did and, together, they lit the flame. And the joy came back to them all.

12

1992
WEEP NO MORE,
MY LADY
Duke–Kentucky

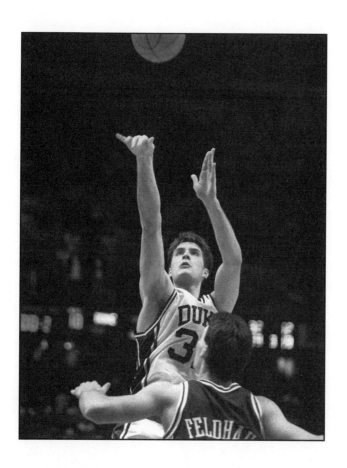

On the evening of March 28, 1992, memories thick with irony accosted four seniors on the University of Kentucky basketball team—Richie Farmer, Deron Feldhaus, John Pelphrey, and Sean Woods —as they came on the floor of the 18,000-seat Philadelphia Spectrum to meet the exalted ones from Duke University. For four straight years the aristocratic institution from Durham, North Carolina, led by its polysyllabic coach, Mike Krzyzewski (try Sha-Shef-Skee), had swept into the National Collegiate Athletic Association's holiest of tournaments, the Final Four, winning its first national championship in 1991. This season Duke, led by its 6-foot-11 All-America center Christian Laettner, its All-America point guard, Bobby Hurley, and its sophomore All-America who played forward or guard, Grant Hill, had started off in the polls at No. 1, and stayed No. 1 all-season long. Now, in these Eastern Regional Finals, they were poised to become the first team since UCLA in 1972 and 1973 to win two straight national championships.

By contrast, the Kentucky seniors were poised for simple redemption, thinking how much a victory over Duke would help to cleanse the past. For the previous four years, while Duke was running off to Final Fours, Kentucky was contending with disgrace. Looking over at the Duke players loosening up, these good old boys from their old Kentucky homes—Manchester, Maysville, Paintsville —couldn't help remembering the only other time they had played Duke, when they were children.

That was in mid-November of 1988, and—wouldn't you know it?—the game was played in Springfield, Massachusetts, which was the birthplace of college basketball. The "Tip-Off Classic," it was called. because it marked the opening of the college basketball season. Duke won it by 25 points.

The troubles had begun in April of 1988, at a Los Angeles airline terminal, when an Emery Air Freight overnight envelope with a videotape case burst open, dropping twenty $50 bills into the hands of the law. The envelope, mailed from the university's basketball office, was addressed to the father of a current high school sensation who had chosen to enroll at Kentucky. One thing spiraled into another, resulting in the resignation of Cliff Hagan, Kentucky's athletic director and a UK basketball immortal; of head coach Eddie Sutton; and severe penalties for 17 violations of NCAA rules. The penalties included three years' probation, no live television games for one year, and no postseason games for two years.

A half-dozen key recruits fled the team for other colleges. Only the four freshmen—Farmer, Feldhaus, Pelphrey, and Woods—hung on. In 1989, when a new coach, Rick Pitino, came on the scene, the first thing he told his charges was: "You guys will have to work harder than you ever worked in your life. And you're going to have more fun than you ever had in your life." And he was right. What could be better than being out there on the floor now, about to play the game of your life against "this perfect team for the 1990s," as Duke was described; its mystique was blowing over the country. Pitino was delighted for his players, who had won 29 games against six losses in the regular season. "It's been the most fun I've ever had as a coach to see them get to this level today," he said before the game. The players also thought they might have some fun. "Down deep," Richie Farmer said, "we felt that we could beat anyone if we executed."

Duke, with its regular season record of 31-2, was favored by seven points. Most observers felt that Kentucky had at best a one-in-ten chance to produce an upset. Mike Krzyzewski, in his 12th year as Duke's coach, took every opportunity when meeting with the press to counter that kind of talk, pointing to Kentucky's strengths. He heaped praise on Kentucky's 6-foot-8 forward Jamal Mashburn, comparing him to the best big college stars of that time—Shaquille O'Neal of Louisiana State, Alonzo Mourning of Georgetown, and his own Christian Laettner. Mashburn, a banger off the boards who could also nail three-pointers, had been the first basketball player from New York City recruited by Pitino. He made the Southeast Conference first team in this, his sophomore year. As Deron Feldhaus put it, "Mash was our scorer, the go-to guy."

Full-court pressure was Pitino's trademark; not staying tight on an opponent man-to-man at half court, but man-to-man from sea to shining sea. He believed in it so strongly that he called his second book *Full-Court Pressure*. (The title of his first book was less modest: *Born To Coach*.) All season long Kentucky had played at full-court pressure. But Duke's Bobby Hurley, the most accomplished point guard of the year in college basketball, expressed no concern about Kentucky's defense. "It's easier for me to concentrate when teams try to press us," he said. "That's when I usually excel."

Well, he would have to wait. Pitino decided to start the game with a two-three zone defense: two guys at the top of the key and three along the backline. He felt that playing man-to-man with a thin bench against a team that ran fast breaks could cause fatal foul trouble, and because his team had a height handicap he needed crushing strength on the boards. It also wouldn't hurt if the unexpected caused a bit of consternation in Coach K's corner. We would soon see. Nine years after the event, Rick Pitino put it neatly: "It was Muhammad Ali vs. Frazier. And who's going to win the fight?"

See the two coaches, sitting at their respective benches before the opening whistle, in their white shirts, Brooks Brothers ties, and somber dark suits, dressed for a funeral rather than a prime-time bake-off. Pitino has a childlike look on his face, not quite able to hide an eagerness to commit mischief. Coach K seems more relaxed, contemplative even, his hand on his chin, as if observing a work of art—this team he created.

To the roar of the crowd, the game began, Christian Laettner winning the mid-court jump over Kentucky's center, Gemel Martinez, a 6-foot-8 sophomore. The ball was taken by the shooting guard, Thomas Hill, who drove in but missed the lay-up.

But what was this down-home team doing on the floor? Len Elmore, the TV analyst, was explaining that "Kentucky has to go out and put pressure all over the court to create those turnovers and to throw Duke out of their rhythm? They also want to *fatigue* them, so they can go out for the second half thinking they have a chance."

Forty seconds into the game, Bobby Hurley failed to excel when Sean Woods, Kentucky's point guard, stripped him of the ball, dribbled, and found an open man, John Pelphrey. *Pop!* Pelphrey nailed the three-pointer. Kentucky led, 3-0. It was early, of course, but it was the first time in the entire tournament that Duke had fallen behind. A moment later, however, Duke's Antonio Lang, driving in, scored, and Pelphrey, trying to stop him, drew a foul.

Still, the Kentucky Wildcats continued their aggressions against a mildly confused Duke team. Woods, running his business high, wide and handsome, swept downfield with the ball, drove, leaped, and scored. Then the ball again came to Pelphrey, standing behind the 3-point line. *Swish!* His second straight three-pointer.

Pitino liked what his guys were doing on threes against Duke's fierce defense. Coming into the game, he felt that if his team could find 20 to 25 three-point opportunities—and could hit on 40 percent of them—they would be in the ballgame. Pitino had become an apostle of three's soon after this radical change in college basketball scoring went into effect in 1986. In Pitino's first season at Kentucky, his players shot 810 threes—an NCAA record—of which they made 281. At the same time he also worked them hard on defending against three's. Pitino's formula was: hold the other team to fewer than 30 percent three-point shots, half the number of three's that his team would take.

What Pitino didn't like, now, was to see Pelphrey, four minutes into the game, pick up his second foul. The coach had to remove his hot shooter, who was also a floor leader, and replace him with his sixth man, Deron Feldhaus. Still, Kentucky continued to play strong. Pitino was particularly pleased with the play of Sean Woods, who stole another one from Hurley, rode half-court, and went up himself, hooking in a beauty. Woods's fancy goal belied what Pitino had told the press the day before—that Woods, who had been one of the keys of the season for his team, had finally come to realize he wasn't primarily a scorer but a play-caller. Well, here he was, doing both for his coach. "I orchestrated a lot of things," Woods later told me. "My penchant was for drawing people out of their dreams."

With half the period gone, Pitino sent Pelphrey back into the game and called for a set play that would free him to let go another three-point missile. This one didn't quite work the way Pitino envisioned it, but the result was the same. Pelphrey, clogged in the middle, passed off to Jamal Mashburn, who floated it in from the corner. Which meant that in their first ten possessions, Kentucky had tried six three-pointers, made four and led Duke 20-12.

Then, suddenly, Duke snapped out of its lethargy. "Okay, they made a run," Grant Hill thought coming off the bench, "now it's our turn to make our run." He became the catalyst. He stuffed a rebound, took a long pass from Bobby Hurley that streaked in net high, and floated upstairs to put it away; made assists, went after rebounds. Hill's explosion produced a 26-11 spurt by Duke and a 38-31 lead.

Duke was turning to its strengths: offensive rebounds, fast breaks, scoring on open-floor opportunities. Kentucky had feared the Duke transition game because they couldn't match Duke's speed and height coming off their own offensive shot, then flying back to attack the Kentucky hoop. Trying to stem the royal blue tide, Kentucky's fouls began to mount. Woods had two, Mashburn two, Martinez two, Pelphrey two.

Late in the period, not wanting Duke to run off and hide, Pitino sent Pelphrey back in, and almost immediately he picked up his third foul. They shoot the ball so well, Pelphrey thought, that you have to go out and challenge them, so you expose yourself to trouble. Leaving the game this time he felt like he was killing his team's chances. But Kentucky refused to fold. Richie Farmer hit a three-pointer. Mashburn, playing strongly on both ends of the court, scored two baskets. Woods tried a three-pointer and missed—he was the one senior not adept at three-point shooting—but he followed his shot in, took the rebound, and snapped in the layup.

History was made with 6:31 left in the first half. Christian Laettner took a pass from Hurley, curled around the basket, shot, and scored. It was his 359th point in NCAA tournament play, breaking the record of the University of Houston Hall-of-Famer Elvin Hayes. Laettner seemed indifferent to his accomplishment, possibly because he was in such a fire zone of his own. He hadn't missed a shot yet, field goal or foul.

Three minutes and 15 seconds before the half, Antonio Lang made a brilliant play, grabbing an offensive rebound and tipping in the shot. With two minutes left, Kentucky came back, closed the gap to two points. As the first-half buzzer echoed through the arena, Bobby Hurley exploded with a three, his first score of the game, and Duke held a 50-45 lead.

A five-point deficit wasn't so bad, the Kentucky players told themselves as they rested, considering that Duke had hit on 18 of 25 of their shots, a sizzling 72 percent average. Kentucky had averaged 50 percent. What was keeping them alive was what Pitino had asked for: making three-point shots. Kentucky had made 6 out of 12, Duke had made only three. Mashburn led the Kentucky scoring parade with 11 points, Woods had 10. Kentucky had also forced 11 turnovers—which almost never happened to Duke. But Pitino wasn't satisfied. He told his team they had to play a more complete game, had to do better getting back on transition. They were also getting killed on the offensive boards. The zone defense had worked all right but it hadn't held down fouls; Kentucky had picked up 12 personals. Pitino didn't want to get in worse foul trouble, so he decided to stay with the zone for a while longer before putting in the full-court press. But he couldn't help thinking: if our press doesn't work, we won't win.

For his part, Coach Krzyzewski was concerned by Hurley's play; even without a press to deal with, the point guard had been stolen on four times. But he had also made seven pinpoint assists to teammates; he would rouse himself. Christian Laettner needed no rousing. He was his usual commanding self, all over the floor on defense and five-for-five on field goals, all on layups and dunks. Grant Hill, coming off the bench, had shot five-for-seven, 11 points in all, with five rebounds and three assists, and Duke also made 12 of its 13 foul shots. Krzyzewski urged his players to start the second half with a spurt—a spurt that would put Kentucky away maybe for good.

And that's what almost happened. Eighteen seconds into the new period, Kentucky's Gimel Martinez picked up his third foul. Then Woods took a third foul. Then Martinez got a fourth; he had to sit down and that put the burden on Mash, who was in foul trouble himself. Early in the second half, when Laettner went up for a shot, Mashburn, fearing another foul, backed off. In one six-minute drought, Kentucky made only one field goal. Now it was 56-48, an eight-point lead for Duke. Kentucky tightened it quickly—56-51—when Mashburn punched in a three-pointer: 56-51.

After a television timeout Martinez, back in the game, was called for setting an illegal screen on an inbounds play. It was his fifth foul; he wouldn't be heard from again. Then, in a melee under the basket, Duke's Butch Davis came up with the ball, scored, and was fouled by Pelphrey—his fourth. Out he went and Pitino got in his face, berating him for watching the ball instead of his man in the dust-up. Pelphrey sagged on the bench. It was Sean Woods who kept Kentucky alive, dribbling into Duke territory, then accelerating and hitting a gorgeous one-handed basket.

But Duke came storming back, Laettner hitting from the corner—"three-ee-ee!" the Duke radio announcer bellowed. Woods answered with a two-point layup. But Bobby Hurley, hot now, dropped in a three over the head of substitute Travis Ford, which gave Duke a 12-point lead, its biggest of the night.

With 11:08 left, Pitino called time. "All right, enough!" he said as he crouched around his players. "We're going after these guys. From now on, we give them our best shot." And for the first time he called for the full-court press.

Krzyzewski, anticipating that Kentucky would come storming out and try to make a run, told his team: "Now we have to try to put them away. If you can beat them at this point, you break them."

College basketball took root in the Southern section of the United States in the early years of the twentieth century and has flowered there ever since, nowhere more passionately than in North Carolina and Kentucky. Blue-collar athletes at blue-collar colleges in North Carolina felt that Duke was snobby—that it always went after kids with a genteel streak, well-spoken and sophisticated kids whose parents stood behind them. But that changed in the 1980s with the arrival of Mike Krzyzewski, whose recruits were not all that genteel.

Krzyzewski was a graduate of the U.S. Military Academy and captain of its basketball team in his senior year. After a five-year hitch in the Army, he was hired by the University of Indiana as an assistant at Indiana to his mentor, Bobby Knight; it was Knight who had originally recommended Krzyzewski's appointment to the Academy. After Indiana he coached the West Point basketball team for two years and then, in 1980, went to Duke. Now 45 years old, he was being compared to John Wooden of UCLA—the John Wooden whose teams had won *ten* NCAA titles between 1964 and 1975, including two back-to-back. Krzyzewski was said to have much in common with Wooden, especially in the way he established authority over all matters related to his team. But where Mr. Wooden was controlling but detached," Fred Andrews wrote in the *New York Times*, "Mr. Krzyzewski wraps his charges into a family-like cocoon of demanding affection. Under game pressure, he says, there is only time enough to speak the truth."

Krzyzewski had baked the truth into a program that was ideally suited to Duke. As he explained in his book, *Leading With the Heart*, he sought kids who were "of strong character—not necessarily kids with great talent who can play, but great individuals who are willing to be part of a team and who are coachable." But having great talent did help. Coach K traveled through the land, an attractive and articulate pied piper, plucking his favored individuals from any environment—upperclass, underclass, or anything in between. The class of '92, now doing battle on the floor at the Spectrum, was a reasonable reflection of the coach's reach. A sturdy example of the "genteel" Duke student-athlete was Grant Hill, one of six African-Americans on the squad, the only child of parents who adored him and always offered him wise counsel. His mother, Janet, was a mathematician; his father, Calvin Hill, had been an immortal running back at two diverse institutions, Yale and the Dallas Cowboys, then established a thriving business career. Grant didn't want to go to Yale and rub against his father's reputation. Though coveted by many colleges, he chose the one that refused to offer him the world. "I'm not going to promise you anything," Coach K told Grant when they first met. "If you choose Duke, you have to come in, work hard, and earn everything you receive."

Bobby Hurley was recruited in an entirely different way—Coach K had to convince the father. Bob Hurley, Sr., was the coach of St. Anthony's High School in Jersey City, New Jersey, which, year after year, produced one of the most successful basketball programs in the country. Krzyzewski assured the father that he was only going to recruit one point guard that year and it would be Hurley. The boy, with his father's blessing, accepted Duke.

The third prodigy was Laettner, the son of a printer for the Buffalo *News*. He had played for an elite upstate prep school, was a good student, and was also a good size, 6-foot-11, 250 pounds, with an array of shots that took your breath away. Laettner was different from the usual Krzyzewski recruit; he was something of a rascal, cocky, could be surly, and sometimes played with an unbecoming hauteur. But Krzyzewski wanted Laettner and the boy wanted Duke. He fit in right away, becoming one of the peerless clutch shooters of the era. In 1990, with 1.6 seconds left in a regional final against the University of Connecticut, Laettner, bumping hard against an opponent, made the basket that sent Duke to the Final Four. In 1991, Duke faced the University of Nevada at Las Vegas, which had won 45 straight victories, including a 102-73 blowout of Duke the year before. This time the score was tied with 12.7 seconds left, Laettner at the foul line. He calmly hit on both free throws. UNLV was done, and Duke went on to beat Kansas and win its first national championship.

But while this Duke team fitted its image in a part of the country where basketball tradition flourished, it was not like the University of Kentucky. In Kentucky, basketball was a cult. The *New York Times* columnist, George Vecsey, who lived in Kentucky for several years as a reporter, recalled that he "saw Kentucky Wildcat calendars hanging in every gas station from Viper in the east to Monkeys Eyebrows in the west, from Warsaw in the north to London in the south." No other college in the commonwealth could command such loyalty from its people. But when the NCAA struck with its penalties in 1989, and a half-dozen blue-chip basketball players left the team, loyalties wavered.

And yet the four freshmen stayed on. Three of them—Farmer, Pelphrey, and Feldhaus—were purebred Kentuckians; the fourth, Sean Woods, was the most conflicted. He had played his high school basketball in Indianapolis, had been one of the country's 30 top high school players, could have gone to Purdue, Indiana, Georgia, Iowa. But he'd always spent his summers with his mother and grandmother, who lived in Lexington. "I kinda fell in love with the Kentucky basketball tradition," he told me. He also liked the idea of playing with a school that got all that national television time. throughout the season. But when the NCAA ax fell, Woods felt that he would never have a chance at a national championship and considered going elsewhere. But his mother said, "You're not going to play without adversity in your life." He stayed.

For the other three it was an easier decision. "How could I leave?" Richie Farmer told me. "As a kid I stayed up late in my bedroom listening to Cawood Leford announcing the Wildcats games on the radio." Farmer's feelings were echoed by John Pelphrey. "The true Kentucky boy," his wife, Tracy, told me, "grows up with dreams of playing Kentucky basketball." As for Deron Feldhaus, his father had been a star at UK. Where else would the son want to go?

The irony was that the deposed coach, Eddie Sutton, hadn't really wanted any of those guys on his team. When Pelphrey was a junior star in high school, mulling offers but waiting to hear from the college he loved, Sutton told him, "We'd love to have you walk on, unrecruited, that is." Richie Farmer was mildly recruited at best. "Eddie Sutton didn't want me there," he told me, "because I would be competing with his son, Sean." But when both Pelphrey and Farmer, who were a year apart, led their teams to the state championships and became Kentucky "Mr. Basketball" players of the year, Sutton had to take them. Deron Feldhaus got in mainly because of his father's reputation as a tough defensive basketball player, and a star in baseball at UK in the early 1960s. The day after Pelphrey was signed with Kentucky was when the money popped out of the envelope. In that long first year of revelation after revelation—money being slipped to the players by enthusiastic "boosters," rigging of grades and other academic indiscretions—Kentucky suffered its first losing season in 90 years. The players, weighed down by a collective inferiority complex, began to feel they should have left with the others.

Hope was restored in June of 1989 when Kentucky's new

athletic director, C. M. Newton, ransacked the New York Knicks and made off with Rick Pitino. The first thing the new coach told an impatient Sean Woods was, "Just be patient, we're going to win, and win right away."

But he added an *if*. His kids would have to get in shape if they wanted to play for him. He wasn't kidding. He took one look at Feldhaus, who had played at 202 pounds in high school and was now up to 218, and said, "Your legs are too big." Farmer, who wore a bristly cop moustache, had played at 170 pounds in high school and now weighed in at 188. "The Pillsbury dough boy," Pitino called him. "I thought I was on a track scholarship for awhile," Farmer told me. He and the other players were made to run on the track every day, do sprints, distance running—run till they were drenched. He also put them on a diet. Feldhaus was thick-legged no more and back down at 202; Farmer got down to 170. "Coach liked the athlete who could run and jump, get quick to the ball, and had great anticipation," Farmer said. "He willed us to do it, and we did."

Pitino, a native New Yorker, was 25 when he took his first head coaching job, at Boston University. In five years, he made that college a winner. Next, he led an underdog Providence College to the Final Four in 1987, and then had a two-year stint as head coach with the New York Knicks. When he moved on to Kentucky, the game he would coach would be a game of discipline and mental toughness. But he wanted more. Pitino wanted kids who could go 40 minutes, playing under full-court pressure, stifling the opponent, advancing the three-point game on offense, never letting up. He took the job knowing the team he had inherited—what was left of it—was not a team full of prodigies like Duke. But he vowed to teach them how to play beyond what they thought they could do.

During Pitino's first year, when he was trying to introduce a new system while the team was under probation, everyone in Kentucky said it was going to be a nightmare—that the Wildcats would be lucky to win five games. But his guys were in superb shape, averaging almost 35 minutes of playing time at full court pressure. And Pitino did make it fun for them; he had his players throwing three's all the time. "He was the first coach to use the three-point shot as the center of his system," Feldhaus said.

In that first year the team went 14-14. In Pitino's second year, still under probation, Kentucky vaulted to 22-6, including a top 14-4 performance in the Southeastern Conference, a number 9 national ranking, and a national coach-of-the-year award from *The Sporting News.* In 1991–92, free at last, Kentucky became Southeastern Conference tournament champs, and Pitino took them to the NCAA tournament, and their current confrontation with Duke. "Pitino told us that if we could defend relatively well against Duke and just break even on the glass," Pelphrey said, "we could win because our offense was so good." Pitino also told them: "Don't be afraid to fail."

It was 67-55, Duke, with less than nine minutes remaining in the game, and it was Kentucky that came out stompin'. Dale Brown, a junior from Mississippi, was having an outstanding game springing off the bench to replace his foul-stricken teammates. There he was, *alone* under the paint, and Sean Woods, finding himself being mugged by two Duke hand-slappers, rifled the ball in and Brown stuffed it. Duke took over on the backline, but the inbound pass was picked off by Deron Feldhaus, who could play either small forward or power forward; "I grew to like coming into that role," he told me. Feldhaus winged it to Jamal Mashburn behind the key, and Mash stroked in the three-pointer. Within 50 seconds, Duke's lead had been cut in half—67-60—and Krzyzewski called time to regroup.

But nothing had changed. As soon as Duke came back on the floor, Kentucky's Mashburn burned another three-pointer. Then, within seconds, he found himself under the glass, ringed by the enemy. He flashed a pirouette left, then right, and flung in the post-up basket —Mashburn 8, Duke 0 on this run. Even with four fouls on him, Mashburn was feeling unstoppable. One of Duke's co-captains, Brian Davis, who had been playing a brilliant defensive game, was thinking: Mashburn is the only person who can beat us. We've got to get him out of there.

The freshman Aminu Timberlake, 6-foot-nine but a scrawny 195 pounds, came in to give Mashburn a blow. Without Kentucky's go-to guy, Duke staged a revival. Bobby Hurley started it with a three-pointer. Then Thomas Hill hit a pull-up jumper. And Duke, in transition once more, swept downfield, Hill scoring again on a layup and adding a point after being fouled by Timberlake. That run ended when Dale Brown nestled a three into the hoop.

Still, Duke held a 73-68 lead, and Christian Laettner had the ball—Laettner, who had been perfect so far, sinking all his field shots and all his fouls. He moved towards the basket and jumped, and Timberlake leaped up after him. But Laettner, arching his back, bumping against Timberlake, dropped the ball in. Timberlake hit the floor and lay there on his back. The foul had been called on him, but that wasn't enough for Laettner. As he looked down on the ground, Laettner was not seeing Timberlake. He was seeing Mount Everest, it was *there*, and he wanted it. Laettner lifted his large, sneakered right foot onto Timberlake's chest, stomping without delicacy, and sauntered away.

Everyone who caught the Laettner act was stunned. Timberlake didn't know quite what to do; the freshman stood up, unhurt, and smiled, either out of embarrassment or because he felt that Laettner would be thrown out of the game for committing that outrage on his body. But Laettner was assessed only a two-shot technical foul. Looking cool, Timberlake strode to the foul line for his two shots and, twice, the ball hissed in. Richie Farmer, Kentucky's best free thrower, then took his turn but could only click on one of the two technicals. There was a pause before the players came back onto the floor. Pitino, shuffling players in and out, hadn't seen Laettner's action. If he had, he said later, he would have demanded his ouster. Krzyzewski, incensed by Laettner's behavior, got into his star's face. "That was unbelievably stupid of you," he said. Years afterward Laettner explained his behavior on ESPN's Classic documentary of the game: "I wanted Timberlake to know I wasn't going to take any crap, and it didn't hurt to help add spice to the game."

In the stands, Duke fans were on their feet going ga-ga over the big guy's melodramatics. It was different in the Kentucky section—boos for Laettner mingled with exhortations to their team. In any case, the uproar seemed to energize Duke and deflate Kentucky.

With 7:29 left, the unrepentant Laettner sank two foul shots and Duke's lead was again ten points, 79-69.

Just as Duke fans sat back, self-satisfied, and Kentucky fans began to twist and turn nervously, Kentucky made a breathtaking 12-2 run. Dale Brown, squeezing through a lane between All-Americas Laettner and Hurley, hit the layup, was fouled, and sank his third point. Then John Pelphrey, playing free and easy despite his four fouls, drew a foul on Hurley for charging and sank his two points. But Laettner picked off an offensive rebound and matched Pelphrey's two points. Coach K was thinking that the game had become a shootout, but not a battle between individuals, like the classic matchup between Larry Bird and Magic Johnson in the 1979 NCAA championship game. It was a battle of teams—appropriately, Krzyzewski felt, because it was Duke against Kentucky, a distinguished rivalry that dated back to 1930.

Duke's lead was 81-76 when Mashburn pumped a jumper over Grant Hill's outstretched arms. Then Pelphrey was fouled by Brian Davis—a one-one situation; he would have to make the first foul shot to get the second. He made them both. Kentucky's run reached a crescendo when Sean Woods nailed a three-pointer from the top of the circle. The game was tied, 81-81.

The shootout continued, Duke regaining the lead on two foul shots by Thomas Hill; Mashburn hitting another layup to restore the tie; Dale Brown, from the right corner, swishing in a three-pointer with 2:50 left. That gave Kentucky its first lead since way back when it was 20-17. But the you-make-one-I-make-one pattern continued. Duke's Brian Davis scored on a shot that Dale Brown thought he had blocked, but he was called for goaltending. Then Duke regained the lead when Bobby Hurley sank one of his foul shots, and Thomas Hill hit a jumper. But Pelphrey and Feldhaus worked one together: a Pelphrey feed to make it 89-89. The two teams traded baskets and it was 91-91. With 1:09 remaining, Thomas Hill scored on a 16-foot jumper: Duke, 93-91.

Now Pelphrey had it, taking the ball downcourt, looking for the shot that would tie it up again. He found a good look, fired from 14 feet out, but missed. Deron Feldhaus grabbed the rebound, twisted, turned, somehow was able to outposition the Duke gang who were all over him, went up and laid the ball in: 93-93.

Bobby Hurley had 33.6 seconds in which to play with the clock while searching for an open man. But the Kentucky defenders were pressing everybody, so with six seconds left Hurley drove into the middle of the scrum himself and tossed up a ten-foot jumper. The ball eluded the hoop and rebounded into the hands of Mashburn.

Overtime.

In the second half, Duke had shot a 59.1 average. Kentucky had shot at a 66.7 clip. Richie Farmer had been so focused on what he had to do—cover Thomas Hill or Brian Davis—that it took him a while to realize what this game was amounting to: "a lot of individuals from both teams were making *great* plays back and forth." And for the first time the thought entered Rick Pitino's mind that his Cinderella kids might get into the Final Four.

As the overtime period began, Jamal Mashburn tried another three-pointer. This one didn't make it. Duke took the ball and Grant Hill tried a jumper that also didn't take. From that moment to the final tick of the clock, almost every shot did take.

With four minutes left, the ball was in John Pelphrey's hands. Pelphrey still remembered the misery of his early days at Kentucky, when all the marquee players had quit; when the new coach, Pitino, had him and the other players running and dying on the track; when he wondered what it was all for. Now he knew, and, calmly, from behind the key, he swished in a three-pointer. Then he induced a charging foul by Brian Davis, his fifth, so the tough Duke defender, who had five rebounds along with his 13 points, was out of the game.

With Kentucky leading by three, Duke began to feel the urgency of the situation. Bobby Hurley, who had attempted eight three-pointers and hit four, tried a ninth, but the ball caromed off the glass and directly into the hands of Grant Hill. Hill, remembering Coach K's admonition that a missed three-pointer opens people up if you can get the offensive rebound, lined it back to Hurley, who was wide open. This time the elite point guard did not miss the three-pointer. Allowing that second-chance shot agonized Pitino, and he said to himself, It's over—we're done.

But Pelphrey, going flat out with his four fouls, found a lane, drove between Laettner and Grant Hill, and feathered the ball into the basket. Kentucky: 98-96. Then Christian Laettner, all business now, took over. Going up for a score, he was fouled by Jamal Mashburn—Mashburn's fourth. Laettner's two successful free throws tied the game at 98.

Kentucky now had to be careful. Mashburn had four fouls, Woods had four, Pelphrey had four, Dale Brown had four. With one minute and 16 seconds left, Woods missed a jump shot over Hurley, and Laettner grabbed the rebound. There were 54.5 seconds left, and Coach K called time.

When play resumed, Dale Brown stole the ball in front of the Duke bench. But he couldn't control it. With the 45-second shot clock down to five seconds, Laettner had it, twisting and turning eight feet from the goal. He swam by Pelphrey, guarding him on one side, and by Mashburn, guarding him on the other side, and, as he started to turn and fall back, flung a line drive up towards the glass. The ball exploded off the backboard, and rattled into the basket. Duke, 100-98.

Both teams were just clawing away at each other. With 19.6 seconds left, Grant Hill and Antonio Lang were on Pelphrey, who was coming out from a Mashburn screen. Pelphrey saw that the big guy was free and whistled a pass to him. Mashburn drove along the left baseline, scored, and was fouled by Lang. He completed the three-point play by sinking the foul shot: Kentucky 101, Duke 100.

After Mashburn's heroics, Pitino called a timeout. He told his players to double down on Christian Laettner—they were going to him all the time. "But don't foul and give up the three-point play." Kentucky didn't give up a three-pointer, but the valiant Jamal Mashburn fouled out.

I've looked at the film sequence of that moment over and over again. It was a long pass, arc to arc, from Hurley to Laettner. Laettner scrambled in and seemed to be all over Mashburn, even flinging an arm across his opponent's body. But the referees wouldn't call a charge on Laettner; they ruled that it was Mashburn who had reached in trying to strip the ball from Laettner. So Laettner was allowed the two foul shots, and he sank them both. Now it was

Duke, 103-101, and Mashburn left a hero for Kentucky. In 43 minutes of feverish play, he had scored 28 points that included three out of four three-pointers, three for three on foul shots, ten rebounds, and three assists. As Mashburn moved to the bench, Duke's Grant Hill remembered thinking, "We got the game now." Richie Farmer came in for Mashburn, and Kentucky had all of its four seniors on the court from that forlorn freshman team of 1988, plus Dale Brown, who had scored 18 points.

With 7.8 seconds left, Duke two points up, Rick Pitino called his last timeout. His go-to guy, Mashburn, was gone, and he felt he had to regroup. He told his players he wanted Kentucky to retain the final shot, not to lose the game in the last possession. He appointed his point guard as the team's executor. Sean Woods would control the ball; penetrate, Pitino told Woods; don't take the shot yourself, find someone else to take the shot.

It was always dicey inbounding against Duke because they were the best *denying* team in the country. But Richie Farmer, with the ball behind the line, managed to feed it to Woods, who faked left, then swung right off a Pelphrey screen that left Bobby Hurley on the seat of his pants. Laettner came out to challenge Woods as he turned the corner. "Everybody else stayed home," he told me. "I could maybe go down low or swing it to Richie Farmer." Feldhaus was in the right corner, 15 feet from the basket, with half an open look. Pelphrey looked like he was clear, too—the three seniors all asking for the ball, the fourth holding onto it for dear life. Finally, Woods took the shot himself. Later he claimed that he shot the ball a little higher than normal so it would hit the back of the rim. "If it didn't go in," he told me, "I would have a second chance to tip it in." I suspect that he went high to avoid the 6-foot-11 Laettner's outstretched arms. Thirteen feet from the basket, almost like a discus thrower, he whipsawed the ball towards the basket and darned if it didn't hit off the glass, and tumble in.

"It maybe wasn't the shot we wanted to take," Pelphrey, a born diplomat, said, "but Sean read the defense, just took off and made a great shot." Others weren't as diplomatic. "How did he have the courage to take that kind of a shot?" Verne Lundquist asked his

TV analyst, Len Elmore. "It was a terrible shot," Elmore answered. Krzyzewski agreed: "There was no way Woods had intended to bank that ball head-on into the basket." Coach K threw a towel to the ground, ran out to meet his players, who had vacant looks on their faces, and tried to figure out how, with 2.1 seconds remaining and Kentucky ahead by one point, to bring them back from despair.

On the Kentucky side, everybody thought the game was over. The cheerleaders were tumbling, the band was blaring, the fans screaming. Pitino understood that Sean Woods's shot would never be called a classic; it seemed to the coach like a gift of providence meant for his overachieving team, meant to take them even farther. As for Woods himself, this appealing young man who liked to draw people out of their dreams was drawing out his own dream: "I thought it was over," he said, "and we were going to the Final Four, and would play Indiana. We had beaten them earlier, and we might be able to go all the way."

Both coaches knew what they had to do. First, Mike Krzyzewski had to turn around the gloom that had befallen his players. "When they got close to me," he would write in his book, *Leading With the Heart*, "their eyes told me they could not win. 'We're going to win,' I said immediately. 'We're going to win.' Finally, they came back to life. They heard me. I could see in their eyes that they were over the shock." Then, as he recalled in his book, "I instantly thought up a play." Actually, he'd always had a play for just such a situation, a "home run" play that his teams practiced all the time and that they had used in one regular season against Wake Forest. Wake Forest held a two-point lead with four seconds left. The play was designed for Grant Hill, the team's premier quarterback; he would heave a long pass downfield to Laettner, who would catch it and take it into the end zone. Hill's pass was a beauty, soaring long and high, except that it suddenly curved towards the sideline. Laettner made the catch, but one foot came down out of bounds. Duke lost the ball and the game, their second of two defeats in the season.

This time the outcome had to be different. Everything was riding on the home run. The throw would again be Hill to Laettner; the best arm putting it up for the best receiver, who would flash from the left corner to take the ball. Tony Lang would be stationed under the basket to screen for Bobby Hurley, who would be up somewhere around half court; if Hill was unable to throw to Laettner he could go to Hurley. The players gathered together, joined hands and chanted their mantra: "We're going to win."

Of course, Rick Pitino knew that Duke would try to find Laettner, 77 feet downcourt; let him make the miracle basket, as he had against Connecticut two years earlier and again last season against University of Nevada at Las Vegas. When his feet were in the fire, Laettner became Duke's mystic firestarter. The only question for Pitino was: should he put a defender on the ball, or play five against four? Pitino had seen films of the Wake Forest game. Grant Hill had been covered before he got the ball off; maybe that had contributed to his throwing the ball that tailed away. The problem was that Kentucky's tallest guys, Pelphrey and Feldhaus, were 6-foot-7. Oh, to have had Mashburn in there! Then it would be O.K. to position a man on Hill. But Mashburn was out of the equation. Five versus four, Pitino felt, was the percentage way to play the situation. So Grant Hill would be unguarded.

Pitino put Pelphrey and Feldhaus on Laettner. "Pelphrey," Feldhaus later told me, "would roam the court like a safety—try to go for the steal or bat the ball down. I would guard Laettner; Pitino wanted to make Laettner catch the ball in front of us. Everyone else was on the wings." Richie Farmer was near the Laettner sideline, guarding Thomas Hill. Sean Woods was on the other wing, his eye on Lang; Dale Brown was back with Bobby Hurley. "All that has to be done is to guard the ball, deflect it," Pitino told his players. If he doesn't get the ball cleanly, we win." The last thing the coach said was, "Do not foul him."

Grant Hill felt good that there was no one in his face; he could concentrate on getting the ball to Laettner without worry. He cranked up his throwing arm and let it go. The ball soared straight and true, zooming in towards Laettner, who was breaking into the middle towards the foul line. At first, Pelphrey thought he had a chance to intercept the pass because it was coming right at him. He jumped, but the ball soared over his head. Feldhaus told himself: hold your ground, and maybe he'll miss the shot. If he didn't hold his ground Laettner could streak in for the layup. Feldhaus held his ground.

Laettner leaped and took the ball chest high, cradling it to his chest. His back to the basket, he put the ball on the floor for a single dribble, faked once, swung low, turned, looked at the basket 17 feet away, ignoring Feldhaus in front of him, jumped and released the ball with a cock of his upraised right arm. The ball lifted off. Laettner was up off his feet, his mouth pursed, his eyes intently following the trajectory of the ball that had left his hands with 00.3 seconds remaining in overtime. Even as the buzzer screamed, the ball seemed to hang up there for an eternity.

Coach K didn't see the ball go in. He didn't have to—from the way his big man had lofted it, he knew it had to go in. Laettner couldn't see it fall either, his vision impaired by the movement of spectators behind the backboard, all on their feet, gyrating wildly. But he knew it had happened. Laettner wasn't going to waste any time, anyway. He was running upcourt, downcourt, everywhere-court, his arms flung out wildly, a look of joy mixed with surprise on his face, as if he had just unwrapped a present he had wanted all his life.

Richie Farmer, who was just behind Feldhaus, remembers seeing the ball come down and hollering, "Was it good? Was it good?" The other three seniors knew it was good. Deron Feldhaus hung his head, devastated; Sean Woods fell to the floor face down, motionless; John Pelphrey walked back and forth aimlessly, thinking: None of us were ready for this. He didn't know where to go.

Mike Krzyzewski knew where to go. In the midst of hugs from his own coaches and players, he looked out on the floor and saw Kentucky's Farmer, the shock and despair on his face. He ran over to the boy and put his arms around him. Farmer has never forgotten that moment. "I was crying, he was crying, and he was telling me, 'You guys are not losers—there were no losers out there tonight.' I thought that showed such class."

Coach K had always taught his Duke teams the etiquette of being good winners. Sure, since winning had become a natural element in their lives. Here was Thomas Hill, arms clasped behind his head, looking for Kentucky players to console. Even the bad boy hero, Christian Laettner, the player of the game with his 31 points, his 20-for-20 record on field goals and fouls, his miracle shot, sought out Kentuckians to hug. He found Sean Woods, who had finally risen from his grave. "Great shot," Laettner said about Woods's miracle toss. Woods smiled. "You, too," he said. "Wasn't it a great game?" Laettner said. Woods nodded his head. Later he would come up with the ultimate rationale: "We lost the greatest basketball game ever played."

"THIS WOULD HAVE BEEN THE GREATEST NCAA GAME IN HISTORY EVEN IF THE LAETTNER SHOT HAD NEVER TAKEN PLACE," the *Boston Globe* columnist Bob Ryan wrote the next day, putting his opinion in caps. Tell that to the Kentucky kids who were still sobbing in the locker room. Rick Pitino went out twice to talk to them, but saw it was still all tears and sorrow. The third time he came armed with a piece of paper. It was the cover of *Sports Illustrated*, May 29, 1989. In block letters were the words: KENTUCKY'S SHAME. "This is where you came from," Pitino told his team. See how far you've come. You've taken Kentucky all the way back from there. You will never have to be ashamed again. You mustn't let the last two seconds of the game destroy your basketball life."

A week later, in the Final Four, Duke beat Indiana, and then beat Michigan to win its second straight college basketball championship. Meanwhile, back at the University of Kentucky, in Lexington, an awards ceremony for the team was held. Thirteen thousand fans turned out to honor their heroes. The last bit of business came at the end of the evening, when athletic director C. M. Newton called the four seniors and their families to come forward. He told the crowd that something special was due these men who had chosen not to run away, but to stay, and by doing that, had helped get the college and its athletic program through the fire.

"Many have scored more points than you have," Newton said to the seniors. "They have won many more individual honors. But no one can match what you've given us by putting your heart into the wearing of the

jersey." Then he said, "Please turn and look up in the rafters as we retire your jerseys." Unfurled were the jerseys of John Pelphrey, No. 34; Sean Woods, No. 11; Deron Feldhaus, No. 12; Richie Farmer, No. 32.

"This was the ultimate moment for us in our careers," Pelphrey told me. "I was in total shock," said Deron Feldhaus. "With all those names of people who had become immortals to us. My Lord, it did more than make me feel good. I will relish it for the rest of my life."

13

1999
AWESOME!
The World Cup
U.S. vs. China

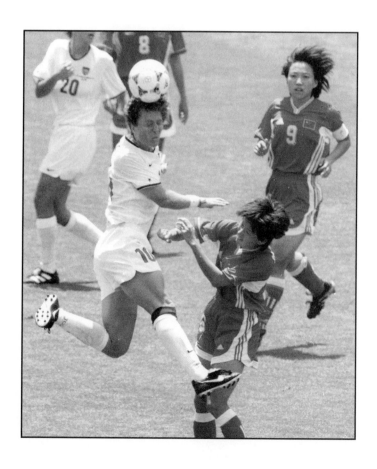

On the afternoon of July 10, 1999, when the national teams of the United States and China marched onto the Rose Bowl field for the World Cup Soccer Final—the climax of a three-week tournament of games that had been held all over the country—the American women, fully aware that this would be the soccer game of their lives, were met by a wind like a hurricane, a wind of applause so hysterical that it made them throw their arms high in the air, waving in delight and wonder at the enormous crowd.

What they saw were girls with braces on their teeth, their faces painted in red, white, and blue, and painted boys' faces and grown-ups' faces, too. They also saw a vast sea of red, white, and blue flags, except for one small section where Chinese fans were waving their country's red flag and banging a drum slowly. There didn't seem to be an empty seat anywhere. The official count was 90,185, including the President of the United States, Bill Clinton, who had been converted to women's soccer by his daughter, Chelsea. That made it the largest crowd ever to witness a women's sports event anywhere in the world. Five months after the event, Michael Bamberger wrote in *Sports Illustrated*, "a million people would swear to you that they were there."

The Chinese team was dressed in basic red, with white trim. The U.S. women were dressed in white—white jerseys, white shorts, white knee socks, with black piping on the hems, their names set in black over black numbers outlined in red. One could easily pick out No. 10, Michelle Akers, 5-foot-10, with a mane of curly hair, the oldest player on the team at age 33, "the last of the dinosaurs," she called herself. In front of her was Julie Foudy, who was co-captain, along with Carla Overbeck. Both were idolized by their teammates. Overbeck was the second oldest player on the team, mother of a two-year-old boy and, said Foudy, "the glue that held us together for years."

Then the ceremonies were over, and the 22 starters rushed to the sidelines to take their final instructions. The temperature was almost 105 degrees. The starting lineups were:

UNITED STATES: Forwards—Mia Hamm, Tiffeny Milbrett, Cindy Parlow; midfielders—Michelle Akers, Julie Foudy, Kristine Lilly; defenders—Brandi Chastain, Joy Fawcett, Carla Overbeck, Kate Sobrero.

CHINA: Forwards—Sun Wen, Jin Yan; midfielders—Liu Ailing, Zhao Lihong, Pu Wei, Liu Ying; defenders—Bai Jie, Wang Liping, Wen Lirong, Fan Yunjie.

There wasn't much to choose between the two goalkeepers; both Briana Scurry and Gao Hong were vying for the best-in-the-world award. Scurry was 5-foot-8, black-haired, broad-shouldered, thick-limbed, muscular, "with eyes," somebody said, "that just glow with intensity." Hong, an inch taller, grew during chairman Mao's cultural revolution, wore her reddish-tinted hair in bangs over her eyes. She was lean, lithe, and acrobatic. Briana Scurry, African-American, a University of Massachusetts graduate who had loved soccer from the beginning, was better at flying from side to side.

The coach of the U.S. team, Tony DiCicco, had been a goalkeeper himself in his playing days; he thought that in the nets Scurry and Hong were very much alike. "They both have shortcomings in their game," he told me. Whoa! Shortcomings? When he was asked what they were he said, "You wouldn't use them for models of how to catch or how to dive. But you would use them for the model of how to be a world-class goalkeeper."

Over the years, the U.S. and China had played each other 21 times, and the U.S had a clear edge, 11-5-5; but 10 of those 16 decisions were by one goal. "We are at the same level now," the Chinese coach, Ma Yuanan, told reporters. "The match will depend on good preparation, good performances, fighting willingness." Tony DiCicco wouldn't argue about that. He felt that his team was "ultimately prepared," by which he meant that his players knew each Chinese player individually—her idiosyncrasies, and strengths and weaknesses, and tendencies. His final decision was to name Michelle Akers, Kate Sobrero, and Mia Hamm as the main "markers" for his team.

Markers? I wasn't up on the term. I have to confess that I'm a latecomer to soccer. I first became a fan in 1993, when a British publisher, Ernest Hecht, who owned a piece of the legendary English team, Arsenal, invited me to his box at Wembley Stadium to watch "the Coca-Cola Cup" final between Arsenal, the home team, and Sheffield Wednesday. My mind was blown by the scene: painted orgiastic faces were the least of it. The great stadium, the equivalent of our Yankee Stadium, seemed to be assembled in "scum" (my host's engaging word) squadrons, each one singing raucous songs a capella. But the play was marvelous. Arsenal came from behind in overtime to win the match, 2-1. The young man who scored the goal was flung in the air by the Arsenal captain, Tony Adams. He landed hard on the turf, broke his arm and had to be carted off the field. Adams was an ebullient captain, once described in the London *Times* as being "the epitome of Arsenal man—rough, tough, uncultured, the leader of a street-fighting football team."

Nobody, however, had told me about marking. So I went for help to *New York Times* columnist George Vecsey, who was a devotee of soccer. "Marking," he told me patiently, "has to do with what soccer is all about. Soccer is a sport of frustration. In basketball you couldn't stop Michael Jordan, you could only contain him. But in soccer you had to do better than just contain someone. Because to say that you held Maradona, the great Argentine scorer, to one goal, or one great pass, isn't going to work. All it takes is one pass in the whole game and Maradona is going to put the ball between the chairs. Marking is when you watch Claudio Gentile staying with Maradona every step of the way and you hear the thump of his shoes on Maradona's shins every time. Marking is stalking, but it's also like stalking in primeval terms—slowing somebody down for the kill."

That turned out to be a perfect description of Michelle Akers when the game between the United States and China began. From the beginning, Akers stalked Sun Wen. It was a thrilling match-up, the two greatest women soccer players of the twentieth century, chopping at each other. But how long could Akers last? She had what she called "a spaghetti knee" and other injuries, plus "chronic energy syndrome," a disease that saps the energy out of the victim. But in the opening minutes of this most crucial match, as Vecsey told me, "All of a sudden she comes out like Big Bird on speed. If somebody had a ball five yards away you'd see Akers come over and take it, and they didn't get the ball away from her. She would go after it like a laser and just beat the crap out of anyone who was in her way."

Both teams were trying to mount serious attacks, but they could only get in so close, then had to fall back to defend the enemy's counterattack. It would be a fierce defensive game, no doubt about that, because both teams had the same strategy: to not let anybody break loose. So the action churned back and forth, probes and pokes, seeking the sliver of light that would enable a telling pass or a speedy attacker to squeeze through those iron curtains. Often, the choreography resembled a George Balanchine ballet, the ballerinas moving with athleticism and lightning-fast grace.

There was Kristine Lilly, twinkling the ball at her feet, eluding a Chinese double-team and, free for a second, booming it back towards the enemy's goal. There was Carla Overbeck, pirouetting all over the field, and Kate Sobrero on the back line, helping to mark Sun Wen. There was Brandi Chastain, whose flamboyance early in her career had earned her the nickname "Hollywood," leaping in the air as a Chinese midfielder plunged into the box, heading the ball away. There were the fastest attackers, Tiffeny Milbrett and Mia Hamm, soaring downfield in early forays.

Mia Hamm, America's Sweetheart, who had personally recruited a national army to women's soccer, who had become their inspiration, their Michael Jordan, seemed to be back in the flow. In the three previous games of the World Cup tournament, Hamm had been unable to score, seemed tight, even unsure of herself. She would have to elevate her play, the critics had said—which was exactly what she was doing now. At one point she was skipping backward from her forward position to her team's 18-yard line to knock a ball from the dangerous Liu Ailing's feet. At another point she was juking forward, faking off one pursuer, cutting the ball back on a breakaway, sweeping downfield with the ball at her feet, passing off until finally the pass was broken up.

Then it was China's turn. In the seventh minute, Foudy was dispossessed of the ball, and here they came, a three-on-one break, Sun Yen streaking in with the ball. But one of her markers, Kate Sobrero, knocked the ball away and Akers cleared it.

Now a foul was called on China. Hamm would handle the free kick from 28 yards out. The clock showed 7:28 when Hamm approached the ball and kicked a long, diagonal serve that bent in towards Michelle Akers, who was roaring into the penalty box towards the far post. Chastain was in there, too, hands up, until she saw Akers sliding. The ball reached Akers with pin-point accuracy just as she fell on her back, legs flung out, desperately trying to reach it. She couldn't quite get there; the ball caught the edge of her foot and dribbled out of bounds.

Coach DiCicco, standing on the sidelines, jumped up from the bench, agony on his face. So close, so close. His assistant coach, Lauren Gregg, spread her hands out, indicating that the ball had been just a foot away from heaven.

The 1999 World Cup tournament began at Giants Stadium, with the United States, the host team, facing Denmark. On the bus taking them to the Meadowlands, in New Jersey, the American women weren't sure what to expect. They weren't nervous about Denmark, one of the weaker teams in the draw. What worried them was whether the gamble of scheduling the games in this huge football stadium would attract a decent audience or would be a major embarrassment.

Tiffeny Milbrett was staring out the window when she noticed that the road had suddenly become congested. Wait a second, she wondered, the Meadowlands is over there, so why is traffic *here* at a standstill? She hollered at the bus driver, "Is there any other major freeway going in this direction?"

"They're going to your game," the bus driver said.

"Holy Moly!" Milbrett said.

"We did it!" Julie Foudy screamed.

When they got out on the field, sure enough, Giants Stadium was full—79,000 people on hand for a *women's* soccer game. The only bigger event at that ballpark had been Pope John Paul II.

Especially moved by the size and the enthusiasm of the crowd were the women who would later come to be known as the "founding players" of American soccer. Most of them had come from the western region of the country, the stories of their beginnings remarkably similar. They had started kicking around a soccer ball at ages six, seven, or eight, while engaging in other tomboy sports. They had no idea at the time that opportunity would finally beckon women so that, if they wanted to, they could make sports a pastime of their lives. Title IX it was called, a federal statute adopted in 1972, prohibiting sex discrimination in education, including athletics, for schools receiving federal funding. Title IX would eventually enable women to attend college with the help of athletic scholarships, and play in intercollegiate sports programs as men always had. "This was the most precious gift we'd ever been given," Brandi Chastain told Bob Costas on one of his television shows. "Because of it I think we changed American culture."

The first women's national soccer team was created in 1985 by its founding father, Anson Dorrance. He was the women's soccer coach at the University of North Carolina, the best college soccer program in the country at the time and ever since. Through regional girls' soccer festivals, Dorrance discovered other amazing players. First came Michelle Akers, a sophomore star at the University of Central Florida; then, in 1986, Brandi Chastain, a freshman at the University of Santa Clara. In 1987, Dorrance struck it rich: 17-year-old Carla Overbeck; 15-year-old Mia Hamm; Kristine Lilly and Julie Foudy, both 16; Joy Fawcett, 19—the core of the national team.

In 1991 they went to China to play in the first World Cup championship tournament, and they won the final with a 2-1 victory over Norway, Akers scoring both goals. Anson Dorrance, happy beyond himself, told the press that Michelle was "the consummate goal scorer." He also said: "I feel that what we've done here is proof to the world we are a developing soccer nation."

A *developing* soccer nation? Akers put it differently: "Girls in the United States can now see women playing a high level of soccer, and they can realize, 'Hey, there is a national team out there and it's the best in the world.'"

The Irish novelist Roddy Doyle once told me that the highlight of his soccer career was "the goal I scored with my face when I was ten, watched and enjoyed by the local hard men." There were no hard men at the Rose Bowl on this July afternoon in 1999. It was a loose, happy, homogenous crowd of well-off soccer moms and daughters, and dads and sons from the suburbs of Los Angeles and Pasadena, clad in fashionable Ivy League outdoor wear. They had been lured by the glamour of this awesome sisterhood of women starring in a world-class tournament.

In the 12th minute, the United States had its second shot on goal. Michelle Akers, 35 yards back, moving away from a Chinese defender, found an open space and let go a mighty kick. It traveled like a Barry Bonds hummer, starting low, riding high and heading out. Akers just missed the home run; Gao Hong, coming off the line, leaped and smothered it in her arms.

Roused by their goalkeeper's acrobatics, the Chinese launched a new attack. Despite the markers around her—Overbeck or Sobrero, Hamm or Akers, or some combination of those players— Sun Wen managed an exotic maneuver. She glided sideways with a delicate, almost sensuous touch, her feet splaying back and forth like a fan, until she found a teammate she thought might escape midfield.

Midfield was the problem for Sun Wen and her teammates because it was under the control of one person. Every ball that came to a Chinese player in the area was being taken away by Akers. Using her height and her inbred recklessness, she kept heading out ball after ball. For Sun Wen, it was frustrating. Halfway through the first period she had but five touches, to Hamm's 11.

Buoyed by Akers' play, the crowd screamed, "USA! USA!" imploring their team to score. At one point the forwards were running past midfield when Akers was brought down hard. She rolled over on the turf so as not to land on her right shoulder, a shoulder she had hurt in a bizarre accident after the only tournament game that she hadn't played in. It was the final preliminary match, against North Korea, in Foxboro, Massachusetts, home of the New England Patriots. The United States had already qualified for the quarterfinal, so DiCicco rested Akers. After the 3-0 shutout she was walking off the field with her teammates, shaking hands with fans in the stands. "I high-fived a guy," Akers said, "and he grabbed my arm and wouldn't let go and dislocated my shoulder."

China's best chance came at the 35-minute mark—a free kick by Sun Yen from 20 yards out. Six U.S. defenders formed a wall ten yards away from the ball. When the whistle blew the Chinese midfielder, Zhao Lihong, as a diversion, crossed over, causing the American wall to tremble, and Sun Wen kicked the ball hard, hitting it with the inside of her left foot to try to bend it around the wall. But her shot was too high, sailing over Briana Scurry's head and over the crossbar.

China soon saw another chance. Space opened up in the U.S. penalty area and 18-year-old Pu Wei raced for the ball, which was heading to the left of the post. Akers beat her to it, headed the ball into the fence and slammed into the fence herself. This time she fell hard on her bad shoulder. She stood up, a grimace on her face. She backpedaled towards midfield, somehow able to endure her exhaustion until that rush of adrenaline, which she had always experienced, took her beyond what she thought possible.

In the last minute of the first half, Gao Hong and Michelle Akers played catch. Hong kicked one deep to midfield and Akers headed it right back to her. They did that once more—Hong to Akers to Hong. The third time Akers went up high to pick off Hong again, just as the whistle ended the half.

It had been a defensive game, for sure—only seven shots in the 45 minutes, five by the U.S., two by China. U.S. had had one shot on goal; China, none. China had committed eight fouls; the U.S., seven. Sun Wen had had nine touches; Mia Hamm, 14. China held possession 55 percent of the time, the U.S., 45. The game was as close as almost everyone had predicted.

The U.S. locker room was unusually still. Co-captains Overbeck and Foudy were consulting with the coaches, then counseling their teammates. Akers was lying on the floor, covered with cold towels. Shannon MacMillan went over to talk with her; but she saw that Akers was not there, was resting in a world of her own.

The question about the second half was whether both teams could maintain the intensity of the game, or would one of them falter? The question was soon answered: there would be no faltering by these two teams. They both swept forward, seeking the kill, the one goal that would decide it, then found themselves being swept back to their own trenches by an ironclad defense. And it was high-octane all the way.

Both teams had opportunities. In the 56th minute, Joy Fawcett hit a great bending ball into the box; Hamm took it but was taken down from behind. The U.S. had its fourth corner kick. Hamm blistered it, but the ball hit the top of the net, and the goalkeeper picked it off. In the next minute came the first substitution of the game. Shannon MacMillan would get her chance, taking over for Cindy Parlow. In the 60th minute, China had another grand chance to score. Sun Yen was in the box by herself, sprinting with the ball towards Briana Scurry. But Brandi Chastain, rushing out of nowhere, made a tremendous save, heading the ball into Scurry's arms.

The heat had intensified in that sunken bowl, and Akers was on the edge. Her head was pounding, but she remembered what it had taken for her to play in this tournament. Way before it started she had resolved to give everything in her life the boot but soccer. "Whatever contributed to my being on the field," she said, "was my life. Whatever wasn't, was out." All she could think of now was to last as long as she could—fight on and *do not quit*.

In the 74th minute, rushing after a drive by Hamm, Akers found a position at the edge of the goalkeeper's haven. She knew that Gao Hong was coming out to get the ball and she decided to challenge her, maybe cause her to lose her focus and drop the ball. At the same moment that Gao Hong was leaping for the ball, Akers was also jumping high, and there was a collision. Hong fell to the ground, writhing in pain, holding her knee. But she got up and shook it off. The referee waved a yellow card in Akers's face, her second of the tournament.

In the last minute of the second half, Akers delivered Part II of her farewell address. It may have been inspired by what had taken place a few seconds before. Zhang Ouying had broken loose in the box, six yards from Scurry, putting her in position to take the shot that could end it all. Kate Sobrero was running laterally, frantic to stop her, but she was too far away. Suddenly, out of nowhere, Brandi Chastain hurtled in, sliding on the ground directly towards the ball—an amazing three-foot slide. One foot caught the ball and knocked it away, and Chastain's contact with Zhang sent her diving head first into the turf.

After the 90 minutes were used up, two minutes of extra time were tacked on, and China found itself with a corner kick. The ball soared towards the center of gravity. Akers went after it. So did Scurry. At the last moment Akers heard her goalkeeper's footsteps, but she didn't want to mess it up in the last seconds of a scoreless game by not going up. So she jumped in front of the goalkeeper, got a piece of the ball, and was struck on the head by Scurry's gloved fist. Akers went down.

Later, she would remember a few things. At that moment, however, she remembered nothing. She only remembered that she was trying to stand up and couldn't make it and that her head hurt. She remembered sitting on the bench, the team now getting ready for overtime, and DiCicco saying to her, "Can you go?" And she saying, "Yeah."

The next thing she knew she was in the trauma room, hooked up to two intravenous lines, with an oxygen mask over her face. When she came to her full senses she understood what had happened to her. It wasn't the collision with Scurry that knocked her out. "I was already out of it," she said. "I was gone mentally, from the heat exhaustion and my low blood pressure. I was already delirious, and I kinda checked out."

That was how the regular 90 minutes ended, 0-0, not with a whimper but with a bang. Next would come the first 15 minutes of overtime—sudden death, "the golden ball," as it is called in soccer—and, if nobody scored, another 15-minute overtime. After that, there would be nothing left but the shootout: penalty kicks.

The first time George Vecsey of the *Times* watched the national women's team play soccer, he became a convert: "The game was good. It was slower than the men's, not as powerful. But the women were so spirited, and they opened up the field. I won't get into the psychology of female athletes as opposed to male athletes, but there was a lot of passing, a lot of teamwork, a lot of energy, a lot of positive vibrations. It was just fun to watch. As a sports fan I said, Wow! And I kept tabs on them."

Almost from the beginning these founding players set out to institutionalize women's soccer, feeling they could create an audience for a sport that Americans had never been able to warm up to. American men who played soccer were still well behind the rest of the world; whereas these women, who had such talent and such ambitions, and such unity between themselves, were not behind the curve; they *were* the curve.

It took awhile for Tony DiCicco, when he became head coach of the national team in 1993, to understand about coaching women. It was Mia Hamm who put it to him early: "Coach us like men. Treat us like women." DiCicco came to learn that what she meant was: "Don't hold back because we're women, train us as hard as you would train the men, as much as you would train any top elite male athlete. But don't get in our face and belittle us and diminish us. Treat us with respect." DiCicco took the advice.

He may have overtrained them in 1995, preparing for the World Cup tournament in Sweden. For six months he had them down in Orlando, Florida, working with hardly a break. "We came out of it just physically fatigued," Julie Foudy said. They failed to reclaim the World Cup; Norway beat them in the semifinals, 1-0. After the game, the American players watched in disbelief as the Norwegian women formed a conga line, grabbing each other around the ankles, and crawled around the field. Her team, Foudy said, would never forget the humiliation of the Norwegians' "centipede crawl."

Revenge came for the United States at the 1996 Olympics held in Georgia. They played Norway in the semifinals and won, 2-1. Akers scored one of the goals on a penalty kick, and Shannon MacMillan's goal got the U.S. into the Finals against China. The game was played in Athens, Georgia, and a roaring crowd of 76,489 witnessed an inspiring 2-1 American gold medal victory. Yet not a minute of it was shown on national television. "They send an NBC crew out on the field *after* the game to get the celebration," Vecsey said. "There's Michelle Akers and all of them, piling on and doing their thing. They show that live and I'm thinking, these hypocrites, they get them cheering, but they won't show them elbowing and diving and tackling and playing and sweating."

It was all right for Michelle Akers being in that pile of happy teammates, because this was spectacular, this was the Olympics! She couldn't help wondering how her mother was feeling at this moment, a woman who had had to fight all-out to become the first woman firefighter in the state of Washington. Women have to fight for every little victory, Michelle thought. Standing on the podium with her teammates, waiting for them to drape the gold medal over her scarred body, she was thinking, oh, my God, I'm going to keel over. But she didn't because, she said to herself, this is AWESOME!

Twenty-three-year-old Sara Whalen replaced Akers. DiCicco knew that Whalen would be nervous because she didn't yet quite know how to play in "the uncomfortable zone," in a game that was so even, and one opportunity, or one mistake, could end it. All the great players, when they found themselves in the uncomfortable zone, where the pressure was intense, performed at a high level. Whalen was having trouble pushing herself in that zone, DiCicco felt, because she didn't yet believe enough in herself, that she could take over a game. But everyone else was tired, and maybe Whalen's speed and her fresh legs would enable her to to get behind the defense once and help win the game for her country.

The strikers, Hamm and Milbrett, made some forays into enemy territory, but now they seemed to be in an uncomfortable zone not of their choosing. They had played more than 100 minutes, offense *and* defense, in intense heat, at high speed. Now both of them felt that their legs were going.

On the other side the Chinese, though exhausted themselves, seemed more emboldened because the demon spirit was gone, the tall one with the deceptive goldilocks, who had been rampaging all over the midfield, striking like a commando, leaving them kicking up their heels in frustration. The other big one, Parlow, was gone, too. China's possessions of the ball increased. In quick order they blasted downfield, firing three shots at Scurry. The first came when Sun Yen stole behind Sobrero, streaked in on Scurry, but blasted wide. The second was shot off the foot of the other striker, Jin Yan; she had made a great run near the post and then swerved into goal, but Scurry was there to take it. The third, the make-or-break play of the game, came in the tenth minute of overtime. It was Sun Wen, breaking through again, streaking down the middle between defenders until, 22 yards from the enemy's goal, she found space. It was a bullet, but Carla Overbeck deflected the ball with her hip, and it skidded out of bounds. China was awarded a corner kick, only its fourth of the game. The kick would come from its left corner.

Julie Foudy, back at the 12-yard line, would remember that moment as frozen in time. Chastain was in the box, as were Fawcett, MacMillan, and Overbeck. Tiffeny Milbrett held the far post. Kristine Lilly was the sentry at the near post. Lilly leaned her left arm casually on the eight-foot white stanchion while she drank water from a bottle, then poured the rest of it over her head. Her close-cropped reddish-brown hair flattened on her scalp. She looked serene.

My wife and I had been watching the game on television, most of the time on the edge of our seats, especially at this moment of sudden death. Corner kicks were dangerous; they could decide a game, a World Cup. We saw Liu Ying's kick lifting off, roaring in towards the goal. We saw a blend of white and red uniforms splashing around the penalty area. We saw the purple-clad Scurry leaping desperately to her right, arms outstretched, failing to intercept the missile that Fan Yunjie headed towards the goal. I stood up, feeling crushed. "It's all over," I said. Scurry had thought the same thing: uh-oh, the ball's behind me.

In the next instant, thoroughly confused, I saw Kristine Lilly clear the ball with her head. Later I studied a color photo of that moment, caught by a *Sports Illustrated* photographer. It showed Scurry flinging herself sideways, her white gloves almost touching one of Lilly's hands. Lilly was playing in her 186th international match, more than anyone else in the world. Her feet were off the ground, her eyes were closed, her arms outstretched. Standing tall, clad in white, she looked like an Old Testament prophet delivering a sermon from the mountaintop. One other element in that photograph: the ball that had been headed by Fan Yunjie was flying back out from Lilly's forehead.

But back in New York, watching on television, I assumed that the ball had gotten beyond the mouth of the goal before Lilly's header. Wasn't it all over? Hadn't Fan Yunjie whipped in the "golden ball"—the ball that would deliver the World Cup to China? Others apparently had the same impression. MacMillan and Overbeck, towards the back of the scrum, had jumped up together to head off the ball. They hadn't made contact, and MacMillan, coming back down, just knew that the Chinese player had beaten them. She didn't want to look. Then she turned her face and saw that it was not over.

But it might immediately *be* over, because the ball was bouncing free in front of the goal, and Fan was rushing forward towards it, seeking redemption. Foudy, seeing what was happening but too far away to do anything, screamed, *"Get it out! Get it out!"* Brandi Chastain was there, in a position she always delighted to be in, in the middle of chaos. Another photo offers evidence: Chastain is horizontal in the air, her left arm braced on the ground, her legs moving separately. The right leg rides high in the air, the left leg dangles towards the goal, almost touching an opponent's hip. She would whip that leg into the ball, and send it flying out of the box. She has executed the bicycle kick, made famous by Pele, the greatest soccer player of them all. Another Brandi Chastain special effect.

But without Kristine Lilly there would have been no bacon to save. After the game, when reporters asked Lilly about her play, she said, "Every time there's a corner kick I'm on the post, and I just shift with the ball. It came right to my head. I was just doing my job."

The first overtime ended without further incidents. China, free of Akers, had outshot the United States, 4-1.

A chill had fallen over the Rose Bowl. The roar of the crowd grew muffled; people stirred nervously in their seats. So many of them had come into the stadium certain about the outcome: the United States would win. How could they not? They were the children of destiny. But 105 minutes had gone by and the U.S. hadn't been able to score. Gao Hong had grabbed every loose ball and kicked away every serious threat. But it was getting late and both teams were tired and susceptible to fatigue mistakes. Whose mistake would give the World Cup away?

Hamm, a feral look on her face as always, but with lines of fatigue showing, too, attempted a run, got into the box but was stripped. MacMillan tried a long pass, but it was knocked down. The Chinese tried their own runs, too, but Chastain was on them, or Carla Overbeck, who seemed to be roaming all over the field, directing her players, inspiring them, never making a fatigue mistake. "You tell your mind to tell your legs to run," she always said.

With six minutes left, the two teams were indistinguishable except for their uniforms: China had had 51 possessions; the U.S., 49.

Here was a pass sent down to Sara Whalen just beyond midfield—just what DiCicco had hoped for. With a burst of speed, she of the fresh legs roared down the middle, shedding defenders along the way. She saw Hamm racing into the penalty area and she fired a cross to her. DiCicco, on his feet, was moaning. If Sara had just taken another dribble and *then* served it, she might have frozen Gao Hong against the line and the ball would have been more dangerous, might have led to a score. But the ball came in too early, and the goalkeeper grabbed it in front of the goal before it reached Hamm's feet.

A minute later, the U.S. picked up a corner kick, only its fifth of the game. MacMillan hit it into the box, but a defender deflected the ball, causing a repeat corner kick. Between kicks DiCicco brought in Tish Venturini for Tiffeny Milbrett. He wanted her fresh legs and heading ability in there for the corner kick; get her up in the air and anything could happen. Milbrett fell onto the bench exhausted, felt like a shell of herself because it had been so draining. Hamm was tired, too, and punched the corner kick high. It was headed out by a defender.

With two minutes to go, China made one last desperate surge, the attackers sweeping past midfield, then bending a pass to Zhang Ouying near the penalty box. Zhang had had two shots on goal in the game, more than any Chinese player, and for a moment she was alone. But Overbeck crashed into the box, freed up the ball, poked it towards the goalkeeper, and Scurry cradled it like a baby.

And the whistle blew ending the 120-minute game. Last act coming up: the dreaded penalty kicks.

Towards the end of regulation play, when it seemed that overtime would be likely and penalty kicks might follow, DiCicco had asked assistant coach Lauren Gregg to draw up the top six U.S. kickers. The one they wanted most, the one who would have kicked first, was unavailable. Five days earlier, they remembered, Michelle Akers had made a brilliant penalty kick that sealed the victory over Brazil. Now she was underneath the stands in the trauma room, hooked up with IV lines on both arms, staring at the television screen that was showing the game. The screen was a blank to her: she could see nothing. She was out.

But DiCicco and Gregg did have reliable kickers, and he pretty much knew who he wanted out there. All he and Lauren Gregg had to do was figure out the sequence.

To start the shoot they would go with someone they absolutely trusted to score first: Carla Overbeck. Overbeck, a mother, wanted to go first, confident that she would make her shot and take the pressure off her teammates. Joy Fawcett, another mother (she had two sons), would go second. Like Overbeck, she was a calming influence, and totally dependable. DiCicco wasn't going one-two with Overbeck and Fawcett because they were mothers, but later it struck him that, hey, if you go through childbirth, taking the penalty kick is no big deal.

The third and fourth kickers, the coaches agreed, would be Lilly and Hamm. But the fifth kicker aroused discussion. Lauren Gregg had written Julie Foudy down. DiCicco wanted Brandi Chastain—which was risky because Chastain had had what DiCicco called "an awful year" on penalty kicks. For the three previous years she had been the best penalty kicker, next to Akers; but now the coach thought Chastain was in a rut, and also had become too predictable. She always took the shot with her right foot, always put it to her left. So, early in the tournament, he urged her to practice kicking left-footed as well. She did, and he decided to take his chances with Chastain, who had done everything right on the field for 120 minutes. She would be the fifth kicker.

The only one of the intrepid five who seemed to have reservations was Mia Hamm. While the players were milling around on the field, trying to keep their legs loose, Hamm said to Shannon MacMillan, "Do you want one?" MacMillan said, "Yeah." Hamm said, "You can have mine." Lauren Gregg, standing nearby, shook her head. "We already submitted the names, Mia, you have to take it."

There was a coin toss to decide who would kick first: China.

The first shooter was Xie Huilin, who had come in one minute before the end of overtime, put into action because penalty kicks were her specialty. Briana Scurry crouched, looking out at the ball that sat 12 yards back. Julie Foudy, on the sideline, stared at the goalkeeper. She was thinking, Bri is so good, so quick, so great laterally, great at shot-stopping. When the referee's whistle blew, Scurry rushed forward, but she was frozen on the spot as Xie kicked it deep into the top left corner of the net.

Then the first big mama, co-captain Overbeck, took her place beyond the ball. As Gao Hong was sprinting to the left, Overbeck banged it into in the lower right corner. She raised a fist high, jumped with joy, ran pell-mell back to her teammates, a see-how-easy-it-is grin on her face.

Scurry didn't watch Overbeck. She was looking the other way, as she would with all her kickers; she was superstitious. She also wanted to concentrate on her own job. Anyway, the crowd would tell her what was happening.

The second Chinese kicker, Qiu Haiyan, had also come in with strong legs, and only played the last six minutes. She was in there to drill a kick. And drill it she did, though it was close. She placed it in the upper left corner. Scurry moved the same way, flung herself at the ball, but it was up and beyond her.

Joy Fawcett, as she approached the ball, offered a stutterstep to Gao, who seemed transfixed by that footwork. She never moved. Fawcett's ball stung the right corner.

The mini-contest was over, the mothers vs. the strong legs: a draw. No more mothers left for the U.S., no more fresh legs left for China.

Enter Liu Ying, a midfielder who had worked hard all 120 minutes. She had kicked all four corner kicks for China. That was her forte; she had powerful legs and was a dependable penalty kicker. But as John Powers would later write in the *Boston Globe*, "She had just spent 120 minutes running up and down the flank in 90-degree heat. The last thing she wanted to do was kick a ball at the world's best keeper with the world watching."

Goalkeepers, who have to cover 192 square feet in their tight little cottage, must also stay put until the ball is kicked. That's the rule: no moving. But with her first two shooters, Scurry had jumped forward. Just how much it was impossible to tell, because the eye of the viewer tends to stay with the shooter. But no flag was thrown by the Swiss referee, Nicole Mouidi Petignat. When it was over she was asked why she hadn't penalized Scurry. She said it was impossible to keep her eyes both on the keeper and on the shooter; she had to concentrate on the shooter. Carla Overbeck told me that Gao Hong had also rushed forward on each kick, but it never showed up on the television screen. That was because the American cameras were on the American kickers, and on the American goalkeeper when China was kicking. Throughout that whole game those TV guys tilted on the side of chauvinism.

Scurry's moves on Liu Ying's shot were caught in still photographs, front and back. There she was, from the front side, guessing right, a purple and white statue on a pedestal, but swaying towards the direction of the shot, that great lateral movement flinging into action, arms up, legs about to slide from under her; but, somehow, before the fall, able to stab the ball with her left thumb and forefinger. You could see a wisp of hair flying from behind the right of her head, and one eye, like the ancient mariner's, fixated on that ball.

From behind there was less to be seen: the ball about to be sent away, Liu Ying's body bent, a question mark on her face because the deed was not yet done, an array of white-clad shooters back there, standing stolidly, except for one, apparently anticipating the result, who had both arms raised. And in the background, a large slice of a crowd, about to erupt.

Scurry certainly did. She stood there, arms out, gloves curled tight, a cry coming from her wide open mouth; by the looks of it, a cry of triumph. As Tony DiCicco always put it, "Goalkeepers, if they make a save on a penalty kick, they're heroes. That's what the best do. They make the vital save." That's what Briana Scurry had done.

But it wasn't over. Kristine Lilly was next up. If she made it, the U.S. would be up 3-2. She made it all right, standing calm and steady, hammering a shot with her left foot that landed high left, over the leaping Gao Hong's head. Then Zhang Ouying tied it with a kick to the lower right side.

Now it was the turn of Mia Hamm, the reluctant kicker who wanted to give her shot to Shannon MacMillan. It wasn't just fatigue that seemed to have blunted Hamm's self-confidence; it was her performance. She, too, had gone cold as a scorer. Hamm was always severely self-critical and tended towards melancholy when she couldn't score. Yet she remained everybody's darlin'. More than 100,000 girls had taken up soccer between 1990 and 1997, many of them inspired by Hamm. But she never craved fame. All she ever wanted was for women's soccer to succeed and become another national pastime in American life.

Now she came up to the line with a frown on her face, and then kicked the ball into the bottom of the net, leaving Gao Hong frozen. She turned and raced back to her teammates and fell into their arms. *"We're going to do it!"* her face proclaimed. The Hamm kick meant that the United States could do no worse than a tie.

The fifth round would be fought between one of the world's greatest players, Sun Wen, and one with a checkered past, Brandi Chastain. Quietly, Sun Wen stepped into the ball and placed it precisely inside the left post to keep the score 4-4.

How much baggage was Chastain carrying when she bent over to place the ball on the spot? A member of the class of '91 that put the first building block in place for women's soccer, she was subsequently exiled by coach Anson Dorrance. Dorrance felt that Chastain wasn't his type of player, that she was a pounder, and lacked finesse; also, she had off-the-field distractions he didn't care for. In 1995, DiCicco brought her back. He had two solid defenders, Overbeck and Fawcett, but he felt he needed another. With her okay, he converted Chastain, a forward, to defender. It was a master move. In the 1996 Olympics, Chastain tore up a knee, but never left the field. Early in 1999, in Portugal, she missed a penalty kick against China. In this tournament, a few days earlier, she had inadvertently flicked in the first goal *for* Germany. That misstep might have haunted her for life, but for the unanimous support she received from her teammates. At halftime Germany led by 2-1, and DiCicco was steaming. "You guys better get your head out of your rear end," he said, "unless you want to go home today." Five minutes into the second half, Chastain scored the tying goal. Fifteen minutes later, Joy Fawcett won it on a header off a MacMillan corner kick.

Chastain, the last kicker—China was finished—understood what a successful kick would mean: victory. She was in place for that moment she had yearned for all her life. The kick was blasted from her *left* foot, aiming for the *right* corner. She drove the ball with the laces of her shoes, an instep drive, designed for power, not accuracy, struck so hard and wide that Gao, going for it, couldn't extend her hand. The ball was in the net.

Then came the other shot, the one that would carry around the world: Chastain, down on the grass on both knees; pulling off her jersey, exposing her black sports bra; holding the jersey in her right hand and flinging up both arms, expelling an immense cry of triumph. Instantly it became everybody's cover shot, one that will be shown over and over again, an artifact of a supremely joyous moment in American sport, the crowning moment for a sisterhood of women who taught the country a lesson about skill, grace, mutual admiration, and love.

Minutes had passed since Chastain's mighty blow, and no one in the Bowl had moved. The 90,000 fans were covered with confetti that had spewed over them from cannons. They sang and cheered and hugged each other and watched their players down on the field, who were doing the same thing. Nobody wanted to leave.

On the field, a television reporter finally nabbed Brandi Chastain, now decorous in the yellow victory jersey that all the players were wearing. Chastain expressed her happiness to the 40 million people who were watching on TV. When she was asked about

Michelle Akers, Chastain said, "She's the goddamn toughest player I've ever played with or against and I'm glad she's on my team."

The only penalty kick Akers saw was Chastain's. She had finally awoken, and they had propped her up so that she could watch it. Then her doctor said, "We're going to helicopter you to the hospital."

"I don't think so," Akers said. "Get this stuff out of me—I'm going out on the field."

They did as they were told. The medics helped Akers fight her way through President Clinton's security force. She was stumbling and felt dizzy and close to collapsing. The medics had her rest, then walk, rest, then walk. Finally, just after her teammates had received their medals and taken a victory lap, she reached the podium and sat down. Suddenly, she heard her buddy and former teammate, Amanda Cromwell, shout up to her. "Do you hear that?" Cromwell screamed. "They're chanting your name."

The crowd had seen her down there on the field—how could they miss that distinctive figure, who wore the mane of a lion. They were all up on their feet, chanting: "Akers! Akers! Akers!"

In its last issue of the year 1999, Sports Illustrated *put the entire squad on its cover as its "SportsWomen of the Year." In an accompanying article by Michael Bamberger that summed up the team's bravehearts, he concluded that "in the final summer of the 20th century, the era of the woman in sports finally arrived." Well, the sisterhood hoped it was so, but leave it to Kristine Lilly to put it in proper perspective. She told a* Boston Globe *reporter right after the game, "This moment is more than a game. It's about female athletes. It's about sport. It's about everything. I don't think we can sustain this level of attention. But people caught on to us and I don't think they're going to let go."*

A week after their victory, the team was received at the White House, and President Clinton told them, "A lot of us who aren't so young anymore were trying to search the whole cluttered attic of our memories to try to think if there was ever a time when there had been a more exciting climax to an athletic event that had meant as much to so many. I'm not sure that in my lifetime there has been."

A New York Times *editorial called the game "an unforgettable portrait of determination and grace," also suggesting that "the excitement they have generated may lead to a formation of a women's professional league."*

Such a league came to fruition in the summer of 2001. It's call letters are WUSA: Women's United Soccer Association. Its major investors, most of them from large cable companies, have guaranteed a $40 million dollar commitment over the first five years of operation. Every one of the founding players, except the injured Michelle Akers, played in the league that first season. Plus 16 elite international players including Sun Wen, Gao Hong, and three other teammates from China.

Three months after the end of WUSA's first season, Akers announced her retirement. In October 2001, the Women's Sports Foundation, an organization founded by Billie Jean King back in 1974, presented Akers with the Wilma Rudolph Courage Award, presented to "a female athlete who exhibits extraordinary courage in athletic performance, overcomes adversity and makes significant contribution to sports."

Awesome.

ACKNOWLEDGMENTS

Late in the Harvard-Yale football game of 1999, with Yale holding a slim lead, I heard a Harvard father sitting behind me say to his young son, "It's not over until it's over—right, Nick?" Nick mumbled, "uh-huh." Sadly, Yale won. Yogi Berra claimed that he chiseled out this vital commandment in 1964, his first year as manager of the New York Yankees. But my friend Marty Appel, who once worked as the Yankees' public relations director and is a close friend of Yogi's, tells me that it entered the lexicon in 1973, the year Yogi managed the New York Mets to a come-from-behind National League pennant. What can I say to Yogi now that *my* game is over except to offer thanks for his most original inspiration?

A book like this, with 13 different stories from 13 different eras in the twentieth century, required the help of many people, and I am extremely grateful for the support I received. For those who answered the call on individual chapters, see my source notes. For those who helped me throughout, I offer my thanks here. I owe a major debt to my brother-in-law, Spike Gordon, and to my young colleague, Nick Scharlatt, for the painstaking research they did for me on every story. Spike plumbed the public libraries of Boston, Lynn, and Salem, Massachusetts, while Nick, who was then on the staff of the *Sporting News*, used all his own extensive sources for the cause. I also received generous reference assistance from the White Plains, New York public library. I am grateful to my friend and fellow writer Ray Robinson who knows how it is and gave me timely help throughout, also allowing me to raid his extensive sports library. Joe Goldstein, a sports publicist of renown, was always there when I called and opened the doors for me to interview Ralph Branca and Bobby Thomson, and also Joe Frazier. This book enabled me to reunite with old friends from my *Sport* magazine days. One was Al Braverman, my last art director at the magazine, who carried on at

Sport when Dick Schaap succeeded me in 1973. Al was able to find stories for me from later issues of *Sport* that were most helpful. Except for "Merkle Forever," I was able to watch every event in the book on film or tape. HBO and ESPN led the way with their rich documentaries. Thanks especially to Steve Buckheit, associate producer of ESPN Classic, for his help. More than once during the years I was working on the book, I sat down with Ed Fitzgerald, my Rabbi from the beginning of my working days. Though he was in poor health he understood my needs. Ed was particularly close to John Unitas in Unitas's glory years, and I was able to tape him about his Unitas recollections. When Ed died in 2001 his wife Liby, a kind and solicitous person always, gifted me with Ed's invaluable bound volumes of *Sport* from its beginning in 1946 through 1960. Spiritual balm came from the monthly revival meetings of a group of single-minded sports aficionados, consisting of Marty Appel, Darrell Berger, Bob Creamer, David Falkner, Stan Isaacs, Lee Lowenfish, Ray Robinson, the sainted Larry Ritter and, from a later generation, my son Brian. George Sullivan, a Boston sportswriter of much wisdom and kindness, came to one of our lunches and we consider him to be a non-resident member of our club. I can't thank George enough for the incredible help he gave me throughout. Sportswriters who I consulted with on various matters and gave willingly of their time, include George Vecsey and Gerry Eskenazi of the *New York Times,* and Dan Shaughnessy of the *Boston Globe.* After writing a dozen or so books on a typewriter, I was able to compose this one on a word processor, thanks to the teachings of Bruce Stark, the computer tutor of my life. I also thank my friend Trevor Bavar, a computer whiz who was always there when I needed him. At Overlook Press, special thanks to Caroline Trefler for seeing the book through with incredible patience and without complaint. Let it be known that it was Peter Mayer, Mr. Overlook Press, whose idea it was for me to do just the kind of book I wanted to do. I am grateful to him for working closely with me chapter by chapter. I owe an uncommon debt to William Zinsser for taking my manuscript in hand and helping me whittle it down to proper size with surgical cuts that left no blood, and for his brilliant line-editing. Finally, I thank my loving wife Rosa for helping to keep me focused and never allowing me to feel sorry for myself. This book would not have happened without her unflinching support and encouragement.

Notes

1908 MERKLE FOREVER

On a late summer Sunday, coming back from a pleasant stay in Vermont, my wife and I stopped at a large and crowded flea market. As was my custom, I wandered around looking for books that were for sale. At my first stop I felt the brush of an angel's wand. My eyes fastened on an unjacketed book that bore this title: *The Greatest Sports Stories From The* New York Times: *Sports Classics of a Century.* It was edited by Allison Danzig and Peter Brandwein, and published by A.S. Barnes and Company in 1951. Sure enough, there was the full account of "The Merkle 'Boner'." *The New York Times's* book also contained stories on the 1923 Dempsey-Firpo battle, and the epic 1937 Davis Cup tennis match between Don Budge and Gottfried von Cramm. For $4, I was on my way.

My account of Christy Mathewson's conversation with John McGraw on the morning of October 8, 1908 comes from Fred Lieb's story in *Sport* magazine of May 1951, titled, "Was This The Greatest Game Ever Played?" For Mr Lieb, the Giants-Cubs playoff game was exactly that.

OTHER SOURCES:
Fleming, G.H. "The Merkle Blunder," from *The Armchair Book of Baseball*, edited by John Thorn, New York: Scribner's, 1987.
Reidenbaugh, Lowell. *The Sporting News Selects "Baseball's 50 Greatest Games."* St. Louis: *The Sporting News* Publishing Co., 1988. (In addition to the Merkle story, this book also includes coverage of my 1951 and 1975 baseball chapters.)
Brown, Mordecai, as told to Jack Ryan. "The Result of Mr. Merkle," from the *Chicago Daily News.* Reprinted in *The Fireside Book of Baseball*, vol. 1, edited by Charles Einstein, New York: Simon and Schuster, 1956.

1923 THE BATTLE OF THE CENTURY

Considine, Bob. *The Firpo Story*. Hearst Headline Series, 1960.

Fleischer, Nat. *The Ring Record Book And Boxing Encyclopedia*. New York: The Ring Book Shop Inc. 1954 Edition.

Kahn, Roger. *A Flame of Pure Fire: Jack Dempsey and the Roaring '20s*. New York: Harcourt Brace & Co., 1999.

Lardner, John. "They'll Never Forget Firpo." *Sport* magazine, October 1951.

Menke, Frank G. "Firpo's Fists Punched Out Boxing's Alger Tale," *The Sporting News*. March 22, 1945.

Sher, Jack. "Fighter From Manassa," from *Twelve Sport Immortals*, edited by Ernest V. Heyn. New York: Bartholomew House, 1949.

1937 A SUPREME DAY FOR TENNIS

I'm grateful to have Bud Collins's *Tennis Encyclopedia,* the third edition edited with Zander Hollander, for its details on the Budge-von Cramm match; also for the help Collins gave me in a telephone conversation. Annette Dumbach, who lives in Munich, Germany, provided me with valuable information on the life of Gottfried von Cramm. Reg Lansberry, a tennis editor and journalist, was helpful in many ways, especially by putting me on to Alan Little, Honorary Librarian of the Wimbledon Lawn Tennis Museum. I thank Mr. Little for providing me with historic details about Wimbledon in 1937. And my thanks to Steve Flink, a noted tennis writer and commentator, for his gracious assistance.

Alistair Cooke, referred to at the time as "the most brilliant of the newest generation of radio commentators," gave an account of the match over New York radio station WEAF, from which I used my Cooke references.

The New Yorker of July 31, 1937, carried a story titled, "Greatest Match in the History of the World." It was credited to "Foot Fault." Who was Foot Fault? I called my friend Roger Angell at *The New Yorker* to ask him if he knew Foot Fault's identity. He didn't immediately, but he said he could look it up, and he did. "It was James Thurber," he told me. Well, of course.

OTHER SOURCES:

Budge, Don, and Frank Deford. *A Tennis Memoir*. New York: Viking Press, 1967.

Engelman, Larry. *The Goddess and the American Girl: The Story of Suzanne Lenglen and Helen Wills*. New York: Oxford University Press, 1988.

Evans, Richard. *The Davis Cup*. New York: Universe Publishing, 1999.

Grimsley, Will. *Tennis: Its History, People and Events*. Englewood Cliffs, New Jersey: Prentice-Hall Inc., 1971.

Tunis, John. "Raising A Racket for Germany," *Collier's* magazine, July 10, 1937.

Drucker, Joel: "The Battle of Wimbledon," *Forbes FYI*, Summer 1998.

Budge, Don, as told to Allison Danzig. "Why I'm Turning Professional," *The Saturday Evening Post,* November 10, 1938.

Grimsley, Will. "Grand Slam of Tennis," *Sport* magazine, February 1960.

1951 THE MOST THEATRICAL HOME RUN

In addition to Ralph Branca and Bobby Thomson, who were generous of their time, I also interviewed Jackie Robinson's widow, Rachel Robinson; 84-year-old Eddie Pellagrini, who was the Philadelphia Phillies' second baseman, for his memories of the last game of the season when Robinson won it for the Dodgers in the 14th inning; and Bill Sharman, the basketball great, who, in 1951, was in the Dodgers' farm system and was called up on the closing days of the pennant race. I am also grateful for the information and illumination provided me by Ray Robinson personally and from his 1991 book, *The Home Run Heard 'Round the World*, published by Harper Collins.

I also read the game stories of the Giants' and Dodgers' drive for a pennant from the *Boston Globe*, the *New York Times*, the *New York Herald Tribune*, the *New York Post*, the *Sporting News*, and the Associated Press.

OTHER SOURCES:

Branca, Ralph, as told to John M. Ross. "They'll Never Forget." *Sport* magazine, May 1952.

Daley, Arthur. *The Arthur Daley Years*. New York: Quadrangle, 1975.

DiLillo, Don. *Underworld*. New York: Scribner's, 1997. A remarkable novel of the period.

Dressen, Charley (sic) as told to Stanley Frank. "The Dodgers Won't Blow It Again." *The Saturday Evening Post*, September 13, 1952.

Durocher, Leo, with Ed Linn. *Nice Guys Finish Last*. New York: Simon and Schuster,1975.

Hodges, Russ and Al Hirshberg. *My Giants*. Garden City, New York: Doubleday, 1963.

Hynd, Noel. *The Giants of the Polo Grounds*. Garden City, New York: Doubleday, 1981.

Kahn, Roger. *The Era*. New York: Ticknor & Fields, 1993.

Robinson, Jackie, edited by Charles Dexter. *Baseball Has Done It*. Philadelphia, Pennsylvania: Lippincott, 1964.

Robinson, Jackie with Alfred Duckett, *I Never Had It Made*. New York: Putnam, 1977.

Thomson, Bobby. "That Home Run Saved Me," *Sport* magazine, April 1952.

1958 SUDDEN DEATH

The late John Steadman was of great help to me on this story, and I will never forget his kindnesses. I'm also grateful for having read John's informative book about the 1958 Colts: *Football's Miracle Men: The Baltimore Colts' Story*. Cleveland, Ohio: Pennington Press, 1959.

In addition to Steadman, I interviewed Don Maynard, Andy Robustelli and Pat Summerall, who played for the Giants that year, and Raymond Berry and Arthur Donovan, Jr. of the Colts. I thank them all for their cooperation. I also spoke with Perian Conerly, the widow of Charley Conerly, who remembered much about that year. Robert Daley, who was the publicity director of the team at that time, graciously opened up his memories to me. I was also helped by Gerry Eskenazi of the *New York Times,* and the photographer, Marvin Newman, who shot that game for *Sport* magazine. And I thank Murray Olderman, a writer and cartoonist for NEA, and an expert on professional football at that time, for the extraordinary help he gave me in my research.

I wrote three magazine stories about the Colts in that period, and called on them for help on this story. "Can The Colts Do It Again?" ran in the October 14, 1959, issue of *The Saturday Evening Post.* It was centered on the late Baltimore coach, Weeb Ewbank, who gave me fascinating tidbits about his team's first National Football League championship (the Colts would repeat in 1959). I wrote "Johnny Unitas: Take-Charge Guy," for *Argosy* magazine; it was published in September 1959. "Block, Tackle And Think," was bylined by Johnny Unitas with my assistance and published in *This Week* magazine, October 26, 1958.

For this story I also made extensive use of *Total Football, "Official Encyclopedia of the NFL."*

I also watched with much interest ESPN's Sports Century documentary of the Sudden Death game, and HBO's 1999 documentary on John Unitas.

OTHER SOURCES:

Berry, Raymond. "The Greatest Game." *Newsweek,* October 25, 1999.

Clary, Jack. *Thirty Years of Pro Football's Great Moments.* New York: Rutledge Books, 1976.

Conerly, Perian. *Backseat Quarterback.* Garden City, New York: Doubleday, 1963.

Cosell, Howard. "It Happened In Sports." *Sport* magazine, January, 1964.

Devaney, John. "No One Stands Higher Than Unitas." *Sport* magazine, August, 1968.

Donovan, Arthur, Jr., and Bob Drury. *Fatso: Football When Men Were Really Men.* New York. William Morrow, 1987.

Fitzgerald, Ed. *Johnny Unitas. The Amazing Success Story of Mr. Quarterback.* New York: Thomas Nelson & Sons, 1961.

Frank, Stanley. "The Experts Pick Pro Football's Greatest Game," *Sport* magazine, January, 1969.

Klein, Dave. *The Game of Their Lives.* New York: Random House, 1976.

Linn, Ed. From *Heroes of Sport, Johnny Unitas: The Genius Who Runs The Colts.* New York: Bartholomew House, 1959.

Maule, Tex. "Sudden Death At Yankee Stadium." *Sports Illustrated,* January 5, 1959.

Olderman, Murray. *The Running Backs.* Englewood Cliffs, New Jersey: Prentice-Hall, 1969.

Olderman, Murray. *The Defenders.* Englewood Cliffs, New Jersey: Prentice-Hall, 1973.

Whittingham, Richard. *What Giants They Were.* Chicago, Illinois. Triumph Books, 2000.

1960 HEAD ON, THE GENERATIONS COLLIDE

In addition to the number of golf books either touching on the U.S. Open of 1960 or focusing completely on that year and that event, I also learned much from Lincoln A. Worden's coverage of the 1960 Open in the *New York Times,* and Bud Shrake's in the *Dallas Morning News.* The Golf Channel's double-video documentary on Arnold Palmer, "Golf's Heart and Soul," gave me a ringside seat to the 1960 U.S. Open, as well as details on Palmer's life. I also found helpful ESPN's "100 Years of the U.S. Open". To those who I spoke with—Paul Harney, Palmer's playing partner on that last fateful day; Gene Neher of the Cherry Hills Country Club, who witnessed it all from the first green; Michael Bamberger of *Sports Illustrated;* Arnold Palmer; and, especially, Doc Giffin, Palmer's long-time alter ego—I thank you all.

OTHER SOURCES:

Bisher, Furman. *Arnold Palmer's Golden Year 1960: The Birth of a Legend.* Englewood Cliffs, New Jersey: Prentice-Hall, 1972.

Bisher, Furman. "Is Arnold Palmer The Best Ever?" *Sport* magazine, September 1962.

Brown, George E. III. *Cherry Hills Country Club, 1922-1997.* Englewood, Colorado: Cherry Hills Country Club, 1998.

Cosell, Howard. "Palmer's Greatest Charge." *Sport* magazine, September 1967.

Graubart, Julian. *Golf's Greatest Championship, the 1960 U.S. New York Open.* New York: Donald I. Fine Books, 1997.

Grimsley, Will. "Arnold Palmer's Uphill Struggle." *Sport* magazine, December 1968.

Jenkins, Dan. "Whoo-ha, Arnold!" from *You Call It Sports But I say It's a Jungle Out There.* New York: Fireside Books, 1989.

Nicklaus, Jack, with Herbert Warren Wind. *The Greatest Game of All: My Life In Golf.* New York: Simon and Schuster, 1969.

Palmer, Arnold, with William Barry Furlong. *Go For Broke.* New York: Simon and Schuster, 1973.

Palmer, Arnold, with James Dodson. *A Golfer's Life.* New York: Ballantine Books, 1999.

Paquin, Jim. "Palmer's Finish Wins Open." *Professional Golfer,* August 1960.

Sampson, Curt. *The Eternal Summer: Palmer, Nicklaus and Hogan in 1960,* Dallas, Texas: Taylor Publishing Co., 1992.

Sampson, Curt. *Hogan.* Nashville, Tennessee: Rutledge Hill Press, 1996.

Sommers, Robert. *The U.S. Open: Golf's Ultimate Challenge.* New York: Oxford University Press, 1996.

Wind, Herbert Warren. "Destiny's New Favorite," *Sports Illustrated,* June 27, 1960.

1964 CHOSEN BY THE GODS

In the spring of 2000 Billy Mills and I met at Disney World in Orlando, Florida. Mills would be speaking at a banquet honoring the national high school cross-country finalists; they would be competing that weekend for the young women and men's national championships, the event sponsored by the Foot Locker shoe company. Between his various appearances, Billy and I sat together and talked about Tokyo 1964 and the race that would define his life. Later, over the phone, I interviewed Billy's wife and partner, Pat Mills, who was open and informative. I also spoke with Billy's prime opponent, Ron Clarke, in Australia. I interviewed Bud Greenspan, the filmmaker of stirring documentaries about every Olympics since World War II. Greenspan also put me in touch with a Japanese sportswriter, Yoichi Furukawa, who covered the 1964 Olympics for the Hoichi newspaper. Furukawa not only became a source, but a friend. I also spoke with Ian Frazier, author of *On The Rez* (New York: Farrar, Straus and Giroux, 2000), his moving story of life among the Oglala Sioux in Pine Ridge, South Dakota. Thanks to Frazier, I was able to speak with Chick Big Crow, a relative of Mills who lives in Pine Ridge. I'm grateful to Tyler Dunkel of the University of Kansas sports information department for providing me with pertinent information on Mills's sports career at Kansas. My brother-in-law, Spike Gordon, an ex-Marine himself, found material on Mills's Marine career from the U.S. Marines' museum in Washington, D.C. I especially want to thank Craig A. Masback, the Chief Executive Officer of the U.S. Track and Field organization for his advice and for putting me in touch with Mills.

Among the newspaper accounts of the race, the one I treasure is Red Smith's in the *New York Herald Tribune*, which won a prize as the best news-feature story of the year.

OTHER SOURCES:

ESPN Information Please Sports Almanac. New York: Hyperion, 1999.

Frank, Stanley. "Great Olympic Upsets," *Sport* magazine, October 1968.

Glanville, Brian. *People In Sport.* London, Great Britain: Secker & Warburg, 1967. This book contains Glanville's feisty *London Sunday Times* coverage of the 1964 Olympics.

Horgan, Tim. "The Sportswriters' Greatest Moments," *Sport* magazine, December 1971.

Mills, Billy, with Nicholas Sparks. *Wokini: A Lakota's Journey to Happiness and Self-Understanding.* Carlson, California: Hay House, 1999.

Quercetani, Roberto. *Athletics: A History of Modern Track and Field Athletes (1860-2000)* Milan, Italy: SEP, 2000.

Shecter, Leonard. "Billy Mills: Upset Star of the Olympics," *Sport* magazine, May 1965.

Sports Illustrated 2001 Sports Almanac. New York: Bishop Books, 2000.

Time. "The Olympics," October 23, 1964.

Track & Field News. October-December 1964.

Underwood, John, "We Win The Five and Ten." *Sports Illustrated,* October 26, 1964.

1968 THE GAME OF GAMES

I got the right start on this story when I went to Cambridge, Massachusetts, to see John Rosenberg, editor of *Harvard Magazine.* He gave me a warm entrance to the world of the Ivy League, and I am grateful to him for his suggestions and insights about the event, and for seeing to it that I received all the articles on the Game that had run in his magazine over the years. I am grateful for the cooperation I received from participants in the Game: Brian Dowling and Calvin Hill from Yale; Pat Conway, Vic Gatto, Stephen Ranere, Pete Varney, and Frank Champi from Harvard. I spent the most time with Champi and I am grateful to him for his willingness to burrow into his complex and bittersweet memories of that time.

I also want to thank John Veneziana, the Sports Information Director at Harvard, and Steve Conn, the Sports Information Director of Yale, for their help. John Ryden, who runs the Yale University Press, gave me much needed assistance about the "big blue" side of the story. I thank Gerald Eskenazi, one of those who covered the game for the *New York Times,* for sharing with me his special memories of that assignment. And special thanks to Stanley Silbert, a close friend from my boyhood, and a deep-rooted Harvard alumnus, especially when it comes to the university's sports program. Silbert provided me with all kinds of clues as to where to go and who to talk to, and helped open various doors for me.

I was given a long-playing record that featured highlights of the game from the radio coverage on station WHDH. It was narrated by the play-by-play radio announcer, Ken Coleman. Also, courtesy of Harvard, I received video coverage of the last 42 seconds. I spent a lot of time watching those seconds tick by. I also read the coverage of the game in the *New York Times, Boston Globe,* and *New Haven Register.* I thank John Powers of the *Globe* for unearthing newspaper stories of the game for me that I probably would have missed. And special thanks to Powers's uncle, George Sullivan, who was a water boy for the Harvard team that Bobby Kennedy played on, before becoming a bat boy at Fenway Park. These youthful occupations fired his ambitions to write about fun and games without regret, also enabling George to offer me rare snapshots of both institutions. I am grateful for his help.

OTHER SOURCES:

American Heritage. "Most Underrated Newspaper Headline," May-June 2000.

Bergin, Thomas G. *The Game: The Harvard-Yale Football Rivalry, 1875-1983.* Yale University Press, New, and London, 1984.

Cozza, Carm. *True Blue: The Carm Cozza Story.* New Haven, Connecticut and London, Yale University Press, 1999.

Farnham, Willard, ed. "Hamlet, Prince of Denmark" from *The Pelican Shakespeare.* New York: Penguin Press, 1970.

Glassman, James K. "A Dream Game Ends A Dream Season." *Harvard Alumni Bulletin,* December 2, 1968.

Goodwin, Lee David. "The Game." *Inside Sports,* December 1983.

Harvard Magazine, November-December 1983. "Endless Replays, the 29-29 Tie, 15 Years Later,"

Harvard Magazine, September-October 1998; "30 Years Again, 1968—Harvard "Beats" Yale 29-29," Joe Bertagna:

Harvard Magazine, November-December 2000: "The Saga of a Great Headline," Alan Schwarz.

Horn, Miriam. *Rebels in White Gloves: Coming of age with Hillary's class—Wellesley '69.* New York: Times Books, 1999.

Powers, John. "Carm." *Harvard Football News*, November 23, 1996.
Yale Daily News. "Yale-Harvard Instant Headline." November 29, 1999.

1971 THEY LEFT IT ON THE TABLE

In June of 2001, I was privileged to be driven to Canastota, New York, just south of Syracuse, the home of Boxing Hall of Fame, for its annual induction weekend. My driver, and companion, was Bert Randolph Sugar, the longtime Pericles of boxing as a writer, a publisher of magazines about fistiana, a laugh-a-second Toastmaster General and, bless his soul, a forthcoming source about the sweet science as it was during the Frazier-Ali era. Because of Sugar's assurances that I was legit, I was able to speak with these fight figures at Canastota: Angelo Dundee, Jimmy Ellis, Eddie Futch (Futch died four months after we talked, at age 90), Kid Gavilan, Ken Norton, and Joe Frazier. I thank Joe Goldstein for sharing with me his memories of the fight. Roger Kahn was gracious about offering his own ringside views of that memorable evening. I also want to thank writers Stan Hochman, Jerry Izenberg and Sandy Padwe for being open to my queries. I interviewed photographer George Kalinsky, who was close to Frazier and Ali in those days and created a legacy of photographs of both fighters. And HBO's excellent documentary, "Ali-Frazier: One Nation Divisible," was of much help.

OTHER SOURCES:

Cannon, Jimmy. *Nobody Asked Me But: The World of Jimmy Cannon*, edited by Jack Cannon and Tom Cannon. New York: Holt, Rinehart & Winston, 1978.

Cooke, Alistair. *Fun And Games: On Sports and Other Amusements.* New York: Arcade, 1994.

Kram, Mark. *Ghosts of Manila: The Fateful Blood Feud Between Muhammad Ali and Joe Frazier.* New York: Harper Collins, 2001.

MacCambridge, Michael. *A History of* Sports Illustrated *Magazine.* New York: Hyperion, 1997.

Pepe, Phil. *Come Out Smokin.' Joe Frazier—The Champ Nobody Knows.* New York: Coward, McCann, 1972.

Playboy "Interview." November 1975.

Roberts, James B. and Alexander G. Skutt. *The Boxing Register.* 2nd edition. Chicago, Illinois: McBooks Press, 1999.

Schulberg, Budd. *Loser And Still Champion, Muhammad Ali.* Garden City, New York: Doubleday, 1972.

Wolf, David. "A Very Close Look At Joe Frazier." *Sport* magazine, May 1971.

1975 BODY ENGLISH

In 1975, Dan Shaughnessy was 22 years old and working in Boston as a stringer for the Associated Press. Because of that connection he was allowed to buy World Series tickets. He took his sister to the sixth game. They sat in section 27, where the bend is between third base and leftfield. They couldn't actually see the Fisk ball hit the pole because the roof was over their head. They just saw the ball come down, thinking at first that George Foster had caught it. Three years later, Dan went to work for the *Boston Globe* and has become one of the paper's key sports columnist. When I was working as an editor at Viking/Penguin, I was lucky enough to inherit *The Curse of the Bambino,* helping to put the finishing touches on a book that will probably never go out of print, at least while the curse still hangs over the Red Sox. In his book Dan wrote a commanding section on the sixth game which, I confess, I paid close attention to. Dan was also kind enough to allow me to interview him for this story. *The Curse of the Bambino* was published by Dutton in 1990, and the paperback edition was published by Penguin Books a year later.

I thank Dwight Evans and Fred Lynn for talking with me, Kevin Shea, publicity director of the Red Sox, for his efforts, and Jeff Idelson of the Baseball Hall of Fame for his courtesies while I was in Cooperstown. I learned much about the game from the ESPN Classic Video, also from Joseph Durso's game coverage in the *New York Times,* and *Boston Globe* daily and evening stalwarts on the Series: Mike Barnicle, Bud Collins, Peter Gammons, Ray Fitzgerald, Leigh Montville, Jerry Nason, John Powers, Ernie Roberts, Francis Rosa, Bob Ryan, and Larry Whiteside. One more salute to George Sullivan for sending me stories on the game from sources I otherwise would have missed. He also presented me a precious copy of his sixth game Scorecard. What more could you ask for from a baseball man?

OTHER SOURCES:

Allen, Maury. "An Event For The Ages." *New York Post*, October 9, 1975.

Anderson, Sparky, with Dan Ewald. *Sparky.* Englewood Cliffs, New Jersey: Prentice-Hall Press, New Jersey, 1990.

Anderson, Sparky, with Dan Ewald. *They Call Me Sparky.* Chelsea, Minnesota: Sleeping Bear Press, 1998.

Angell, Roger. *Once More Around The Park: A Baseball Reader.* New York: Ballantine, 1991.

Beech. Mark. On Bill Lee, from *Sports Illustrated* feature, "Where Are They Now?" July 31, 2000.

Cannon, Jimmy. *Nobody Asked Me But.* New York: Henry Holt, 1978.

Lee, Bill "Spaceman," with Dick Lally. *The Wrong Stuff.* New York: Penguin Books, 1985.

Montville, Leigh. "A Sporting Life," from "The Boston Collection," *Sports Illustrated*, 1998.

Reidenbaugh, Lowell. "Fisk's Shot Floors Reds," *The Sporting News*, November 8, 1975.

Sugar, Bert. "The Greatest Game Ever Played," from *Baseball's 50 Greatest Games.* New York: Exeter Books, Books, 1986.

Sullivan, George. *The Picture History of the Boston Red Sox.* Indianapolis, Indiana and New York: Bobbs-Merrill, 1979.

Zimmer, Don, with Bill Madden. *Zim: A Baseball Life.* New York: Sports Illustrated and *Total Sports,* 2001.

1980 DO YOU BELIEVE IN MIRACLES?

Mike Eruzione was both analytical and articulate when he talked to me about that time in his life, and I'm grateful for his cooperation. Other players I interviewed were Dave Christian, Rob McClanahan, Jack O'Callahan, Dave Silk, and Mark Wells. They were most helpful. I also thank Howie Schultz, president of Grand Stand Sports, for inviting me into his office the day a group of 1980 players were busy signing their names to photographs and other memorabilia. Larry Millett, a friend and fellow author, who lives in St. Paul, Minnesota, provided me with game stories from the *St. Paul Pioneer Press* and the *Minnesota Herald-Tribune.*

I was able to watch three versions of the U.S.–Soviet Union game: ABC's telecast; the HBO documentary titled, of course, "Do You Believe in Miracles?"; and the ESPN Classic documentary on the 20th anniversary of the game. I also read miracle-game coverage from *People* magazine, *The New Yorker, Newsweek,* and *The Readers' Digest.* E.M. Swift covered the game for *Sports Illustrated,* and also wrote the year-end story when the team became *Sports Illustrated's* "Sportsmen of the Year." In the February 20, 2000, *New York Times,* Dave Anderson wrote a fascinating anniversary column on the game, aptly titled: "When All of America Skated On Golden Pond."

OTHER SOURCES.
Carter, Jimmy. *Keeping Faith: Memoirs of a President.* New York: Bantam Books, 1982.
Powers, John, and Arthur C. Kaminsky. *One Goal: A Chronicle of the 1980 U.S. Olympic Hockey Team.* New York: Harper & Row, 1984.
New York Times. The Staff. *Miracle On Ice.* New York: Bantam Books, 1980.
Total Hockey, 2nd edition. Kingston, New York: Total Sports Publishing Company, 2000.

1992 WEEP NO MORE, MY LADY

Grateful thanks to Richie Farmer, Deron Feldhaus, John Pelphrey, and Sean Woods, the four hometown Kentucky seniors whose jerseys hang on the rafters among the University of Kentucky's elite athletes, for their vivid memories of the game. I was pleased, too, to talk about the game with Pelphrey's wife, Tracy. I thank Brooks Downing, Sports Information Director at the University of Kentucky, for helping me contact those players, and for all the valuable files on the game that he shipped to me. Duke's Sports Information Director, Jon Jackson, also provided me with various stories in the Duke archives pertinent to the game.

I learned much about the game from the following newspapers: *The Paducah, Kentucky Sun,* the *Cincinnati Enquirer,* the *Louisville Courier-Journal,* the *Lexington, Kentucky Herald-Leader, and the Philadelphia Inquirer.* I read *Sports Illustrated's* May 29, 1989 issue, with its "Kentucky Shame" cover that broke open the scandal at Kentucky. In the later years of recovery at Kentucky, Alexander Wolff wrote four stories for *Sports Illustrated* on the Duke-Kentucky rivalry, all of them with a fine writer's flair. And Bob Ryan of the *Boston Sunday Globe* of March 29, 1992, wrote a featured story that captured the thrill of the game. I watched ESPN's classic documentary, and a friend, Michael Collina, who grew up in Charlotte, North Carolina, gave me his own tape of the game. Collina claims he was "the happiest, most obsessed guy in the world" about college basketball in his state. A composer by profession, he was watching Duke–Kentucky while he was working in a sound studio. When Laettner hit his shot, Collina said, "I jumped high up in the air with both arms upraised, and knocked a bunch of ceiling tiles to the ground." Nothing odd about that in the world of basketball in North Carolina.

OTHER SOURCES.

Grundy, Pamela. *Learning To Win: Sports, Education and Social Change in 20th century North Carolina.* Chapel Hill, North Carolina & London: University of North Carolina Press, 2001.

Hill, Grant. *Change The Game: One Athlete's Thoughts on Sports, Dreams and Growing Up.* New York: Warner Books, 1996.

Krzyzewski, Mike, with Donald T. Phillips. *Leading with the Heart: Coach K's Successful Strategies for Basketball, Business, and Life.* New York: Warner Books, 2000.

Pitino, Rick, with Dick Weiss. *Full-Court Pressure: A Year in Kentucky Basketball.* New York: Hyperion, 1992.

Sports Illustrated. *Sports Almanac.* New York: Little, Brown, 1997.

1999 AWESOME!

I started my research on this last story in the right way, by interviewing Tony DiCicco, the coach of the World Cup winners. For me, the session was like going to Berlitz to try to learn another language. The language DiCicco taught me was that of international soccer played by women as best exemplified by his 1999 team. I thank him for being such a good teacher. With DiCicco's wisdom seeping into my head, I went on to interview these founding members of the national team: Michelle Akers, Julie Foudy, Shannon MacMillan, Tiffeny Millbrett, and Carla Overbeck. They were all articulate, candid and helpful. I also thank Dave Schifrin of the Founders Cup staff for arranging interviews for me in Boston during WUSA's "founding" 2001 championship game festivities. Aaron Heifitz, a guru of soccer, was magnanimous when I had to bother him for help. George Vecsey was the other one, beside DiCicco, who helped pass on his passion for the game to me. Michael Bamberger, who covered the World Cup for *Sports Illustrated,* offered me wise advice about my research and what to look for. I'm grateful to him. I also found Jere Longman's game coverage for the *New York Times* invaluable, as well as Alex Yannis's in the same paper, and John Powers's World Cup stories in the *Boston Globe,* along with his colleague, Shira Springer. Just about every weekly magazine ran cover stories on the game, and the ones I found most interesting were *Sports Illustrated, Time,* and *Newsweek.*

OTHER SOURCES.

Hamm, Mia with Aaron Heifitz. *Go For The Goal: A Champion's Guide to Winning in Soccer and Life.* HarperCollins: New York, 1999.

Longman, Jere. *The Girls of Summer: The U.S. Women's Soccer Team and How it Changed the World.* HarperColllins: New York, 2000.

List of Illustrations

Cover/Frontispiece
Nothing beats the thrill of the crowd! (*photo © Pascak Rondeau/Tony Stone Images*)

p. 13 MERKLE FOREVER
A one-time "boneheaded" play on the field immortalized first baseman, Fred Merkle.
(*photo © Brown Brothers*)

p. 29 THE BATTLE OF THE CENTURY
After being knocked down seven times in the first round, Luis Firpo struck the blow that
turned the fight to myth. (*photo © Bettman/CORBIS*)

p. 49 A SUPREME DAY FOR TENNIS
Don Budge performed at his glorious peak in the must-win Davis Cup match of 1937, at
Wimbledon. (*photo © AP/Wide World Photos*)

p. 69 A MOST THEATRICAL HOME RUN
"I'm seeing the ball! I'm seeing the ball!" And Bobby Thomson got out in front of it.
(*photo © AP/Wide World Photos*)

p. 99 SUDDEN DEATH
Untouched, Alan Ameche secured the sudden-death championship for the Baltimore Colts.
(*photo © AP/Wide World Photos*)

p. 125 HEAD ON, THE GENERATIONS COLLIDE
Seven strokes back, with 18 holes to play, Arnold Palmer made the charge of his life at the 1960
U.S. Open—and reacted as he should have, with pure joy. (*photo © AP/Wide World Photos*)

p. 147 CHOSEN BY THE GODS
He felt the divine thought: "*I can win, I can win.*" And Billy Mills, a 1,000-1 underdog,
showed them all that he could. (*photo © AP/Wide World Photos*)

p. 173 THE GAME OF GAMES
A two-point catch by Pete Varney, with no time left, allowed Harvard to "beat" Yale, 29-29.
(*photo © Jerry Cooke/Sports Illustrated*)

p. 193 THEY LEFT IT ON THE TABLE
In the 15th round, Joe Frazier's left hook, going "all the way to home," made Muhammad
Ali the loser. (*photo © AP/Wide World Photos*)

p. 213 BODY LANGUAGE
Carlton Fisk saw to it that his 12th inning drive stayed fair, and became a most celebrated
World Series home run. (*photo © AP/Wide World Photos*)

p. 233 DO YOU BELIEVE IN MIRACLES?
The U.S. team went mad after upsetting the supposedly invincible Soviet Union.
(*photo © Bettmann/CORBIS*)

p. 259 WEEP NO MORE MY LADY
With no seconds left, Christian Laettner flicked in Duke's game-winner over Kentucky.
(*photo © AP/Wide World Photos*)

p. 283 AWESOME!
Michelle Akers resolved to last as long as she could—"fight on and do not quit." That she
did, heading out ball after ball until she had nothing left. (*photo © AFP/CORBIS*)